HOMEN/
A
ALEXANDRINO SEVERINO

HOMENAGEM A ALEXANDRINO SEVERINO:
ESSAYS ON THE PORTUGUESE SPEAKING WORLD

edited by

Margo Milleret
Department of Spanish and Portuguese
Vanderbilt University

Marshall C. Eakin
Department of History
Vanderbilt University

HOST PUBLICATIONS, INC.
AUSTIN, TEXAS

Published by
Host Publications, Inc.
Austin, Texas

© 1993 Host Publications, Inc.

Printed in the United States of America
Design and Layout: Joe W. Bratcher III

For information, address Host Publications, Inc.
2510 Harris Blvd., Austin, TX 78703

Library of Congress Catalog Card Number: 93-77309
ISBN 0-924047-09-7

To Dorothea, Sandy, Cornelia, Roger Katherine and Julia

CONTENTS

BRAZILIAN LITERATURE

LITERARY THEORY AND HISTORY

Preface

This project began in the late spring of 1992 when Alex Severino was compelled by poor health to retire from the Vanderbilt faculty. With the encouragement of Christopher Maurer from the Department of Spanish and Portuguese, we sent out a preliminary call for essays in June. By the end of September our desks were covered with essays, and we were overwhelmed, but pleased, by the response from scholars in the United States, Brazil, and Europe.

Financial constraints limited our selection to about one-third of the essays submitted. With an eye toward thematic coherence, we chose essays that reflect a broad range of interests and scholarship in the Portuguese speaking world. Our goal was to organize a volume of essays that both would make a contribution to the field, and honor Alex and his distinguished career.

In organizing this volume, we have gained an even greater sense of respect and admiration for Alex and his pioneering role in establishing Luso-Brazilian studies in the United States and at Vanderbilt. For nearly three decades, Alex has inspired his students, engaged his colleagues, and enriched the lives of all those who have known him. May this volume convey our gratitude to Alex for his work and his influence on us.

Margo Milleret and Marshall C. Eakin
December 1992
Nashville, Tennessee

viii

Acknowledgements

We would like to recognize the contributions of time and expertise given by Helen Church of the Department of Spanish and Portuguese, Norma Antillón of the Center for Latin American and Iberian Studies, and Johnny Tharpe of the Micro-Computer Laboratory at Vanderbilt. Our appreciation goes to Christopher Maurer, Chair of the Department of Spanish and Portuguese for encouraging us to pursue this project.

We are grateful to the University Research Council, the Department of Spanish and Portuguese, and the Dean of the College of Arts and Science for providing us financial assistance.

We would especially like to thank the many loyal colleagues and friends who wrote to express their concern for Professor Severino and to support this project: Norwood Andrews, Buddy Arrington, Joanna Courteau, Jorge Fernandes da Silveira, Pedro Fonseca, Rodolfo Franconi, Marga Graf, Leland Guyer, Robert Hayes, K. David Jackson, Linda Ledford-Miller, Fábio Lucas, Helder Macedo, Naomi Hoki Moniz, Gerald Moser, Terry Palls, Susan Quinlan, Monica Rector, Peggy Sharpe, Vera Regina Teixeira, and Yara F. Vieira.

Alexandrino Eusébio Severino:
A Life in Letters

True to his Portuguese heritage, Alex Severino has been a transatlantic scholar. His life and work have taken him to four continents on both sides of the Atlantic world. He has written and taught about English and American literature in Portugal and Brazil, and about Luso-Brazilian literature in the United States and Africa. His life has been shaped by his love of learning and literature.

A native of Olhão, Portugal, Alex's father emigrated to the United States in 1912 with his first wife and a daughter. Like many of his countrymen in the fishing business, he moved back and forth across the Atlantic many times in his life. After divorcing his first wife he returned to Portugal in the 1920s and married another *olhense*. In 1926 his wife gave birth to a daughter, Stella. In 1930 he returned to Olhão for a few months, leaving once again before the birth of his son, Alexandrino Eusébio, on July 17, 1931.

The elder Severino never returned to Portugal. Young Alex grew up in Olhão during the Depression and the Second World War. Reared by storytellers and lovers of poetry, his upbringing left indelible marks on him. His mother died in 1940 leaving Alex and Stella in the care of her relatives. When his father married for a third time, he sold his house to purchase tickets to fly Stella and Alex to the United States. Alex became a U.S. citizen in 1946.

Alex attended Rogers High School in Newport, Rhode Island, and also worked as a hospital orderly at night. His father also worked as an orderly at the same hospital, after leaving the fishing business. A high school English teacher, impressed with Alex's hunger for knowledge, encouraged his interest in literature, especially poetry. After graduation from high school in 1950 he received a Rotary scholarship to attend a teacher training school, but decided to turn it down. Instead, he worked as a nurse's aide at a local hospital, and began taking pre-medicine classes at the University of Rhode Island.

1

A draft notice in 1952 interrupted his studies, and for the next two years he spent most of his time near Richmond, Virginia working in Army intelligence. He often entertained himself on long training marches by reciting poetry. Alex managed to save up $2,000 during his service, and when discharged in August 1954, he took a ship for Portugal, intending to enroll at the University of Coimbra. Frustrated with both his work and his studies, he abandoned his plan after less than a year and returned to Rhode Island. Over the next three years he finished his B.A. at the University of Rhode Island, majoring in English and Spanish.

Alex then enrolled in graduate school at the University of Rhode Island, and on the advice of a professor, he applied for and won a Fulbright fellowship to study Portuguese in Brazil. This naive, young graduate student arrived in Rio de Janeiro on Fat Tuesday, 1959. Both fascinated and frightened by the tropical exuberance of *carnaval*, he almost turned around and headed home. His fascination overcame his initial fears, and he stayed on, although he quickly decided to study in São Paulo rather than staying in Rio.

While teaching at the binational center in March 1959 he met Dorothea Bresslau, the daughter of German immigrants. Her grandfather had founded the zoology department at the University of São Paulo in the 1930s, and her father was an engineer and architect. Dorothea learned English while an American Field Service high school exchange student in Dallas, Texas. In 1960, Alex's acceptance of an offer to organize the English department at a newly-created *faculdade* in Marília complicated their courtship. After their marriage in January 1961, Dorothea transferred from the University of São Paulo, and finished her degree in Marília. Over the next five years she taught English at a local high school and gave birth to three children: Sandy (1961), Cornelia (1962), and Roger (1965).

During the early sixties Alex built his department and cultivated his great love for English literature. When he decided to pursue doctoral work, he naturally sought out a mentor at the University of São Paulo. Rebuffed by the professor who should have been the most likely sponsor for his work, he managed to convince a professor of Portuguese philology to serve as his advisor. As his dissertation topic, he chose to write about the South African experience of Fernando Pessoa. Although much had already been written on Pessoa by the early sixties, very little had been done on his formative years.

While his studies progressed and his family grew, Brazil slid into political chaos and the military imposed a dictatorship. Feeling increasingly uncomfortable in post-coup Brazil, Alex began to look for an academic position in the United States. Despite his love of English literature, he decided that his best chance for securing a job would be in a Portuguese department.

In 1965 he discussed his plans with Earl Thomas, a prominent Portuguese language specialist at Vanderbilt University, and an old friend. The two had met by chance on a boat to Portugal in 1954, and they had corresponded for years. They met again in 1959 at a symposium in Salvador, Bahia. Thomas promised to help Alex, and the next year he was offered a job at the University of Texas. On August 25, 1966, he defended his dissertation on Pessoa before an audience of fifty, and then he and his family moved to Austin.

While Fred Ellison taught Brazilian literature, Alex taught Portuguese language and literature courses, something he had never done before. After two years in Austin, he was promoted to associate professor with tenure, and he finally severed his ties with the university in Marília. In 1969 he received two job offers—at Tulane and Vanderbilt. Once again, Earl Thomas played a key role in his life, persuading him to move to Nashville.

Over the next three decades, Alex helped make the Portuguese program at Vanderbilt one of the best in the nation. He taught everything the department offered, from introductory to advanced language classes to the literature of both Brazil and Portugal. Perhaps his favorite courses, however, were not even in Portuguese. For many years he offered a humanities class in great literary works. The class allowed him to combine his two great loves—English and Portuguese literature. Much to his delight he found he could teach both Melville and Camões to undergraduates in the same course.

Whether he was teaching beginning language courses or the great books of the western world, Alex captivated his students with lively classes. With a preference for discussion over lectures, he had a knack for making students comfortable talking about literature and language. He became famous for his recital of poetry, and the songs he taught his introductory Portuguese classes. During his years at Vanderbilt, he trained eight Ph.D.s, four of those in his last five years on the faculty.

In 1975 he was promoted to full professor. Dorothea gave birth to their fourth child, Katherine, the same year. An active organizer and administrator, he chaired the Department of Spanish and Portuguese from 1975 to 1979, and he served as the Fulbright representative on campus throughout the 1980s. In 1980 he directed a National Endowment for the Humanities Summer Seminar on American and Brazilian literature. In 1983 he organized the Second International Symposium on Fernando Pessoa, held at Vanderbilt.

Always the international scholar, Alex spent 1970-71 on leave in Brazil and Portugal. In addition to visiting appointments at Middlebury (1974) and in Rio de Janeiro (1981), he taught for a semester at the University of Rennes, France (1990). One of his proudest moments was a trip to South Africa in 1986. At the invitation of the António de Almeida Foundation in Portugal, he went to Durban and spoke at the unveiling of a statue of Fernando Pessoa. He then edited a volume produced in honor of the occasion.

In addition to his books on Pessoa, Alex published articles on a wide array of topics from language teaching to English literature. Perhaps because of his origins, he has been especially interested in images of the sea, particularly in the works of Pessoa, Camões, Melville, Guimarães Rosa, and Clarice Lispector. For Alex, the sea was a wonderful metaphor for life.

Failing health over the last decade slowed his research and writing. He began having trouble with his eyes in the 1970s that turned out to be early signs of retinitis pigmentosa. The same disease had struck Dorothea in the early 1960s and had advanced rapidly, destroying her eyesight. In the late 1980s, Alex's vision deteriorated slowly, a cruel fate for a man so devoted to a life of books and reading. Nonetheless, it was his most productive time in mentoring graduate students.

Crueler still, a tumor began to grow in his brain. The first signs of danger appeared in 1989 when Alex developed flu-like symptoms that he could not seem to shake. While in France the next year he suffered seizures. Not until the spring of 1991 were doctors able to pinpoint the problem—a growth near the thalamus. The seizures became more frequent and severe in late 1991 and early 1992. Radiation treatment in April and May failed to help, and after 23 years at Vanderbilt, Alex reluctantly retired on medical disability. He spent his last months at home with his family. Alex died quietly in his sleep on April 25, 1993, a few days before his sixty-second birthday.

Alex Severino was a wonderful colleague, an inspiring teacher, and a highly respected scholar. A charming and gracious man with a wry sense of humor and a quick smile, he always exuded dignity, almost courtliness. He considered himself fortunate to have lived in and loved three countries, and to have had the opportunity to pursue a life of letters. His hunger for knowledge and love of literature made a young Portuguese immigrant into a worldly man of letters, and one of the most prominent exponents of Luso-Brazilian literature in the Americas. We are fortunate to have known him.

Marshall C. Eakin

Alex Severino
Selected Publications

Books

Fernando Pessoa na Africa do Sul: Contribuição ao Estudo de Sua Formação Artística. 2 vols. Marília: Faculdade de Filosofia, Ciência e Letras de Marília, 1969-70 (actually published in 1973).

Fernando Pessoa na Africa do Sul. 2nd. ed. Lisbon: Dom Quixote, 1984.

Fernando Pessoa and the Portuguese Sea. Durban and Porto: António de Almeida Foundation, 1988.

Chapters in Books

"The Brazilian Short Story: Reflections of a Changing Society." *Brazil in the Sixties.* Ed. Riordan Roett. Nashville: Vanderbilt UP, 1972. 376-396.

"Clarice Lispector." *Latin American Writers.* 3 vols. New York: Charles Scribner and Sons, 1989. 1303-1311.

"Portuguese Poetry." *Princeton Encyclopedia of Poetry and Poetics*, 3rd ed. Ed. Alex Preminger. Princeton: Princeton UP (in press).

Articles

"A Presença de Milton em Uma Ode de Alvaro de Campos." *Luso-Brazilian Review* 7.1 (1970): 34-45.

"La Formación Artística de Fernando Pessoa." *Insula* 297-298 (July-August 1971): 12-13.

"A Primeira Publicação Literária de Fernando Pessoa." *Hispania* 54.1 (1971): 68-72.

"Tendencias principales del desarrollo del cuento brasileño." *El Cuento Hispanoamericano ante la Crítica.* Ed. Enrique Pupo-Walker. Madrid: Editorial Castalia, 1973. 358-370.

"'Os Lusíadas' a Luz da Nova Crítica," *Luso-Brazilian Review* 17.2 (Winter 1980): 207-212.

"Fernando Pessoa: A Modern Lusiad." *Hispania* 67 (March 1984): 52-60.

"The Metaphor of the Sea in *Grande Sertão: Veredas*." *Transformations of Literary Language in Latin American Literature: From Machado de Assis to the Vanguards.* Austin: U of Texas P, 1987: 111-115.

"Coleridge and Pessoa: Poetry to the Fifth Degree." *New Canadian Review* 2.1 (1989): 159-162.

"Was Pessoa Ever in South Africa?" *Hispania* 72 (September 1991): 526-530.

HOMENAGENS

Alexandrino Severino's Love of Literature

On several occasions, during my nearly nine years at Vanderbilt, I have heard colleagues in the Department of Spanish and Portuguese remark that Alex Severino truly *likes* literature. Now, to say that a professor of literature *likes* what he or she teaches may seem to state the obvious. On the other hand, there are those who maintain that these days some teachers of literature truly disdain the subject they profess.

Robert Alter, for example, in his *The Pleasures of Reading in an Ideological Age*, relates an incident involving a student in his undergraduate comparative literature course at Berkeley. It seems that in previously-taken courses two separate professors of English had told this student that *Moby Dick* was a bore and reading the novel was a waste of time. Alter, who in his own comparative literature course devotes three weeks to Melville's classic, makes the following observation with regard to his colleagues' dismissal of the work: "It is hard not to construe this as a discouraging sign of the times, a confirmation of the suspicion that literature faculties may be increasingly populated with scholars who don't particularly care for literature."[1]

As the title of his book suggests, Alter takes issue with the idea that literature can be relegated to pure ideology; he also inveighs against jargon-ridden, often abstruse postmodernist theory. Moreover, Alter complains that rather than read literary works many of today's students and scholars prefer to read about literature.

But how does Alexandrino Severino fit into this equation? Does he scorn those who follow the lead of the likes of Lacan, Derrida, and Foucault, to say nothing of such neo-Marxist critics as Terry Eagleton? To my knowledge, Alex bashes neither "trendy" theorists nor berates socio-historical critics (and, incidentally, I count myself among the latter). On the other hand, Alex undoubtedly derives pleasure from the intrinsic aesthetic and human values of individual literary texts.

Before attempting any further characterization of Alex Severino as a scholar and teacher who loves literature, in general, and Luso-Brazilian letters, in particular, I would first like to indulge in some personal reminiscences about my colleague and friend. To tell the truth, I do not

9

remember exactly when we first met, but it seems as though I have known Alex all of my professional life. Coincidentally, although our paths did not cross there, we were in Brazil at the same time—he in São Paulo, between 1959 and 1966, and I in Salvador, Bahia, from 1960 to 1962. Moreover, for part of that time in Brazil we were both Fulbright fellows. Also in the realm of comparabilities, Alex and I got our Ph.D.s within a year of each other. In all likelihood Alex and I met face to face in the mid- to late-1960s. I was then at the University of Minnesota, and, if memory serves me, we were introduced in Austin, where, at the time, Alex was a faculty member at the University of Texas. Whenever and wherever we met, the fact of the matter is that Alex and I have known each other for about twenty-five years.

Over the course of these years, Alex and I have participated together in conferences and symposia from Minneapolis to New York to Nashville. In 1983, I was privileged to participate in the International Symposium on Fernando Pessoa, which Alex Severino most successfully organized and directed at Vanderbilt, whose faculty I joined a year later. Since that time, Alex and I have maintained a close collegial relationship, and along with our respective wives, Dorothea and Cherie, during these years in Nashville we have also been friends who have enjoyed each others' company on numerous social occasions.

Throughout the years, as might be expected, Alex and I have chatted about many things, including literature. Apropos of these conversations, I think that those colleagues who have commented that Alexandrino Severino really *likes* literature mean that he can rise above the academic politics that seem to dominate many professorial conversations. I do not mean to suggest that Alex avoids those departmental, collegiate, and university-wide political issues that, for better or worse, seem to take up inordinate amounts of our time. What I do mean to imply is that Alex seems to be able to rise above the fray and engage even those with whom he may disagree on issues of collegiate politics in conversations about the pleasures of reading literary works.

I recall a conversation I had with Alex some months ago about the future of the Portuguese program at Vanderbilt. After reiterating his interest in language pedagogy and eagerness to continue to teach introductory and intermediate Portuguese, he stated that in his view literature was, however, the "salvation of humankind." Taken at face value such a statement might strike some as sarcastic, a joke, or ingenuous. On the other hand, taken in context, and allowing for a measure of poetic license on Alex's part, the statement has relevance for one who loves to read and who sees literature, and art in general, as transcendent. Consider what Terry Eagleton has to say about the English Romantics' view of literature's role in society: "The literary work itself comes to be seen as a mysterious organic unity, in contrast to the fragmented individualism of the capitalist marketplace: it is 'spontaneous' rather than rationally calculated, creative rather than mechanical."[2] I don't mean to suggest that Alex Severino is a neo-Romantic nor that he understands literature to be, as Eagleton claims it was for the English Romantics, "a whole alternative ideology" (p. 20). Alex Severino's idealistic conceptualizations of the "creative imagination" and "imaginative creation" are thoroughly modern, probably grounded in his having come of age as a scholar during the heyday of Anglo-American formalism and the New Criticism. (I confess to not knowing for sure how Alex's doctoral training at USP may have influenced this grounding.) But to the extent that, as Eagleton would have it, we are all post-Romantics (p. 18), Alex certainly is one who sees in the literary artist the possibility of transcending history and capturing in his or her work that which most ennobles humankind.

On another occasion I remember Alex telling me what a thrill it was to have his own son as a student in one of his undergraduate literature courses. What a source of satisfaction it was, he told me, to read *Aspects of the Novel* with his son. Forster's very durable work, published in 1927, was, of course, one of the mainstays of Alex's and my generation of budding literary scholars. This landmark critical work is, indeed, as Judith Ruderman writes in her encyclopedia entry on the British writer, "an idiosyncratic and engaging discussion of the novel as art form" as well as "an invaluable guide to F's own novels."[3] And according to Ruderman, "F's fictional works are moral guidebooks that juxtapose classes or cultures in order to enlarge perspective and achieve liberation from rigid social and national distinctions" (p. 122). One of these days I must ask Alex if he has read any of Forster's short stories or novels. But even if he hasn't read Forster's fiction, Alex's regard for *Aspects of the Novel* and his above-quoted remark about literature's redemptive value would suggest that he also equates moral guidance with the "imaginative creation."

Although Alex certainly sees the products of "creative imagination" as something other than ideological commodities, he also is not a strict proponent of art for art's sake or of the artist as socially disengaged or politically uncommitted. A case in point is "Was Pessoa ever in South Africa?," one of Alex Severino's most recent articles. The article's concluding sentence answers the question posed by the title: "Yes, Fernando Pessoa did live in South Africa and reacted, *nobly and persuasively*, to the social and political ills of the day" (emphasis added).[4]

The social ills of the day had to do with the aftermath of the Boer War. According to Severino, "the question of what the British should do with the defeated Boers was the great issue of the day, and not racial conflict, the topic that engulfs South Africa today" (529). Pessoa decried, in verse and essay, British treatment of the vanquished Afrikaners. And, Severino writes, "[h]ad Fernando Pessoa been alive today, living in twentieth-century South Africa, it is likely that he would have reacted in a similar manner against those who promote white racial supremacy" (529). Alex's sentiments are as "noble" (he frequently uses this adjective and the corresponding noun and verb) as those he ascribes to Pessoa and, indeed, to poets in general. In fact, in view of Alex's conceptualization of the "creative imagination," it comes as no surprise to read his assertion that "[t]hroughout his life, Fernando Pessoa had the objective stance of the poet, a duality between himself and the outer world which was perfected in him through the experience of having lived in South Africa at such a tender age and having absorbed that country's British culture so completely" (527). Severino also ascribes objectivity and even aloofness to Pessoa during his thirty years in Portugal. What Severino means, of course, by the "objective stance of the poet," is the latter's ability to become detached from reality in order to transcend its historical immediacy and then recreate it in terms that convey the noblest of human ideals (no need to comment here on the notion that the "poeta é um fingidor").

Finally, whether or not one is in total agreement with Alexandrino Severino's conceptualizations of literature and his critical approaches to the "creative imagination" and to "imaginative creation," one has to admire his belief in art's ability to ennoble humankind. Although Alex may not again grace the classroom, at least not on any regular basis, I join with his colleagues and former students in hoping that he will continue to write and otherwise contribute to that which he loves and, by doing so, ennobles. I myself shall continue to seek his counsel and prize his friendship.

Russell Hamilton
Vanderbilt University

Notes

[1] Robert Alter. *The Pleasures of Reading in an Ideological Age*, New York: Simon and Schuster, 1989, 12.

[2] Terry Eagleton. *Literary Theory: An Introduction*, Minneapolis: University of Minnesota Press, 1983, 19-20.

[3] In *Encyclopedia of World Literature in the 20th Century*, Vol. 2, New York: Frederick Ungar Publishing Company, 1982, 123.

[4] Alexandrino E. Severino. "Was Pessoa Ever in South Africa?," *Hispania* 74.3 (September 1991): 530.

* * *

Dear Alex:

As I was preparing to mail off "Europe and the Invention of Fernando Pessoa" as my contribution to this volume, I found myself shaking my head: "But Alex won't like it." There then ensued an internal debate. Cataclysmic, Sousa against Sousa: "Isn't it improper to participate in an honorific publication with a contribution that the person being honored would disagree with?" "Of course not; what's important is to participate in the honoring of Alex." "But even so. . ." The argument went back and forth or, depending on how we think we talk to ourselves, maybe around and around. No matter, though, for I came to realize that I wasn't really talking to myself as much as I was talking about you. Let me, then, tell you what that *controversia intestina* made me see clearly.

What I both respect and admire is your ability to give support to others in such a way that your own convictions both inform that support and at the same time do not interfere in it. Much more than the relationship between the two of us, I think of your treatment of students, a goodly number of which we have in one way or another shared over the years. I comprehend our relationship, despite its ironies (you certainly *can* talk about Pessoa as a historically-determined construct of literary-critical practice!). And I am grateful for that relationship — with all its irony. The students, however, have received from you something in some senses similar but ultimately quite different from what I have received, something quite rare: support pure and simple for the efforts they make to attain their goals. Not an uncritical support, for that would lack any guiding force. Instead an unconditional support—in the sense that criticism implies no lessening of the support but instead is a part of that support.

In practical terms, I recall marvelling, in retrospect, when, on one of your visits here, I asked if you would spend an hour or two with our students, who were at that time feeling quite abandoned, it being a moment in our program's history when only one advanced graduate student and I were available to a large number of aspiring Portuguese language students, majors, and beginning graduate students. Not only were you interested in spending the time with the students, but you insisted then and there on learning as many details as possible. Instead of going to lunch as we had planned, the two of us sat in my car for the next hour going over the situation and discussing the students' studies; you even tried to memorize some of their names without yet having met them. The ensuing visit played an important part in carrying us to a point where the program could be revitalized.

Now as you know, Alex, I don't believe in that proposed transcendental ground called "humanity" which we supposedly can let transcend our own personal interests and make contact with the correlative "humanity" in other "human beings." It's a cultural myth—indeed, in its current form, one only a few hundred years old. It is, however, my conviction that interpersonal commitment can exist, in various manners and forms. To your commitment to me I am greatly indebted. A large number of people, your students, are similarly indebted to your efforts on their behalf—students who won't have the opportunity to say this to you. Let me, for all of us, thank you.

O abraço de sempre,

Ron Sousa
Minneapolis
October 1, 1992

                              *   *   *

Remembering

It was strange to have started out our
friendship by my knowing the details
of your quotidian life (it seemed)
even before meeting you by design
at the U.S.I.S. library in São Paulo,
on Avenida Paulista, not yet friends,
measuring away at one another, Americans
in our near-native land, thinking
thoughts, folding away impressions.

Over years, over months: family visits exchanged, introductions, dinner in a New York restaurant of some sort of South-American cuisine when you talked of Camões and Melville and recited Pessoa, another talk in Pittsburgh on your discovery of Pessoa's rubaiyat, a stay-over at my old farmhouse in Burrillville, Pessoa conferences — in Providence, Nashville, Lisbon, São Paulo — the AATSP in Mexico City, offprints exchanged, recommendations written, books inscribed, plans for Pessoa books revealed. Scholars talking up dreams in the fetid air of conference rooms, shaking down aspirations that gnaw at well-being.

And yet, and yet. . . I knew more about the dust and detail of your life before I met you, when everywhere I went in the city, Rio, Marília (your old stamping grounds)—I heard the innocent gossip that fills out an outline, that colors in a portrait. Fitting that when we did meet—a meet not exactly of the Stanley and Livingston sort— we met as Americans in a place dangerous to us— an American library—in the Conjunto Nacional across the passageway from the bank (where over a weekend inflation ate up my small get-away's balance)—a sitting duck for the machine-guns of the urban guerrilla, a target for the sharp-shooter Lamarca. I did not envy you your trip to Durban, but thought it a nice quid pro quo for your long devotion to Pessoa, to old Jennings.

George Monteiro
August 27/September 16, 1992

* * *

I have known Alex Severino for almost twenty years, as a matter of fact during my entire professional career. He has always helped all of us in the field of Luso-Brazilian studies, not only as an academic mentor, but also with his time and patience in dealing with the personal and professional interests of his friends. I am indeed privileged to have him as a friend; there are no words to describe my gratitude for the many favors that he has so willingly granted me. I can think of nobody more deserving of this *Homenagem* than Alex Severino.

Celso L. de Oliveira
Professor of Portuguese and Spanish

* * *

Alexandrino on My Mind

Long before I learned to say *bom dia* correctly, Portuguese held a peculiar attraction for me. Perhaps it was an old friend who had expostulated on the beauty of its lyric poetry. Or the sound of the language. Whatever, I decided to audit basic Brazilian Portuguese during my first doctoral year at Tulane, at the end of which I applied for and was awarded an NDEA Summer term in Portuguese at the University of Texas (Austin) in 1967.

My election was a happy one; the teachers were all-stars, all the way from the lab instructors and conversation leaders to the classroom professors.

Figuring prominently in this structure was our friend Alexandrino

Severino, literature professor extraordinaire, a teacher's teacher even as a young man, a friend to his students.

Now, twenty-five years later, I still see Alexandrino presiding over our afternoon classes of about forty—also my age at the time—good naturedly engrossing us to the point of our forgetting the time of day and the sweltering Austin summer heat, in so many fine moments of Luso-Brazilian literature like the conflicting personae of Fernando Pessoa (*o poeta é fingidor*), or the case for his innocence on the part of Dom Casmurro, or the vagaries of Carlos Drummond de Andrade's poetry (*no meio do caminho tinha uma pedra*).

I was to meet Alex thereafter at yearly regional language and literature conferences during the seventies and early eighties. Occasionally we shared a happy hour together, sometimes in the company of Earl Thomas, of Vanderbilt, that fine scholar and gentleman.

Oh, yes, I left Alex's class at Austin with the resolve to make Luso-Brazilian a significant area of my studies. And I did.

Thanks, Alexandrino. *Até logo.*

Warren Hampton
University of South Florida
September 1992

*   *   *

Recordação de Vanderbilt

No verão de 1980, doze professores de Português se reuniram em Nashville para um seminario de Literatura Comparada Brasileira e Norteamericana, em Vanderbilt. Nosso director, Alexandrino Severino, era tambem o organizador do seminario para a National Endowment for the Humanities. Preparara-o com entusiasmo e carinho e se propunha a tratar os participantes a pão-de-ló—o que realmente fez.

Segundo ele, os treze eramos colegas, dedicados ao exame de figuras e obras comparáveis em ambas as literaturas. Assim, o Pe. Vieira se contrapunha a Jonathan Edwards, através dos sermões de ambos; Machado de Assis era examinado com a mesma lente que Henry James; *As vinhas da ira* de Steinbeck revelavam paralelo com as *Vidas secas* de Graciliano; Autran Dourado então já deixava transparecer que Duas Pontes tomaria as proporções do Yoknapatawpha County faulkneriano. O entusiasmo do diretor contagiava os doze "fellows". Estes, Alexandrino nos revelara, distribuiam-se simetricamente: seis homens e seis mulheres, repartidos entre posições geográficas quanto a suas universidades e a origem ao Norte ou Sul do equador.

A nossos olhos, Nashville passou a ser (que ele nos perdoe), não a terra de Elvis, mas a sede de nosso seminario de literatura. Líamos, estudávamos e reuniamo-nos diariamente nas salas do departamento e na biblioteca. Nas poucas horas em que não estávamos estudando ou escrevendo, passávamos bons momentos reunidos em nossas respectivas casas, restaurantes, ou bares e nos parques, em piqueniques. A primeira das festas, uma feijoada completa que marcou epoca, foi-nos oferecida por Dorothea e Alexandrino em sua casa. Foi ai que os "fellows" se conheceram ou se reviram, na vespera do inicio do seminario. Ainda me lembro da salada de frutas saborosíssima.

Do diretor aos alunos, todos os membros do seminario tínhamos o luxo de dedicar nossa inteira atenção aos autores de nossa preferência. Que delicia poder ler Machado e James horas e horas e dias e dias! Alexandrino, entusiasta de Osman Lins, de quem era amigo e tradutor exaltava *Avalovara* (no que ele alias era seguido pelos alunos). Tão marcante era seu entusiasmo que encomendamos um bolo comemorativo a uma padaria de Nashville. Deveria ser decorado com um dos simbolos gráficos de Avalovara (o circulo com ponto no centro), uma mulata a lembrar a Gabriela de Jorge Amado, uma baleia em honra a Melville e finalmente, um papagaio, como aquele da interjeição predileta do nosso diretor.

Na padaria, explicamos nosso conceito artistico a uma funcionaria perplexa se bem que atenta. No final da explição, ainda meio perdida, ela apontou para o simbolo do O de Osman e disse, com certo enfado, "Oh, you mean a boob..." O bolo foi servido em uma de nossas ultimas festas em Nashville.

Ainda me lembro do seminario que abriu caminho para nós, ao dar-nos oportunidade de debruçarmos sobre as duas literaturas. Varios de nós continuamos a trabalhar com autores e movimentos que viemos a conhecer em Nashville sob a direção segura e generosa de nosso amigo Alex.

Maria Angélica Guimarães López
University of South Carolina

*   *   *

Alexandrino E. Severino

Colleagues of the caliber of Alexandrino E. Severino are a rare commodity in American higher education—individuals of unquestioned competence, superb academic training, a sense of modesty, a willingness to listen, and finally, a trenchant sense of generosity in sharing both his love for Luso-Brazilian culture and the means toward a goal of intellectual attainment. He has done many things both wisely and well, never with a spirit of personal aggrandizement, but rather as part of an aspiration to lift human existence to a higher plane.

During my lengthy tenure as Executive Director of the American Association of Teachers of Spanish and Portuguese, I knew that I could count on Professor Severino for sane, dispassionate advice on the state and prospects of Luso-Brazilianism within the Association. I also learned that I could have confidence in his judgment and assessment of individuals who could lead the "P" in the AATSP to greater prominence, something long overdue both within the AATSP and in the United States. It is ironic that he stayed as a worker largely behind the scenes, being elected to the Association's Executive Council only in 1991.

I need not detail Professor Severino's many accomplishments in the academy. He is one of a rather small number of deeply-interested individuals who has been responsible for the renaissance of Luso-Brazilian studies which is beginning to emerge today. It has been a pleasure to know him, to share in his generosity, and to express these words of gratitude for his *homenagem*.

Richard B. Klein
University of Mississippi

*   *   *

"Sete anos. . ."

. . .—Mais servira, se não fora
Pera tão longo amor tão curta a vida.
— Camões

In the fall of 1981, I arrived at Vanderbilt to work with Professor Severino at what I consider a very exciting time in the study of Portuguese in the department. That fall, we had eight students enrolled in Professor Severino's seminar on Fernando Pessoa, a class that was full of lively discussion. Although I felt that I was in over my head, having never studied Pessoa before, at the end of that semester Professor Severino made the first of two key phone calls in my academic career, assuring me that I had "made the grade" in his class. That same fall, he also encouraged me to apply for a Fulbright scholarship. I told him that I was interested in going to Brazil, and we worked on a project on Brazilian modernism and convinced the Fulbright Commission to send me to São Paulo for the following academic year. Professor Severino's letters of introduction and contacts in Brazil helped me a great deal, especially his choice of Professor Antonio Dimas of the University of São Paulo as my advisor. I maintain regular contact with Dimas to this day, a special connection I owe to Alex Severino. Upon my return to Vanderbilt, I was able to speak Portuguese more fluently and could enjoy the discussions in Professor Severino's seminar on the contemporary Brazilian novel. Other memorable classes of his included the Brazilian short story and a seminar on the lyric and epic poetry of Camões. Professor Severino was equally qualified and comfortable teaching prose or poetry, but his first love was clearly poetry, which he could quote effortlessly from memory. In those years, I appreciated the fact that we had to write in Portuguese, and I admired his patience with my errors at that time. I also recall that Professor Severino's reputation was in part responsible for the distinguished visiting professors in Portuguese at Vanderbilt: Massaud Moisés, Fábio Lucas, and Benedito Nunes.

At the same time, Professor Severino's help, knowledge, and encouragement extended outside the academic setting. Besides always inviting students and visiting professors to his home for dinners and parties, he maintained a sincere personal interest in the well-being of his students. During a particularly difficult time in my own life, he suggested that I take a trip to Portugal, where I could meet his nephew, Ramires, and his wife, Ana Paula, and her family. Their hospitality and good spirits helped me through a rough period, and I have pleasant memories of that experience.

Professor Severino's suggestion that I go to Portugal in 1985 began an important phase of renewal in my own graduate school career. The trip helped me to face the prospect of qualifying exams and writing the dissertation, a process that took me nearly three years. Professor Severino helped me choose a dissertation topic, and although I managed to write the proposal and submit most of the dissertation on a regular basis, I was blocked as I tried to write the conclusion. Almost out of the blue Professor Severino called me in San Antonio, Texas (the second of the two key calls), and encouraged me to write the conclusion and to set a date for the defense. At that time, I was especially thankful that I was in a small program and grateful to Professor Severino for his personal attention.

In July of 1988, I returned to the Vanderbilt campus with the defense date set and still no conclusion. Professor Cathy Jrade lent me her computer and the final chapter finally emerged. I hope Professor Severino felt pride at the defense, because he had pulled me through the seven-year process. As I think back to those seven years, I can still hear his resonant voice quoting Camões's sonnet "Sete anos de pastor Jacó servia. . ." Those seven years (1981-88) that I worked with him "foram aos (m)eus olhos como poucos dias" to misquote the Bible from the story of Jacob, whose "servitude" was actually a labor of love.

M. Elizabeth Ginway
University of Georgia

*   *   *

I met Alex Severino in 1964 in the offices of the Fulbright Commission in Rio de Janeiro. I was spending the academic year 1964-65 as the Fulbright Lecturer in American Literature at what was then called the University of Brazil. Alex was lecturing at the university in Marília and meanwhile writing his dissertation on Fernando Pessoa at the University of São Paulo. He extended an invitation to me to visit Marília, but I was never able to fit it into my schedule. We were both participants in a seminar on American literature at São Paulo in January 1965. After that I don't believe we saw each other for several years. He was teaching at the University of Texas; I was back at South Carolina. But after he moved to Vanderbilt we saw each other either in Nashville, where I had a circle of friends from my days as a graduate student, or at conferences in Atlanta and elsewhere. I quickly became aware that he was greatly respected in Luso-Brazilian academic groups in the United States. His career has coincided with the great interest in Fernando Pessoa that has developed in this country, and certainly he has contributed a lot to it. It was a pleasure to hear, a few years ago, that he was being invited to Durban, South Africa, to lecture on his favorite subject; Durban, of course, was where Pessoa had spent his formative years. Alex has always been very generous with his time, especially when younger people have sought his assistance. He is one of the few of my contemporaries to whom I could easily apply the term "courtly"—such dignity of manners is infrequent these days.

Ashley Brown
Professor of English
University of South Carolina

PORTUGUESE AND LUSOPHONE
LITERATURE

"A Fala do Velho do Restelo": Heterodoxia?

Massaud Moisés

1. A "Fala do Velho do Restelo", que ocupa as estâncias 94-104 do Canto IV de *Os Lusíadas*, constitui um dos seus mais importantes episódios, razão por que os comentaristas da obra camoniana nela se debruçam com mais demora. E não só pela beleza intrínseca das palavras proferidas, senão também pelos problemas interpretativos que envolvem. Como explicar que, antes de Vasco da Gama e os seus comandados se lançarem ao mar em busca do caminho marítimo para as Indias, "um velho, de aspecto venerando" (est. 94) levantasse a voz para imprecar contra eles? Como admitir sem discussão que um discurso veemente se erguesse para atacar uma jornada heróica, precisamente numa epopéia destinada a exaltá-la? Contradição interna? E nesse caso como interpretá-la? Será que Camões falaria pela voz do Velho? Veiculará o seu rasgo tribunício uma censura à política expansionista de D. João III? Denunciará os males acarretados para a Nação pelas navegações e as conquistas no ultramar?[1]

Este breve ensaio, sem retomar e sem discutir as várias hipóteses arquitetadas em resposta a tais indagações, visa a sugerir a existência de uma outra faceta no quadro cênico proposto pelo verbo inflamado do Velho do Restelo. Situado "nas praias, entre a gente" (est. 94), ele desenrola uma longa invectiva, enfileirando argumentos que denotam uma retórica especial. Não é a retórica livresca, em que pese à notação mitológica (est. 103-104) e às reminiscências de Horácio, Ovídio, Aristófanes, Catão, Virgílio, Tibulo, do *Cancioneiro Geral*, de Sá de Miranda, Gil Vicente, da Bíblia e mesmo de *Orlando Furioso*.[2] Evidenciava, diz o poeta, um "saber só de experiências feito" (est. 94), o que faz supor, notadamente se atentarmos para o restritivo "só", que não ostentaria o conhecimento escolar nem o dos livros, e, sim, o que a vida ensina, quer por ter vivido muito, quer por ter observado outro tanto. E, tirante a hipótese de Camões falar pela voz do Velho, o que explicaria os traços cultos da arenga na praia do Restelo, o seu saber, ainda

23

quando acusasse influência clássica, seria todo caldeado pela experiência. Por seu intermédio, Camões negaria o saber pelo saber, o mero conhecimento dos livros. Orçaria, quem sabe, pelos 60 anos, idade em que, naqueles recuados tempos, um homem se consideraria ancião. Teria assim nascido pouco depois da conquista de Ceuta, em 1415, com que teve início a grande fase das navegações portuguesas; e teria, provavelmente, presenciado outras largadas de navios, nenhuma no entanto do porte da que demandava o extremo Oriente.

A experiência do Velho, além de oriunda do viver cotidiano, não seria exclusiva, única: viria de um saber que é do povo, em meio ao qual alçou "a voz pesada" (est. 94). Homem do povo, "homem da rua", contrariamente ao parecer de Hernani Cidade, estava ali como o seu representante, como o seu símbolo. Imaginá-lo de outra classe obrigaria a manobras forçadas para lhe justificar a presença junto aos populares; e, mais ainda, para lhe justificar as palavras de censura. Se a multidão era constituída de gente do povo e, quando muito, da burguesia embrionária dos comerciantes e artesãos, mas nunca a fidalguia e a nobreza, por meio do Velho fala o povo, cujo saber somente poderia ser o "de experiências feito". Ele é porta-voz do povo, uma vez que apenas o povo discordaria da partida das naus para as Indias, pelas conseqüências fáceis de profetizar ou de fantasiar. Não esqueçamos que ainda se estava na Idade Média, embora às vésperas do Renascimento, e as navegações já haviam deixado um saldo negativo em vidas e em matéria de relaxamento dos costumes.

2. O Velho é, assim, porta-voz popular numa época em que ainda não despontara o sol da Renascença: o seu discurso é medieval, quando muito pré-renascentista, pelas idéias antropocêntricas que ali esvoaçam, pelo apoio fugaz na mitologia grega e pelas reminiscências assinaladas. Na verdade, quanto mais descortinamos em sua fala os valores medievais, mais nos damos conta do seu caráter heterodoxo. Do prisma do homem medieval, a arremetida para as Indias seria sinônimo de aventura insensata, norteada pela

> /. . ./ glória de mandar, /. . ./ vã cobiça
> Desta vaidade, a quem chamamos Fama! (est. 95).

Para garantia de tão sombrio diagnóstico, já que o resultado eram "mortes, /. . ./ perigos, /. . ./ tormentas, /. . ./ crueldades" (est. 95), lançava mão do referido "saber só de experiências feito". A seqüência da fala parece mostrar que tal saber mergulha raízes na tradição cristã: a imprecação é de fundo moral, ético, religioso. Ele censura a ambição, o gosto da fama e da glória, tudo resumido na dilatação da Fé e do Império, que serve de emblema para a epopéia e que se tornaria apanágio do Portugal renascentista. Se é pela lei de Cristo que vão pelejar os navegantes, argumenta o Velho (est. 100), por que não combatem o mouro em Africa? Sua diatribe parece de um cristão inconformado com os rumos tomados pelos seguidores de Cristo: guiado por uma visão medieval de vida, opunha-se ao caráter mercantilista, utilitário e militante que a religião viria a assumir no século XVI, especialmente em sua feição jesuítica.

3. Por outro lado, como explicar que a fala do Velho seja a mais eloqüente de todas as que pontilham *Os Lusíadas*? A dúvida sobe de ponto se considerarmos que ele não era uma personagem histórica, nem mitológica, nem da estirpe dos navegantes, entrevistos como uma espécie de argonautas renascentes. É certo que Camões acabou criando, com o episódio, uma cena mítica, das mais impressionantes do poema, mas também é verdade que o protagonista não encerra nenhuma das características que, como representante de classe, poderiam distingui-lo do povo em Belém. Talvez resida justamente nesse aspecto o vigor que emana da sua figura, de resto sucintamente delineada, e de suas frases candentes.

A razão dessa força retórica, que no leitor de hoje ainda ressoa, provém do seu lastro emocional: repassa o discurso uma emoção escaldante, mais poderosa que a da réplica suplicante de Inês de Castro (Canto III, est. 120-135) ou da plangência amorosa do Adamastor (Canto V, est. 37-60). E tal emoção resulta de ele não falar por si, mas por todo o povo sem voz, como que fazendo reverberar em suas palavras toda a revolta surda e os padecimentos que trespassavam os populares reunidos na praia do Restelo (est. 88-93). Aquece as palavras do Velho uma indignação de fundo mais emotivo que racional: nutria, possivelmente, a esperança de comover os nasvegantes cujas

Mães, Esposas, Irmãs, que o temeroso
Amor mais desconfia, acrescentavam
A desesperação e frio medo
De já nos não tornar a ver tão cedo. (est. 89)

Como fosse insuficiente o espetáculo de dor, o Velho se dispôs a imprecar contra a expedição de Vasco da Gama, crente de que através da fala emocionada, de amplo espectro, à maneira do coro das tragédias gregas, como a crítica já assinalou, seria possível abalar a certeza dos navegantes. Em vão: as palavras não os enternecem, muito menos os demovem, enfebrecidos que estavam pelo anseio de riqueza, glória e fama.

4. Por que Camões o fez? Não haveria contradição nessa passagem, dado que a epopéia se propunha a exaltar a façanha de Vasco da Gama?

Salta aos olhos que o episódio funciona como contraste, contraponto dialético do arcabouço renascentista do poema. Por seu intermédio, o poeta pretenderia reforçar o sentido heróico do feito lusitano: os navegantes arrostariam, nas palavras oraculares do Velho, os inúmeros perigos do mar, razão suficiente para lhe justificar a verrina anti-expansionista. Mas também, ao menos implicitamente, a sua fala constrói uma dificuldade de última hora que os navegantes tiveram que enfrentar. É muito plausível que as suas ponderações tão-somente ecoassem o sentimento do povo, igualmente norteado por um "saber só de experiências feito", ou seja, experimentado de sobejo em circunstâncias semelhantes, mas tendo de calar-se por motivos óbvios.

Escudado no seu porte olímpico e na idade provecta, o Velho arvora-se em legítimo advogado do povo, sem medo algum de sofrer a punição correspondente a tal ousadia. No movimento pendular, de um lado ele exorta os navegantes ao bom senso; de outro, a sua imprecação consiste em mais um obstáculo que os navegantes deparariam antes de cortar as amarras e abandonar-se ao desconhecido. Ultrapassando os argumentos emotivos que acabavam de ouvir, contrapunham-lhes o seu reverso, ou seja, a mesma ambição e cobiça, execradas pelo Velho, como resgate para a consciência. Daí que o discurso, não obstante recamado de ardente eloqüência, tenha sido inútil, mesmo porque, se houvesse alcançado o seu objetivo, nem haveria a conquista das Indias, nem a epopéia que Camões engendrou. Não esqueçamos de sublinhar que tais hipóteses são falaciosas, inclusive pelo fato de a figura do Velho do Restelo não ser histórica: apenas no interior do poema é que se lhe explica a presença, fazendo supor um intuito dialético por parte do poeta, evidente no recheio das palavras do Velho e na inutilidade do seu generoso esforço.

Outra força, ou outro ideal, impelia os navegantes. O povo, que emprega o Velho como seu fiel intérprete, ainda se conduzia por padrões medievais, e por isso não podia compreender que os seus patrícios se atirassem aos perigos marítimos por dinheiro, glória e fama, sujeitos a morrer de mil formas. Deixar o certo pelo duvidoso, a ordem pelo acaso, a paz pela guerra, cultivando "em tanta quantidade / O desprezo da vida"? (est.99) E se o motivo fosse combater os incréus,

> Não tens junto contigo o Ismaelita,
> Com quem sempre terás guerras sobejas?
> Não segue ele do Arábio a Lei maldita,
> Se tu pola de Cristo só pelejas? (est. 100)

Nenhum argumento estremece por um instante sequer os nautas determinados. E com isso o enaltecimento da Pátria, que constitui o fulcro do poema, sai engrandecido, graças ao confronto entre o velho e o novo, o passado e o progresso, entre o medieval e o renascentista. E não importa que o tempo acabasse dando razão ao exaltado orador popular: os perigos enfrentados, as mortes sofridas não impediram que Vasco da Gama arribasse às Indias e que Portugal se tornasse o colossal império do século XVI. E quando o comandante da missão ao Oriente retoma a narrativa, nos primeiros versos do Canto V, ocorre-lhe dizer que

> Estas sentenças tais o velho honrado
> Vociferando estava, quando abrimos
> As asas ao sereno e sossegado
> Vento, e do porto amado nos partimos.

onde o reconhecimento da solene figura do Velho é chocantemente contrastada pelo verbo "vociferar", que diz bem do modo como ele e os demais navegantes recebiam a melancólica saudação de despedida. Seria demasiado imaginoso entrever, nas palavras acrimoniosas do grande herói, qualquer coisa como uma acusação? Vasco da Gama dá margem a se acreditar que considerava o venerando orador um colérico, um néscio, um senil. E assim, com um julgamento superficial e preconceituoso, vencia o derradeiro entrave à sua peregrinação ao Oriente.

5. Falaria Camões pela boca do Velho do Restelo? Se bem lhe interpretamos as palavras, o texto sugere uma resposta negativa: afigura-se contraditório que ali se transmitisse a voz do poeta; negar-se-ia o tom e o sentido grandiloquente da epopéia, bem como a sua maior razão de ser. Na análise desse pormenor, é comum que nos lembremos do epílogo de Os Lusíadas, visto que a fala do Velho e as palavras finais de Camões semelham ligadas por um fio ideológico. Acontece que essa aproximação, sendo necessária por imposição da analogia, é ilusória: ali, exprime-se o povo através de uma figura simbólica, figura de sacerdote beatificado por jejuns e penitências, silhueta de eremita, talvez concebido à luz dos velhos apóstolos bíblicos; aqui, o poeta derrama-se em lamento, não pela viagem às Indias (o que o situaria no mesmo nível do Velho do Restelo e comprometeria toda a mensagem ufanista do poema), mas pela decadência do império:

> No mais, Musa, no mais, que a Lira tenho
> Destemperada e a voz enrouquecida,
> E não do canto, mas de ver que venho

Cantar a gente surda e endurecida.
O favor com que mais se acende o engenho
Não no dá a pátria, não, que está metida
No gosto da cobiça e na rudeza
De uma austera, apagada e vil tristeza.

Por que "gente surda e endurecida"? Por não ter ouvido as advertências
judiciosas do Velho do Restelo, ou por que, "metida/No gosto da cobiça"
etc., naufraga em luxo e ócio indigno, assim ocasionando a decadência do
império? Se a cobiça é censurada nas duas passagens, diverso é o contexto
e o significado: ali, a cobiça incitava à viagem ao Oriente, "donde vem
tudo, o dia e a fé", diria mais tarde Fernando Pessoa; aqui, denuncia-se a
cobiça, que se tornara regra de costumes na Pátria. Poderia Camões invectivar
a cobiça nos mesmos termos do Velho do Restelo sem tombar noutra
contradição, negadora do sentido exortativo do poema? A mesma cobiça
que gerou o império, agora o destrói: é isso que o poeta lamenta.

Na voz do Velho repercute o sentimento do povo, que não atina
com a razão da viagem, pois paga com a vida de muitos dos seus o preço do
cometimento, nem pode avaliar a importância que terá para o
desenvolvimento da Nação a chegada marítima às Indias. Escusa lembrar
que tampouco auferiria dos lucros que a empresa pudesse amealhar. Tudo
se passa como se alguém, em nossos dias, bradasse em praça pública,
verberando o crime de gastar somas vultosas em usinas nucleares, viagens
em ônibus espaciais, sondas interplanetárias etc., enquanto milhões morrem
à míngua, de fome e de miséria. Nessa perspectiva, o Velho representaria o
pensamento retrógrado, assim como alguém que hoje agisse desse modo;
ser progressista, colocar-se na linha da vanguarda, mirando o futuro com os
olhos da utopia, consistiria em optar pelos padrões renascentistas emergentes,
de que o caminho por mar que levasse às Indias era o signo mais perfeito,
até porque repleto de sentido mítico, assim como o progressismo da
atualidade pressuporia uma dose de utopia, ou de antevisão idealizante dos
séculos vindouros. Não percamos de vista que o paradoxo implícito nesse
quadro, em que as posições ideológicas se diriam maquiavelicamente
invertidas, não surpreenderá a quem tiver em mente as linhas cruzadas e as
ambiguidades da cultura e do pensamento ao longo do século XVI.

Um argumento que parece fortalecer essa hipótese vem de onde
menos se espera: de Baco. No concílio submarino, que se organiza logo
depois que as naus, arrancando de Melinde, singram na direção de Calicute,
Baco toma a palavra para obstar o prosseguimento da viagem. E diz:

Vistes que, com grandíssima ousadia,
Foram já cometer o Céu Supremo;
Vistes aquela insana fantasia
De tentarem o mar com vela e remo;
Vistes, e ainda vemos cada dia,
Soberbas e insolências tais, que temo
Que do Mar e do Céu, em poucos anos,
Venham Deuses a ser, e nós, humanos.

como se reproduzisse a chama oratória do Velho do Restelo: o argumento é semelhante, a razão invocada gravita na mesma órbita, mas o objetivo é diverso. Baco tentativa inutilmente opor dificuldades à chegada dos nautas lusitanos às praias indianas, pois que lá reinava soberano. Encobrindo o seu verdadeiro desígnio, Baco verbera a "grandiosíssima ousadia" e a "insana fantasia", à maneira do homem do Restelo.

6. Com a diferença de que a fala do Velho ressuma de tal emoção que se diria ensombrada por sentimentos metafísicos, tangenciada por qualquer coisa como o fantasma da senectude e da insanidade. E nesse caso Vasco da Gama e os seus companheiros de aventuras teriam percebido de pronto o que se passava na mente do orador de bíblico perfil: como hostilizar a viagem, e os seus propósitos, se ela representava o progresso? Na sua voz, a Idade Média emotiva, cristã, cavaleiresca, então nos estertores, falaria mais alto, antes que a Renascença entrasse em cheio em terras portuguesas. Derradeira e veemente tentativa de impedir que uma nova era se abrisse para a Europa e o mundo. Como censurar a expedição ao Oriente, em sã consciência, se ela significava o progresso, o futuro etc.?, indagaria o herói da epopéia, num recanto obscuro de sua mente.

O tempo virá a dizer que os navegantes tinham alguma razão, assim como o Velho reunia as suas, na medida em que o progresso custará muitíssimo em vidas e em valores. Mais catastrófico seria perder tudo quanto os navegantes conquistaram, — pensaria Camões —, mas isso nos reenvia para o desfecho de *Os Lusíadas* e para as forças que provocaram a derrocada do império: é uma outra e complexa história, que nos obrigaria a reavaliar os movimentos culturais do século XVI, centrados nas disputas entre a Reforma e a Contra-Reforma, com todas as suas amplas e profundas conseqüências.

Notas

[1] A respeito, ver Cidade 123-126, onde se encontra uma resenha das principais teorias acerca da interpretação do episódio do Velho do Restelo. Ver também Saraiva 123-125, Tavani 77-84, Melo 341-345.

[2] Tavani 82-83.

[3] Cidade 125.

Obras Citadas

Cidade, Hernani. *Luís de Camões. II. O Épico.* Lisboa: Revista da Faculdade de Letras, 1953.

Melo, Gladstone Chaves de. "Uma Interpretação do Episódio do Velho do Restelo". Coimbra: *Revista da Universidade de Coimbra* 33 (1985): 341-345.

Saraiva, António José. *Luís de Camões.* Lisboa: Publicações Europa-América, 1959.

Tavani, Giuseppe. "A Proposito del Vechio del Restelo." *Studi Camoniani 80.* Ed. Giulia Lanciani. L'Aquila: Japadre Editore, 1980.

Binary Structure in the
Auto Da Mofina Mendes

J. Richard Andrews

One of the interesting problems in Gil Vicente's *Auto da Mofina Mendes* concerns its organization. The problem is already evident in the naming of the work. In the sermon-prologue (131 lines) that introduces the *Auto*, the mock priest tells us it is called "os mysterious da Virgem." But the popularity of the Mofina-episode resulted in the Mofina Mendes title which appears in the *Copilação de todalas obras*. From this difference between the internal and the external titles, one might suppose that the work offers a confusion of focus, with the subject being split between the Virgin and the shepherdess Mofina. Such is not, however, the case.

The *Auto* is a Christmas play, first performed for King John III at the Christmas matins in 1543. Since it comes at the end of Gil Vicente's career, being his next-to-last play, we might assume that it demonstrates a creative skill built up through many years of experience. It does. Although this is not the place to substantiate this claim fully, the following remarks will show that the playwright was very much in control of blocking out his material. We notice, for example, that the play uses two performance spaces, which I shall call the rear stage and the front stage, also imagining that the action takes place predominantly on opposite sides of these spaces; say, for example, on the left of the rear stage and on the right of the front stage. These two performance areas deal with two orientations for the audience's attention, the hieratic and the pastoral, with the Virgin dominating the rear stage and Mofina being featured in part of the action on the front one.

The play begins on the rear stage. Four angels playing musical instruments enter, followed by Mary and her four Virtues: Poverty, Humility, Faith, and Prudence. After sitting down, the Virtues report to Mary on their reading concerning the prophesies about, and the prefigurations of, a

Virgin who will give birth to the Messiah. The Angel Gabriel enters, greets Mary, and announces that she has been chosen to fill the Virgin-mother role. After expressions of confusion, Mary acquiesces to the will of God. Gabriel leaves while the four Angels play music, after which the curtain is drawn on the rear stage.

At this point the shepherd André enters the front stage, lamenting the loss of his father's donkey. Next Payo Vaz enters looking for Mofina Mendes, a shepherdess in his employ. In the ensuing conversation about her, it becomes evident that she is Misfortune personified (as her name indicates). The shepherd Pessival now enters and turns the conversation again to the problem of the lost donkey. Payo Vaz suggests that Mofina Mendes probably knows its whereabouts and has André call her on-stage. After she enters, the play focuses entirely on the disasters that have befallen the animals in her care and on her demands for pay. Payo Vaz, to avoid further ruin, finally pays her off with a pot of oil, which Mofina manages to break after imagining her rise to wealth, marriage, and happiness through its sale. She exits with a song prophesying human unhappiness. Three shepherds now enter, and one of them reports that he has found André's donkey. The shepherds lie down on stage and go to sleep.

Now the curtain opens again on the rear stage and the Virgin, her four Virtues, and Joseph prepare for the soon-to-be-born Christ. After the birth takes places, the action on the rear stage ceases with a cradle song sung by the Virtues.

At this point, an Angel comes onto the front stage, awakens the sleeping shepherds, and sends them to pay homage to the Virgin and the Christ child. The play ends with music, singing, and dancing.

In considering the material summarized here, scholars have tended to see in it a three-part organization. Carolina Michaëlis de Vasconcelos, for example, described the play as an "auto de simbolismo religioso em cujas duas cenas (Anunciação e Natal) está entremetido o . . . Passo profano da Morfina Mendes."[1] Oscar de Pratt wrote "Este auto é um lindo tríptico quinhentista."[2] And António José Saraiva wrote, "O episódio da Mofina Mendes está colocado entre as duas partes simbólicas da obra."[3] It seems to me however, that a more detailed consideration of the organization of the auto requires a different analysis.

Gil Vicente himself has invited us to recognize a two-part division in the play. The prologic priest, after explaining that the audience should consider

       isto ser contemplação
       fóra da historia geral
       mas fundada en devação,

describes the entrance of the Virgin's Virtues and then says:

> E virá a Virgem com ellas,
> com mui fermosa apparencia.
> Será logo o fundamento
> tratar de *saudação*
> e depois deste sermão
> hum pouco do *nacimento*.

This statement concerning the *nacimento* is later verified in the *didascália* that heads the Nativity scene: "e logo se segue a segunda parte, que he hũa breve contemplação sobre o Nacimento."

Gil Vicente has, then, clearly marked out a two-part structure for the work, has named the parts with regard to their principal action (the Annunciation and the Nativity), and has indicated the point of demarcation between them. What he has not told us, and what we must find out, is how he handled the internal organization of these two parts. It is immediately evident that he divided each part into two scenes, with the first scene of each part dealing with the divine world and the second scene of each dealing with the shepherd world. But the binary segmentation does not end there.

Looking at the first part (the one the mock priest called *saudação*), we see that scene one is itself divided into two segments, the first dealing with the delineation of a Virgin-mother role and the second with the identification of Mary as that Virgin. Each of these segments is in turn divided into two subsegments. In the first segment, the first subsegment presents the prophesies and prefigurations (72 lines) while the second presents Mary's reaction to those prophecies (10 lines). In the second segment (which begins with Gabriel's entrance), the first subsegment presents Gabriel's announcement and the Virgin's humble confusion (95 lines), while the second presents her acquiescence (5 lines).

Turning now to scene two of the first part (the shepherd scene, performed on the front stage), we find that it also is divided into two segments, one dealing with the lost donkey and the other with Mofina. But it is to be noted that the Mofina segment is embedded (or nested) inside the lost-donkey segment. Since the lost-donkey segment thus serves as a frame for the Mofina segment, it is obvious that it is divided into two subsegments. Its first subsegment (20 lines) presents the loss of the donkey, and its second one (15 lines) presents the report of its having been found. Inserted between these two discontinuous subsegments is the second segment, the part of the play that features Mofina Mendes. Its first subsegment is further divided into two sections, the first of which prepares for Mofina's appearance (60 lines) and the second of which brings her on stage where she presents her report of services rendered and her request for pay (50 lines); the second subsegment of the Mofina segment presents the pot of oil sequence (49 lines).[4]

The first segment of the first part consists of 18 lines, the second of 194 (see Figure 1).

Figure 1.

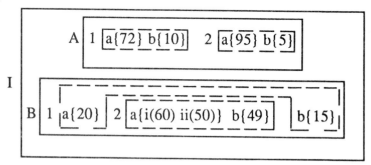

I = First Part = Annunciation
   A = hieratic scene = 182 lines
     1 = characterization of the Virgin
      a = 72 lines = prophecies and prefigurations
      b = 10 lines = Mary's reaction
     2 = annunciation
      a = 95 lines = Gabriel's announcement
      b = 5 lines = Mary's acquiescence
   B = shepherd scene = 194 lines
     1 = lost donkey
      a = 20 lines = report of loss
      b = 15 lines = report of recovery
     2 = Mofina
      a = characterization of Mofina
       i = 60 lines = preparation for Mofina's entrance
       ii = 50 lines = Mofina on stage
      b = 49 lines = pot of oil episode

Looking now at part two of the *Auto* (the part the mock priest referred to as "hum pouco do nacimento"), we see that its first scene is divided into three segments, the first deals with the imminent birth, the second with the search for light (a motif centered on the metaphorical meaning of Christ: ". . .o Senhor qu'ha da nacer / he a mesma claridade"), and the third with the call for praise for Christ. Here the third is embedded in the second and the second in the first. The first segment is divided into two subsegments, which in their discontinuity serve as the frame for the other segments. Its first subsegment consists of an address by Mary to the unborn Christ (12 lines), and its final subsegment presents the birth (marked by a baby's cry) and lullaby (the words for which are not given). Although this second subsegment is lineless, the stage business it presents is climactic to the work. The second segment is also divided into two discontinuous subsegments: the search for light (23 lines) and the aftermath of the search (96 lines). In contrast to the two discontinuous segments, the third segment (the centrally embedded one) has no subsegments, being a psalm in which the Virgin, Prudence, and Humility call on all things to praise Christ (31 lines, with 7 occurrences of *louvae*, 5 of *laudate,* 1 of *lauda*, and 1 of *louvar*).[5]

And finally, when we turn to scene two of the second part (i.e., the shepherd scene, with attention again focused on the front stage, but with no mention of the curtain being closed on the rear stage), we find that it consists of two segments, the first of which deals with the summoning of the shepherds (41 lines), while the second suggests the movement of the shepherds from the front stage to the rear stage (30 lines, starting with "Pastores, ide a Belem"). The final *didascália* indicates that the play ends with the Angels playing their instruments, the Virtues singing (the words for their song are not given), and the shepherds dancing.

The first segment of the second part consists of 162 lines, the second of 71 (see Figure 2).

Figure 2.

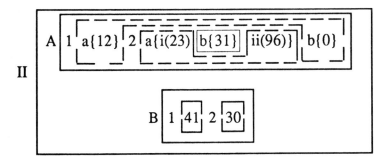

II = Second Part = Nativity
 A = hieratic scene = 162 lines
  1 = nativity
   a = 12 lines = Mary's address to baby in the womb
   b = [baby's cry; lullaby]
  2 = praise for Christ
   a = the problem of light
    i = 23 lines = Faith sent for light
    ii = 96 lines = Faith's report
   b = 31 lines = psalm calling for praise
 B = shepherd scene = 71 lines
  a = 41 lines = summoning of shepherds
  b = 30 lines = trip to manger

This generalized description of the parts, scenes, and segments makes it evident that Gil Vicente has exploited the binary principle on both the upper and lower levels of the work's structure and has used a chiasmic arrangement in the sequencing of the segments, using in the first part concatenation and embedding, followed in the second part by embedding and concatenation. But as the line count for each of the various parts indicates, this binary segmentation is not mechanical. There is no attempt to give an equal number of lines to parts, to scenes, to segments, or to subsegments. Nor should it be thought that this binary segmentation represents an appeal to conflictual opposition. One of the most characteristic aspects of Gil Vicente's theater is the avoidance of presenting conflict.[6] This play is no exception. The closest we come to struggle is found in Mary's inability to accept the announcement that she is the one chosen to fill the role of the Virgin-mother. And Gil Vicente has refused to present even that struggle dramatically, since he has played down the function of the character Humility, even to the point of emptying that allegorical figure of any real meaning.[7]

Gil Vicente's interest in the binary principle is further witnessed by his handling of the relationship between the rear-stage scenes of Annunciation and Nativity. As is implicit in the Biblical source story (Luke 1 and 2), the latter scene serves as the fulfillment of the former. Gil Vicente has repeated this promise-and-fulfillment relationship on a smaller scale in the first scene by having its second segment, the identification of Mary as Virgin-mother-to-be, come as a fulfillment of the first scene, the delineating of a Virgin-mother role.

It is this interest in the binary principle that also stands behind the relationship between the first and second scenes of the first part, that is, the relationship between the Annunciation scene and the shepherd scene that includes the Mofina segment. The contrast between the two scenes is severe. Not only is there a shift from the rear stage to the front stage, with a total change in characters that involves a shift from high tone to low tone as the hieratic, "aristocratic" (the Virgin is dressed as a queen), serious quality of the first scene is replaced by the pastoral, comic quality of the second, there is also a shift in time placement, with the first scene being located in the past (with tendencies to a-temporalism) and the second in the "present," shown in the mention of contemporary events (the sack of Rome, the capture of Francis I of France, and Charles V's threat against the Turks) and the use of anachronistic exclamations (such as *nome de Jesu*), in spite of the fact that these shepherds will later visit the new-born Christ child. Furthermore, the religious symbolism of the first is replaced by a folkloric symbolism in the second, a contrast accompanied by a change in allegorical technique: the first scene personifies personal moral characteristics (that is, Mary's four Virtues) while the second scene personifies an abstract concept (that is, Mofina as Misfortune Itself). A final contrast lies in the difference in the pace and strategy of speeches and the interaction of characters in the two scenes. For example, in regard to entrances, the first scene brings characters on in a group while the second brings them on one at a time.

Such a large number of contrasts should not be seen as putting in jeopardy the unity of the play. Given Gil Vicente's aesthetic convictions, these contrasts actually justify the juxtaposition of the two scenes. In other words, the purpose of the juxtaposition of these scenes lies precisely in their contrastive nature. And the center of the contrast lies in the figures of the Virgin and Mofina. This can be easiy demonstrated by taking into account the following considerations concerning the deliberate strategy behind Gil Vicente's artistry.

The presence of shepherds in the play was required by the Biblical source. But that source only justifies their appearance in the second part, that is, in the scene following the Nativity scene. The introduction of the shepherd scene following the Annunciation scene is therefore totally a matter of Gil Vicente's invention, and it comes in answer to his interest in the structural principle of a binary arrangement of parts. This is true not only with regard to the abstract level of structure but also with regard to the concrete level of meaning. The content of the first shepherd scene is centered upon the lost donkey and Mofina, with the latter brought into the

play by way of the former. The strategy behind this is somewhat obvious
and its implementation graceless. The Mofina segment carries the thematic
burden of the second scene, but since Mofina cannot remain in the play
after the end of the segment (her figure represents a contradiction to the
Christ principle), Gil Vicente needed, for the sake of continuity and
harmony, to motivate her departure from the stage. He forced the shepherd
situation to serve as the Mofina segment's container by inventing the lost-
donkey segment. Being more intimately a part of the shepherd world, this
lost-donkey problem can be resolved before the shepherds go to sleep and
still leave André on stage to be awakened by the summoning Angel. The
degree of force Gil Vicente used in putting this strategy into action is
evident in the fact that André, who calls Mofina on stage to ask her about
his donkey, never speaks to her after her entrance; furthermore, the lost
donkey is never mentioned in the Mofina segment. The excuse for Mofina's
entrance is, therefore, not justified. . .not, at least, on the surface level.

There is, however, a thematic motivation. The point of the lost
donkey appears in the lines:

> E s'ella não parecer
> atás per noite fechada,
> não temos hoje prazer. . .

The loss of happiness is the frame segment's thematic link with the Mofina
segment, since, as Mofina's final song shows, human unhappiness is the
moral of that segment:

> Por mais que a dita m'engeite,
> pastores, não me deis guerra
> que todo o humano deleite
> como o meu pote d'azeite
> ha de dar consigo em terra.[8]

Mofina Mendes, as Misfortune personified, is a figure abandoned by *a dita*
("good luck," "happiness"). Not only is she unfortunate and unhappy
herself, she brings misfortune and unhappiness to others.[9] Her momentary
happiness, when she plans the wealth to be gained from the pot of oil, is
illusory. She stands, then, in contrast to the Virgin, who is represented as
the fortunate one, the one chosen by God to bring hope and happiness to the
soul of man. Gabriel greets Mary with:

> Oh! Deus te salve, Maria,
> cheia de graça graciosa
> dos pecadores abrigo!
> goza-te com alegria. . .

In contrast to Mofina, Mary is *ditosa*. It is Prudence who offers us the key to understanding the relationship that Gil Vicente established between the two contrasting figures when she says:

> He tão zeloso o Senhor,
> que quererá o seu estado
> dar ao mundo per favor,
> per hũa Eva peccador,
> hũa virgem sem peccado.

While Mofina does not tempt with forbidden fruit, she is nevertheless an Eve-figure in that she brings misfortune and unhappiness to mankind. The Virgin, on the other hand, brings the possibility of joy.[10] Because of her, the shepherd André can say to another shepherd:

> . . .vamos ver os prazeres
> que eu nem tu nunca viste.

The contrast, then, serves to highlight the meaning of the Virgin. Gil Vicente had the prologic priest say that the work is a "contemplação" and refer to the Annunciation scene as a "sermão." In the *didascália* before the Nativity scene, that scene is called "hũa breve contemplação sobre o Nacimento." These descriptive labels suggest that Gil Vicente meant the audience to pay attention to the meaning latent in these scenes rather than to their surface action. One way he had of bringing the meaning of the first part into focus was to juxtapose the scenes of the Virgin and Mofina.

It is interesting that we have a test of the importance for Gil Vicente of this contrast of the Virgin and Mofina. His two-part division places the Mofina segment in the first part, while logically the shepherd scene should belong in the second part since it is chronologically associated with the Nativity because it obviously takes place earlier on the same night as Christ's birth while the Annunciation occurs months earlier (the *didascália* makes this clear: "Juntão-se os Pastores *pera o tempo do nacimento*"). In other words, chronological considerations would lead to an unbalanced one-versus-three arrangement, with scene one in the first part and scenes two, three, and four in the second part. Gil Vicente has contradicted that time-governed arrangement and has chosen a meaning-governed two-versus-two grouping.

But, in spite of his interest in the *contemplação* project, which is seen in the careful strategic manipulation of his material as well as in the heavier investment in lines for the hieratic segments (344 lines) than in those for the shepherd segments (265 lines), Gil Vicente apparently overplayed his hand when he, perhaps unwittingly, made Mofina a more interesting figure than the Virgin, so that the logic of the structuring of the parts and the symbolic function of their interaction came to be overlooked, if possibly not by the royal audience, at least by the populace.

Notes

[1] Carolina Michaëlis de Vasconcelos, *Notas Vicentinas* (Lisboa), p. 467, m. 471.

[2] Oscar de Pratt, *Gil Vicente: Notas e comentários* (Lisboa), p. 27.

[3] António José Saraiva, *Gil Vicente e o Fim do Teatro Medieval* (Lisboa, 1942), p. 95.

[4] An alternative way of looking at the Mofina segment would have the first subsegment deal with the preparation for Mofina's appearance (60 lines) and the second subsegment deal with her on-stage presence, with the latter consisting of two sections, the first being her report and request for pay (50 lines) and the second presenting the pot of oil episode (49 lines). In this case the structure would be "a + (b + c)," while the structure described in the main text is "(a + b) + c." The latter was chosen as preferable because of the consistency between the "a" and "b" episodes (the delineation of Mofina as Misfortune).

[5] In addition to the embedding employed both here and in the first shepherd scene, we can see Gil Vicente's fondness for the device of embedding one part in another, in one other, albeit small, instance. In the Annunciation segment, the Virgin seeks Faith's opinion, but before she finishes speaking, Gabriel interrupts her (8 lines). The Virgin responds to him with something of a put-down (2 lines: "Anjo, perdoae-me vos, / que com a Fé quero fallar."), and then continues speaking to Faith (1 line). The pattern of exchange is:

```
        V ——> F (quandary speech)
  G ——> V          (interruption)
  G <—— V          ("put-down")
        ——> F (quandary speech resumed)
      V <—— F (answer to quandary speech)
```

[6] See J. Richard Andrews, "The Artistry of the Plays of Gil Vicente." Diss. Princeton U., 1953. Also see René Pedro Garay, *Gil Vicente and the Development of the Comedia*, Chapel Hill: The University of North Carolina Press, 1988.

[7] Notice that Humility's speech praising the Virgin after Joseph's and Prudence's return without a light would better have been given to Prudence since it is devoid of humility.

[8] António José Saraiva, *op. cit.*, p. 95, quotes these lines as pointing to the symbolic meaning of the pot of oil. It is a symbol of the "mundo movediço e fútil" in contrast to the "simbolismo imóvel, uniplano e irrepresentativo que exprime o mundo da 'resplandecente glória'. . .essa disparidade constituía. . .a própria substncia da unidade do conjunto."

[9] The moral implied by Gil Vicente's use of the fable of the pot of oil is not the usual one of "Don't count your chickens before they are hatched." Sadness and unhappiness have replaced foolish anticipation.

[10] It is interesting to compare Gil Vicente's handling of the antithesis of a source-of-joy-figure (Mary) and a source-of-unhappiness-figure (Mofina) here with his handling of similarly antithetical humility-figure (Mary) and pride-figure (Cassandra) in another of his Christmas plays, the *Auto da Sibila Cassandra*.

Contemporary Responses to the Fragments of a Modenist Self: On the Various Editions of Fernando Pessoa's *Livro do Desassossego*

Ellen Sapega

In the ten years that have passed since its original publication, Fernando Pessoa's *Livro do Desassossego* has received more international critical attention than any other facet of the author's work. This is due, in part, to the Book's relatively recent appearance for the more than five hundred prose fragments that constitute the *Livro* were published only in 1982, more than four decades after Pessoa's death. Although initially projected for publication in the 1960s, in an edition to be organized by Jorge de Sena, overwhelming limitations of an apparently technical order forced the editor to abandon his plans. After many years of anticipation, these fragments came to light at a time when Pessoa's work had achieved great popularity and renown. This led scholars, critics, and readers of Pessoa's poetry to eagerly turn to the *Livro do Desassossego* in hopes of finding, if not a key, at least a new point of entry from which to approach the labyrinth that is Pessoa's poetic universe.

While general consensus has it that these fragments consist of a restatement, in a different voice and a different genre, of the same general ontological questions regarding truth and fiction that are raised time and again in Pessoa's poetry, the *Livro do Desassossego* has nonetheless been the center of some of the most heated polemics taking place in the field of Pessoan criticism today. At the time of its appearance, such well known scholars as Jacinto do Prado Coelho and Georg Rudolf Lind disagreed publicly as to the most appropriate form in which to make these *inéditos* available to the reading public. More recently, Teresa Sobral Cunha and Richard Zenith have argued quite vehemently about the identity of the book's narrator, Bernardo Soares, as well as quarreling over the both the quantity and the organization of the material that may be attributed to him. Bearing in mind that only eleven of the book's 520 fragments were published by Pessoa during his lifetime, the fervor of this debate is not surprising.

As it openly tests the limits of genre, the *Livro do Desassossego* implicates the reader in a series of disquieting uncertainties that must be understood in light of several fundamental questions that bear upon both the identity and the intentions of its author. Due to its very incompleteness, any serious reading of the *Livro do Desassossego* forces the critic to assume a stance of personal responsibility for his or her understanding of the book's content and structure. In the following pages, I will demonstrate how several different readings of the book result when one chooses to foreground elements of the text that refer to the speaker's identity, to what the speaker has to say, and finally, to how the speaker says it. The adoption of these perspectives allows the reader to privilege certain aspects of the text, while down-playing others, thereby signaling the need for a significantly different approach to the organization of the Book's contents. I will then show how this variation is reflected in the many different Portuguese versions of the book that have appeared to date and has, by extension, had a great impact on the three English editions of the book that were published in 1991.[1]

Given both the incomplete and the unpublished nature of the *Livro do Desassossego*, a case may logically be made in favor of ordering its contents in a chronological sequence. In theory, this ordering would allow the reader a sort of "window" from which to accompany the creative process that motivated the book's production. As we shall see, however, this type of organization only serves, at best, to call attention to the many questions that the reader must face concerning the identity of the book's narrator, as well as the fundamentally indeterminate nature of its contents and structure.

First off, one must note that any attempt at imposing a temporal structure on the book's fragments implicitly posits the text as pertaining to the genre of the *diário íntimo*, that is, as constituting a narrative whose apparent point would be to present the reader with a portrait of an individual consciousness. One of the most literal examples of this type of presentation may be found on the front and back covers of a recent translation of the *Livro do Desassossego* by Margaret Jull Costa that appeared in Great Britain last year. I would like to use this edition as a point of departure for my comments on the *Livro do Desassossego* for, it is, in my opinion, the most problematic version of the book to appear to date.

Here, the book's publishers would have us believe that Soares' narrative reflects an individual's perceptions of a more or less plausible or credible reality. After being informed that this book constitutes "The most beautiful diary of the century," the reader is treated to the following summary of the its contents: "Seated at his desk in Lisbon's Rua dos Douradores,

Bernardo Soares, an assistant bookkeeper, writes his diary—a self-deprecating reflection on the sheer distance between the loftiness of his feelings and the humdrum reality of his everyday life." Confidently accepting the narrative authority of Bernardo Soares, this edition clearly seeks to present the text as consisting of a strait forward piece of prose fiction. In a similar gesture, the book's purported verisimilitude is bolstered by the inclusion of a map of Lisbon's *Baixa*, so as to orient the reader unfamiliar with the physical characteristics of the area that Soares frequented.

By privileging the physical, professional, and psychological circumstances that give rise to the protagonist's thoughts, an "innocent" reader of this edition would quite rightly seek to understand the book's contents by appealing directly to the informational aspects of the narrative. These expectations are then met in opening pages, where, in the preface that Pessoa drafted for the *Livro do Desassossego* the reader is presented with a mimetically conceived description of the fictional narrator:

> Era um homem que aparentava trinta anos,
> magro, mais alto que baixo, curvado exageradamente
> quando sentado, mas menos quando de pé, vestido com
> um certo desleixo não inteiramente desleixado. Na
> face pálida e sem interesse de feições, um ar de
> sofrimento não acrescentava interesse, e era difícil
> definir que espécie de sofrimento esse ar indicava—
> parecia indicar vários, privações, angústias, e aquele
> sofrimento que nasce da indiferença, que provém de
> ter sofrido muito.[2]

In the pages that follow this preface, it is not difficult to seek confirmation of Bernardo Soares's existence as a more or less individualized character with a "believable" narrative voice. Indeed, most of the *Livro do Desassossego*'s fragments are frequently supplemented by descriptions of Soares's immediate surroundings and the regular inclusion of proper names, as well as allusions to time and place, situate Soares's narrative in an easily conceived external world that serves as both referent and backdrop to his private musings:

> Hoje, em um dos devaneios sem propósito nem
> dignidade que constituem grande parte da substância
> espiritual da minha vida, imaginei-me liberto para
> sempre da Rua dos Douradores, do patrão Vasques, do

guarda-livros Moreira, dos empregados todos, do moço,
do garoto e do gato. (p. 32)

As he registers the activities that fill his days, Bernardo Soares is remarkably
successful in informing his readers of the trivial or mundane details of his
existence. Due to its very banality, however, we are constantly diverted from
these details because Soares's life contains very little that holds our attention.

Thus, while a good portion of the *Livro do Desassossego* is clearly
triggered by the narrator's apprehension of place or event, one cannot help but
recognize that the most remarkable characteristics of this prose have very
little to do with the contingencies and constraints of the narrator's reality. At
best, the self-portrait Soares offers in the pages of his diary is a static one,
devoid of the psychological motivations or the emotional depth that we
normally ask of diaristic prose. In most cases, Soares's frequent descriptions
of exterior reality only serve to invoke or reflect his deeper, more poetic or
philosophical thoughts. As a result, the passage of time, marked by an
accompanying change in the narrating protagonist, is all but absent from the
pages of the book. This text, or collection of texts, clearly does not adhere to
the traditional dictates of diaristic prose and, when pressed to inquire as to the
narrative point of these passages, one may only conclude that the book's
narrator seems to be variously intent on reflecting upon an idea (essay) or
understanding an event as metaphor (prose poetry).

In light of this tendency for Soares's prose to resemble either the
formal dictates of a personal essay or to take on the lyrical stance of poetic
prose, it is clear that the aim of this book is not that of inventing or
reproducing the contours of an individual consciousness acting in an historical
world. Rather, the author's intent apparently resides in the designation of an
existential problematic which exceeds the constraints of time and place and is
situated, as it were, in the realm of dream. Soares's desire to embrace a reality
that can only be found in the pages of his journal is corroborated by many of
the fragments that bear witness to his need to invent or reinvent himself
through the act of writing. Time and time again, he explains that only when
writing the pages of his diary does he feel that he truly exists: "Há muito
tempo que não escrevo. Têm passado meses sem que viva, e vou durando,
entre o escritório e a fisiologia, numa estagnação íntima de pensar e de sentir"
(II, p. 145). By incorporating the problematic relation between writing and
being into the narrative context, Soares incessantly calls attention to the
predicament that motivates his need to write—in order to exist in this world,
he must abandon it, in favor of his "estado da alma" which can be his only true
"paisagem" (II, p. 202).

When faced with the realization that, for Soares, the only possible answer to the problem of existential truth is to be found in the act of writing, one cannot help but abandon an innocent reading of the *Livro do Desassossego*. Confronted with relentless meditations on the inextricable ties that link fact and fiction, the reader is pressed to delve more deeply into questions regarding the identity of Bernardo Soares. In effect, the striking similarities between the protagonist's predicament and that so often expressed by Soares' "author" or creator, Fernando Pessoa, seem to invite the reader to leave the boundaries of the text and to seek confirmation that Soares's voice is, in essence, that of Pessoa.

If, however, we are to accept that Soares's narrative actually serves as a mask or a cover for his creator's private meditations, one may be led to agree with Alfred MacAdam who, in his American edition of the Book posits that the *Livro do Desassossego* actually consists of Pessoa's own *diário íntimo* (vii). At first glance, this correspondence is confirmed by a rapid inventory of the biographical information contained in the narrative. Many elements of Soares' personal and professional experience bear a distinct resemblance to what we know of the life of Fernando Pessoa—like his creator, the book's narrator leads a modest and solitary existence, working as a clerk in Lisbon's *Baixa*. He has few friends and his activities are limited to work and to writing.

These similarities, although striking, are not sufficient, however, to make a case for identifying the many fragments attributed to Bernardo Soares as constituting Pessoa's own *diário íntimo*. As I have already noted, the content of these narrative passages only minimally fulfills our expectations of diaristic prose and, as such, any attempt at reading these pages as a reflection on Pessoa's own psyche would result in the same impasse regarding the existential problematic of fact and fiction as was described above. In addition, it is clear that although Soares is in many ways similar to Pessoa, the details of his personality differ from Pessoa's in several respects. We must remember, of course, that Soares was enigmatically referred to as a "semi-heteronym" by his creator because, as Pessoa explained, ". . . não sendo uma personalidade minha, é, não diferente da minha, mas uma simples mutilação dela. Sou eu menos a afectividade e o raciocínio" (Quadros, 343). As Jorge de Sena was the first to demonstrate, Bernardo Soares is, in fact, *less than his creator*, not only in the sense that he inhabits a lower social station and has benefited from fewer educational or cultural opportunities, but also because he incarnates a different range of emotions (188). Indeed, the negative and frustrated tone that prevails in the pages of the *Livro do Desassossego*, is markedly lacking in the Pessoa's other heteronymic or orthonymic work.

This contradictory situation, in which Soares' voice is recognized, in effect, as being the same but different than Pessoa's, has led several of the book's critics to conclude that Soares's prose represents the reverse or the "flip side" of the Pessoan project. According to this theory, one may assume that the *Livro do Desassossego* consists of no more (and no less) than a sort of depository for the residue or the *lixo* that was generated as a by-product of Pessoa's poetic invention. As Eduardo Lourenço has pointed out, "Na realidade, são as mesmas intuições capitais, as mesmas metáforas, os mesmos sintagmas, mas ditas, assumidas em nome de outro sujeito, onde se escuta a voz de todos os outros, Caeiro, Campos, Reis, separadas ou amalgamadas, mas também *banalizadas*, à medida exacta de um enunciador que não tem projecto de existência. . ." (353).

By identifying a relationship of similarity and difference between Soares and the three major heteronymic voices of Pessoa's poetry, this theory is particularly useful for Pessoan scholars. In addition to successfully accounting for the disparity of styles to be found in the book's many fragments, this reading also calls attention to Pessoa's changing perceptions of the book's function during the more than twenty years that he intermittently worked on it.[3] It must be noted, however, that this approach to the *Livro do Desassossego*, while providing an astute *description* of the Book, does little to further our understanding of its possible structure. As it avoids the fundamental problem of the author's (unfulfilled) intentions regarding its final form, Lourenço's reading of the *Livro do Desassossego* overlooks one of the most intriguing aspects of the text. This would be the reader's participatory role in the creation of the status and meaning of the text.

By the end of his life, Pessoa appears to have finally decided to prepare this book for publication, attributing the authorship of the *Livro do Desassossego* to Bernardo Soares. In doing so, however, he also recognized, quite lucidly, that this choice would necessarily force him to go back and revise a good deal of material:

> A organização do livro deve basear-se numa escolha, rígida quanto possível, dos trechos variadamente existentes, adaptando, porém, os mais antigos, que falhem à psicologia de Bernardo Soares, tal como agora surge, a essa vera psicologia. Àparte isso, há que fazer uma revisão geral do próprio estilo, sem que ela perca, na expressão íntima, o devaneio e o desconexo lógico que o caractarizam. (I, 57)

Unfortunately, for lack of time or direction, Pessoa was unable to complete this revision and we have no clear indication as to what he may have imagined to be the book's final form. We can only guess as to which fragments would be included or excluded and in what order we should read them.

When confronted with the many versions of the *Livro do Desassossego* that have appeared over the past ten years, we must recognize that the editorial act of selecting and ordering the fragments that have been found in Pessoa's *espólio* ultimately reflects back on each compiler's perceptions of its role in the wider context of the Pessoan project. If Jacinto do Prado Coelho chose to arrange the fragments thematically for the book's first printing, the organizers or editors of the several editions that followed have opted for a variety of approaches regarding the organization of its content matter. Maria Alzira Seixo, while respecting the first editor's thematic ordering of the material, reduced the original 520 fragments to the more "manageable" number of 200, which she states will, nonetheless, provide "uma compreensão geral da índole da obra, bem como a percepção dos seus aspectos temáticos, estilísticos e discursivos mais significativos" (31). Although these two books are then significantly different in terms of length and content, I believe that, in both cases, the emphasis on the thematic similarities of the book's fragments reveals a desire to read the *Livro do Desassossego* as a collection of essays. By privileging the thematic elements of the text, Prado Coelho and Seixo seem to implicitly suggest that these selections constitute a sort of reflection or commentary on Pessoa's poetic project.

In 1986, António Quadros chose to divide the fragments into several different categories, distinguishing between the published and the unpublished and also placing the fragments in separate sections respectively entitled "Confissões" and "Textos Literários." This organization takes its cue from the notion that the *Livro do Desassossego* actually consists of two different books with three different authors—while the later texts attributed to Soares are presented as pertaining to the genre of the *diário íntimo*, the earlier, post-symbolist texts, ascribed to Pessoa or Vicente Guedes, are set apart from this diary, being presented as a series or collection of prose poems. Thus, this edition is apparently much more committed to a reading of the esthetic and ontological questions raised in the *Livro do Desassossego*.

In the most recent and undoubtedly the most complete edition of the *Livro do Desassossego*, published in 1991, Teresa Sobral Cunha has attempted to adhere, as closely as possible, to a chronological sequencing of the fragments she identifies as pertaining to this book. In doing so, she clearly aims to document the book's evolution. Cunha, however, also includes a great deal of new material that has resulted from her thorough archival research. As such, she has been able to publish what may ironically be considered a "prequel" to Soares' text. In effect, the fragments that comprise the first volume, most of which are attributed to Vicente Guedes, take on importance and can only be understood in light of our reading of the book's later material. The final result of this valuable philological exercise is that our attention is drawn to the book itself, which is presented as a process and not a completed narrative.

As this brief overview demonstrates, the goal of the respective editors of the *Livro do Desassossego* is always the same: to create coherence where there is none. Given the incomplete and often indeterminate nature of the most of the Book's contents, every editorial gesture must, by definition, be seen as committed to the creation of a meaningful narrative that we may refer to as the *Livro do Desassossego*. In this sense we must admit that the *Livro do Desassossego* cannot exist as an unmediated work, that is, without a layer of critical interpretation necessarily interposed between reader and text. By extension, the readers of any given edition should always be careful to take into account the editor's selection and organization of the materials that are included in pages of the *Livro do Desassossego*.

As no single reading of the *Livro do Desassossego* is able to posit a definitive answer to the problem of the book's organization or contents, it is not at all surprising that such a wide and varied number of editions should have appeared in such a short time. Indeed, the *Livro do Desassossego* exists and can only exist as a text that is, by definition, incomplete, unfinished, or imperfect. Given this situation, it is up to each reader of the *Livro do Desassossego* to create his or her own version of the text for, as Eduardo Lourenço noted, ". . . este *Livro do Desassossego* é um texto que Fernando Pessoa nunca teve, material, fisicamente, diante dos olhos. Assim e só por isso *sendo dele é ainda mais nosso* do que normalmente são os seus outros textos" (350).

Although this sentiment is expressed to a greater or lesser extent by all the editors who have tried their hand at organizing the Book's contents, it undoubtedly finds its most radical dimension in Richard Zenith's recent translation. Unlike the other English translators of the *Livro do Desassossego*, Zenith goes beyond the mere task of rendering the contents into another language, choosing, rather, to present yet another possible method of organizing the book's contents. After first defending the somewhat anarchistic notion that "ideally, the *Book of Disquietude* should be published in a loose-leaf edition," he goes on to justify his decision to "place the dated fragments from the last phase in chronological order, interspersed with the other fragments." In his reading of the text: "[w]e should imagine. . . that Bernardo Soares is looking back over his life, reading what he wrote a long time ago ('I am the selfsame prose I write') and mentally or literally collating the pieces of his past in between his present journal entries" (5).

Here, it is clear that Zenith has taken more liberties with the text than any of its previous editors. He has also taken a much greater risk, as he consciously seeks to provide the book with a fictional structure that he openly admits to as his own. In effect, Zenith has succeeded in creating such a personal version of the *Livro do Desassossego* that, in many respects, his editorial strategies result in the creation of a "postmodern" text. His is an edition that openly speaks both to and of the era in which it was published. When reading Zenith's introduction, we are forced to examine the question of the narrator's subjectivity from a new perspective and to ask whether or not we are still reading a work that belongs to the Modernist tradition.

It is particularly telling that this book saw its first publication only in 1982. When faced with the many versions of it that have appeared to date, one is indeed tempted to assert that the *Livro do Desassossego* belongs more to the period in which we read it than to the time in which it was written. As I have noted, the differing approaches to constructing the narrator's identity and explaining his purpose for writing lead to significantly different interpretations of the Book's contents. This, in turn has contributed to a proliferation of approaches to the ordering of the book's fragments and, by extension, has given us a notion of the *Livro do Desassossego* as a multiple, open, and ever-changing text.

Fascinating as it may be, however, this critical debate concerning questions about the book's "true" form actually revolves around an aspect of the *Livro do Desassossego* that the author probably never intended to address. Regardless of the manner in which the editor chooses to organize the book's fragments, the reader of the *Livro do Desassossego* eventually is forced to recognize and give in to Pessoa's attempts at constructing yet another substantial poetic identity. Therefore, while it is impossible to ascertain what the final narrative intentions of the "self" that is writing may be, there can be little doubt that the voice that we hear in these pages clearly belongs within the parameters of Pessoa's investigations into the problematics of modernist subjectivity. Whether his author's intention was that of elaborating an essay or series of essays, a *diário íntimo*, or a collection of prose poems, the power of Soares's prose finally forces us to abandon this line of questioning, as the urgency of his quest for identity ultimately leads us back into that textual labyrinth that is Fernando Pessoa's "drama em gente."

Notes

[1] In a recent note, published in *Colóquio/Letras*, 121/122 (1991) p. 282, José Blanco reports on four editions of the *Livro do Desassossego* that appeared in English in 1991. I will refer to three of these translations in this paper: Alfred MacAdam's translation, which is based on the original Atica edition; Margaret Jull Costa's, which follows Maria José de Lancastre's Italian translation of the *Livro do Desassossego*; and Richard Zenith's trans-

lation which proposes a wholly original ordering of the Book's fragments. I was unable to consult the fourth English translation, by Iain Watson (London: Quartet Books) which, according to Blanco, is based on the French edition that was organized by Françoise Laye.

² Cunha, vol I, pp. 63; For the purpose of consistency, I will transcribe all quotations from Teresa Sobral Cunha's recent two volume edition of the *Livro do Desassossego*. Also, given the disparity to be found in the translation of the book's title into English, I have chosen to maintain the original Portuguese title in all references to the text.

³ While most of the texts that have been attributed to Soares carry dates that fall between 1929 and 1934, the well-known piece of post-symbolist prose entitled "na Floresta do Alheamento," published in 1913, was already identified as pertaining to the *"Book of Disquietude*, em preparação." If the author of this text was identified as Fernando Pessoa, other contemporary fragments refer to Vicente Guedes as the Book's author in its earlier phase.

Works Cited

Coelho, Jacinto do Prado, ed. *Livro de Desassossego*. By Fernando Pessoa. 2 vols. Lisboa: Atica, 1982.

Costa, Margaret Jull, trans. *The Book of Disquiet*. London: Serpent's Tail, 1991.

Cunha, Teresa Sobral, ed. *Livro de Desassossego*. By Fernando Pessoa. 2 vols. Lisboa: Presença, 1990/91.

Lourenço, Eduardo. *"O Livro de Desassossego*, texto suicida." *Actas do 2° Congresso Internacional de Estudos Pessoanos*. Porto: Centro de Estudos Pessoanos, 1985. 347-361.

MacAdam, Alfred, trans.. *The Book of Disquiet*. By Fernando Pessoa. New York: Pantheon, 1991.

Quadros, António, ed. *Prosa 1*. By Fernando Pessoa. Vol. 2 of *Obra Poética e em Prosa*. 3 vols. Porto: Lello & Irmãos, 1986.

Seixo, Maria Alzira, ed. *Livro de Desassossego de Bernardo Soares*. Lisboa: Comunicação, 1986.

Sena, Jorge de. "Introdução ao *Livro de Desassossego*." Vol. 1 of *Fernando Pessoa & Cª Heteronímia*. Lisboa: Edições 70, 1982. 177-242.

Zenith, Richard, trans. *The Book of Disquietude*. By Fernando Pessoa. Manchester: Carcenet, 1991.

Fernando Pessoa's Translation of *The Scarlet Letter*

George Monteiro

At this late date one wonders whether it will be possible to recover all of Fernando Pessoa's translations of English and American literary texts —fiction and poetry— into Portuguese. It has long been known that he published translations of Edgar Allan Poe poems and stories, O. Henry stories, an Aleister Crowley poem, and an Ann Catherine Green detective story (Blanco; Rui de Sousa). In recent years, it has been discovered that he also published translations of poems by William Wordsworth, John Greenleaf Whittier, James Russell Lowell, Alfred Lord Tennyson, and Thomas Moore (Pessoa, *Folha* F-4, F-5). He also translated, it turns out, Nathaniel Hawthorne's 1850 novel *The Scarlet Letter*. It is this last title that interests us here, for this essay does not add any new titles to the list of texts known to have been translated by Pessoa. It presents a discovery of another sort: the hitherto unknown publication during Pessoa's lifetime of his translation of *The Scarlet Letter*.

I

It might be useful to begin with a rehearsal of the background material on Nathaniel Hawthorne and the typescript of Fernando Pessoa's translation Hawthorne's great romance. Less than three years after the critically and financially successful publication of *The Scarlet Letter*, the first novel of his maturity, Nathaniel Hawthorne found himself seeking gainful employment. He wished to secure certain and steady support for his family, and having been most recently a federal employee in the Salem custom-house, it was not unreasonable to think that a diplomatic post abroad would

53

do the trick nicely. To that effect he wrote to his publisher, James T. Fields, on December 11, 1852: "Do make some inquiries about Portugal—as, for instance, in what part of the world it lies, and whether it is an empire, a kingdom, or a republic. Also and more particularly, the expenses of living there, and whether the minister would be likely to be much pestered with his own countrymen" (*Centenary* 625). His request was both serious and tongue-in-cheek. After all, besides working at the local custom-house, Hawthorne was a native of Salem. In the early story, "Drowne's Wooden Image," he had even introduced a mysterious dark lady from Fayal in the Azores, and, among his readings, as we know from charge-books at the Salem Athenaeum, figured *Os Lusíadas*, Luiz Vaz de Camões's epic in the William Julius Mickle translation of 1798.

Soon after writing to James T. Fields, however, Hawthorne began to have second thoughts about the post in Lisbon. "I hope [President Franklin] Pierce will not offer it, for I cannot answer for myself that I shall do what really seems to me the wisest thing—that is, refuse it" (Wagenknecht 23).

Had Hawthorne gone to Portugal as chargé-d'affaires in the 1850s, instead of assuming the consulship in Liverpool, as he did eventually, it is likely that *The Scarlet Letter* would have been translated into Portuguese long before Fernando Pessoa had the occasion to do it. Had there been a single such translation in existence, moreover, it is unlikely, moreover, that Portugal's great modern poet would have tried his hand at a new one.

Typed on two-hundred-twenty numbered half-sheets, Fernando Pessoa's translation of *The Scarlet Letter* rests among the his papers in the National Library in Lisbon. It carries the call numbers 83-1—113, 84-1—106 and 74-B-27. The last number, as it turns out, is assigned to the last page of the novel, a single sheet inadvertently separated from the rest of the typescript. Why this manuscript had not hitherto attracted the attention of scholars, I shall not try to fathom. When in 1988 I telephoned Pessoa's first biographer, the late João Gaspar Simões, to ask him questions about the typescript, he expressed surprise. He said simply that not only had he not known of the typescript's existence but that he had not known—until that moment—that Pessoa had even done such a translation.

There are many questions regarding this manuscript that I cannot answer. But they are worth posing. For starters, when did Pessoa do this translation and why did he translate this book? Did he decide on the book himself or was it suggested to him by a friend or a publisher? Did he do the translation on speculation, hoping to find a publisher for the completed work? Was he paid to do it? Why wasn't it published when he finished it or at any later time? Why is there no record of his having dealt with a publisher or, if an original agreement fell through for some reason, with some other publishers? And why, on at least two occasions, did he start to write what appears to be an introduction or preface to *The Scarlet Letter*, only to break off, in each case, after a few sentences? Although, as I have said, I cannot answer these questions, there are two points that can be made with some surety. The first one is that given the fact that the complete translation survives in fair copy with only minor holograph revisions, it is safe to say that Pessoa had hopes for publication until sometime after he had typed the text for the printer. (I am assuming that there existed an earlier version of the translation, possibly in holograph.) The second point is that given the fact that the "introduction" survives only in two fragmentary texts—both of them seem to be beginnings—it is unlikely that the translation was ever set in type.

II

Much of what I have written so far I have largely said elsewhere, principally in the introductory essay I prepared for the edition of Pessoa's translation of *The Scarlet Letter* published in Lisbon in 1988 by Dom Quixote as volume 34 in its "Biblioteca do Bolso" series ("Introdução" 9-27).[1] Now it is time to take up the new information regarding Pessoa's translation of *The Scarlet Letter*.

Subsequent to the appearance of the Dom Quixote edition I learned that a Portuguese translation of *The Scarlet Letter* had appeared in print as early as the 1920s. It had been serialized in the Lisbon magazine *Ilustração*. This information came to me by way of Dr. Mario Mesquita, then the editor of the *Diário de Lisboa*. The acquisition recently of a copy of the Dom Quixote edition of Pessoa's translation, Dr. Mesquita informed his friend Onésimo T. Almeida (my colleague at Brown University), had caused him to recall that he had once seen a translation of *The Scarlet Letter* in an old magazine in his father's library. The magazine he had in mind was the *Ilustração*, a volume of which he now owned, having inherited from his father. That much I learned in June 1990. Dr. Mesquita kindly offered to bring the volume now in his possession to the offices of the *Diario de Lisboa* where I might examine it at my leisure. But by then I had virtually run out of time on that particular trip to Portugal, and I could not get to his office any sooner than the morning of the day on which I was to return to the United States. In the few minutes I could spare for the task I managed to take some sketchy notes. The "volume from his father's library" was indeed the *Ilustração*, the first volume. The journal began publication, fittingly enough, on January 1, 1926. There, in the first number, starting step-by-step with the magazine itself, was the first installment of *A Lettra Encarnada*, described as a "sensational American novel, the extraordinary success of which is attested to by its 2,700,000 copies printed in the United States" ("Sensacional romance americano, cujo extraordinário êxito se avalia pela tiragem de 2,700,000 exemplares atingida nos Estados Unidos" [*Ilustração* 26]). It is no matter that the figure—2,700,000—is grossly exaggerated. As recently as 1922, Hawthorne's American publishers, Houghton Mifflin, had determined that sales over the first seventy-two years the book was in print totaled 340,000—certainly a success by contemporaneous standards, but a far cry from the figure reported by the Portuguese magazine (Monteiro, "Introdução" 19-20). Nowhere in the pages of the magazine—including in the front and back matter—could I find a credit line for the translation. Nor would I discover, in any of the subsequent installments, any clue whatsoever to the identity of the anonymous translator. Incidentally, the magazine itself is apparently not considered important enough (or, more likely, sufficiently literary) to warrant space in Daniel Pires's 1986 *Dicionário das Revistas Literárias Portuguesas do Século XX*.

I did not return to Lisbon until January 1991. But when I did it was at the Biblioteca Nacional that I searched for the *Ilustração*. Fortunately, they had a full run of the magazine. I was able to trace its serialization of Hawthorne's novel in translation through to its completion in the issue for February 16, 1927.

This publication in 1926-1927 makes it, apparently, the earliest known Portuguese translation of Hawthorne's *Scarlet Letter* to achieve print. But the big question for me was: is it Pessoa's translation? Except for a second "t" in the spelling of "Letra," the title is translated the same way, *A Letra Encarnada*. Such is not the case in the five other Portuguese language translations I have located, all of which carry the identical title of *A Letra Escarlate* (Viana, Mielnik, Rodrigues, Pinto de Carvalho, and Navarro de Oliveira). Further comparison of the *Ilustração* text and the Pessoa typescript in the Biblioteca Nacional reveals that although they are not identical word for word, they show all the signs of being two versions of the same translation. Significant, too, is that the occasional changes inked into the typescript all appear in the magazine version of *The Scarlet Letter*. And while the *Ilustração* serialization omits Hawthorne's opening essay "The Custom-House," which does appear in Pessoa's typescript and is mentioned by him in print in another context in the same year (1926) ("'Régie," *Obras* 642, *Oeuvres* 307), it is notable that twenty of the twenty-four chapters (with some changes in orthography) bear identical titles. Of the four titles that are in any way different, two of them omit a single word (*seu* [chapter 10]; the article *a* [chapter 23]); one substitutes a word (*encontro* for *entrevista* [chapter 4]); and the fourth substitutes a phrase (*O Feriado* becomes *O Dia de Festa* [chapter 21]). When we put these four titles back into the context of the entire list of twenty-four chapter titles, the total picture indicates a single principal author was responsible for the texts of the Pessoa typescript and of the *Ilustração* serialization.

(Typescript)	*Ilustração*
A Alfandega	[not printed]
I. A Porta da Cadeia	I. A Porta da Cadeia
II. A Praça do Mercado	II. A Praça do Mercado
III. O Reconhecimento	III. O Reconhecimento
IV. A Entrevista	IV. O Encontro
V. Hester Trabalhando	V. Hester Trabalhando
VI. Pearl	VI. Pearl
VII. O Vestibulo do Governador	VII. O Vestibulo do Governador
VIII. A Creança e o Padre	VIII. A Criança e o Padre
IX. O Physico	IX. O Físico
X. O Physico e o Seu Doente	X. O Físico e o Doente
XI. O Interior de um Coração	XI. O Interior de um Coração
XII. A Vigília do Padre	XII. A Vigília do Padre
XIII. Outro Aspecto de Hester	XIII. Outro Aspecto de Hester

When we turn to the very last sentences of the novel, moreover, we find that the translation of the engraving on the slate monument with which Hawthorne concludes his narrative is rendered the same in both instances (except that the typescript Pessoa doubles the *t* in *lettra* and omits the circumflex over the *e* in *prêto*): "Em campo prêto a letra A em sanguinho." That this is neither merely coincidental nor a case of the inevitability of two translators having to come up with pretty much the same translation is reinforced when we look at three other, quite different, published translations of the same monumental words: "Sobre um camp negro, a letra vermelha" (Mielnik), "Num campo severo, imenso, negro e triste,/ Gravada a vermelho, a letra A subsiste!" (Rodrigues), and "A letra A a vermelho em campo escuro" (Navarro de Oliveira).

In almost every paragraph informative comparisons can be made between the *Ilustração* and typescript versions of Hawthorne's novel. In this respect the opening paragraph of the book's first chapter is not exceptional:

Pessoa's typescript

> *Um grupo de homens barbados*, de fatos de cor triste e *chapeus cinzentos em chaminé*, misturados *com mulheres, algumas de coifa, outras em cabello, estava reunido em frente de um edifício de madeira, cuja porta, de carvalho reforçado, era coberta de pontas de ferro.*

Ilustração

> *Um grupo de homens barbados*, vestidos de côres escuras e com *chapéus cinzentos em chaminé*, de mistura *com mulheres, algumas de coifa, outras em cabelo, estavareunido em frente de um edifício de madeira, cuja porta, de carvalho reforçado, era coberta de pontas de ferro.*

The italicized passages are identical, and in one of the instances in which there are differences the difference is a change from *misturados* to *de mistura* while the other changes *fatos de cor triste* to *vestidos de côres escuras*. Obviously, these changes indicate that one text is a revised version of the other rather than the two of them being discrete and independent attempts at translation.

To pin this down further, we can also look at the way this paragraph is handled in three other Portuguese versions of *The Scarlet Letter* (Mielnik, Rodrigues, and Navarro de Oliveira)[2]:

(Mielnik)

> Diante do edifício de madeira, de porta sòlidamente construída de carvalho com pontas de ferro batido, comprimia-se uma turba de homens barbados, vestídos de escuro com seus chapéus copados e mulheres de cabelos soltos ou presos com toucas.

(Rodrigues)

> Em certa manhã de Verão—há pelo menos dois séculos—o tabuleiro de relva existente em frente de cadeia, na prisão Lane, estava ocupado por imensos habitantes de Boston, todos com o olhar ansiosamente preso à porta de carvalho guarnecida com os seus pregos de ferro.

(Navarro de Oliveira)

Homens de longas barbas, roupas de cores sombrias e chapéu alto em forma de torre de campanário, na companhia de mulheres, umas de capuz e outras em cabelo, apinhavam-se defronte dum edifício grande cuja porta enorme de madeira grossa de carvalho era adornada com bicos de ferro.

Notably, in these three later translations there is almost nothing to italicize. With the exception of one phrase—*bicos de ferro* (Navarro de Oliveira)—these three versions not only differ entirely from one another but are in every case markedly different from both of the Pessoa versions of the translation—the typescript and the *Ilustração*.

I should like to take up one other matter. In Chapter VIII of *The Scarlet Letter*, entitled "The Elf-Child and the Minister," Pearl is questioned about her origins—is she a Christian child, or an elf or faery (thought to have been left back in Europe with the other relics of Papistry)? Hester's child answers: "'I am mother's child'" (*Scarlet Letter* 130). A comparison of the various ways in which Pearl's reply has been translated into Portuguese is revealing. Mielnik renders it: "Sou filha de minha mãe"; Rodrigues: "Tenho mãe"; Navarro de Oliveira: "Sou a menina da mamã!"; and the *Ilustração* serialization: "Sou a menina da minha mãe." It is the last of these—Pessoa's *Ilustração* version—that comes closest to the even more Pessoan solution given to the sentence in the typescript in Pessoa's *espólio*, which renders Pearl's answer to the clergyman's hostile question: "Sou a menina da sua mãe." The poet Eugénio de Andrade confesses that tears came to his eyes when he read this sentence, so resonant is it to anyone familiar with Pessoa's widely esteemed poem "O menino da sua mãe." Interestingly enough and perhaps not merely coincidentally, Pessoa's poem was first published in the journal *Contemporânea* in May 1926, even as the very chapter of *A Letra Encarnada* containing Pearl's reply to the minister was appearing in the May 1, 1926 issue of *Ilustração*.

A thorough word-for-word comparison of the typescript text with the *Ilustração* text might be informative in unsuspected ways. But I suspect that it would not modify the evidence indicating that Pessoa's typescript served as the basis for a second, somewhat revised version which became in turn the the copy—or the basis for the copy—used to set in type the magazine version. Almost every one of the few handwritten changes in the lightly corrected typescript appears in the *Ilustração* version. Whether or not Pessoa was in any way responsible for the additional revisions made to the text immediately preceding its publication in the *Ilustração* is not at this time known or, perhaps, even knowable. Yet, for all the unanswered questions, it is gratifying to be able to add the translation of *A Lettra Encarnada* as serialized in *Ilustração* in 1926-1927 to the Fernando Pessoa canon.

Notes

[1] An expanded version of that introduction, in English, appeared later ("Pessoa and Hawthorne").

[2] The three translations I exclude from the comparison are those of Rodrigues, Viana, and Pinto de Carvalho.

Works Cited

Blanco, José. *Fernando Pessoa: Esboço de uma Bibliografia*. Lisbon: Imprensa National - Casa da Moeda/ Centro de Estudos Pessoanos, 1983.

Chiaretti, Marco. "Livreiro descobre e Folha publica cinco traduções perdidas de Pessoa." *Folha de S. Paulo* 26 May 1990: F-1.

Hawthorne, Nathaniel. *The Centenary Edition of the Works of Nathaniel Hawthorne, Volume XVI, The Letters, 1843-1853*. Ed. Thomas L. Woodson, L. Neal Smith and Norman Holmes Pearson. Columbus: Ohio State U P, 1985.

---. *A Letra Encarnada*. Trans. Fernando Pessoa. Intr. George Monteiro. Lisbon: Dom Quixote, 1988.

---. *A Letra Escarlate*. Trans. Sodré Viana. Rio de Janeiro: José Olympio, 1942.

---. *A Letra Escarlate*. Trans. Isaac Mielnik. São Paulo: Clube do Libro, 1949.

---. *A Letra Escarlate*. Trans. Aurora Rodrigues. Lisbon: Romano Torres, [2nd ed.] 1950.

---. *A Letra Escarlate*. Trans. A. Pinto de Carvalho. São Paulo: Saraiva, [1957?].

---. *A Letra Escarlate*. Trans. Maria de José Navarro de Oliveira. Lisbon: Europa-América, 1976.

---. *A Lettra Encarnada*. Trans. Fernando Pessoa. *lustração* I (1926—Jan. 1, 16; Feb. 1, 16; Mar. 1, 16; Apr. 1, 16; May 1, 16; June 1, 16; July 1,

16; Aug.1, 16; Sept. 1, 16; Oct. 1, 16; Nov. 1, 16; Dec. 1, 20 [26-27, 28-29, 26-27, 26-27, 20-21, 20-21, 30-31, 18-19, 20-21, 36, 34-35,26-27, 30-31, 30-31, 28-29, 24-25, 22-23, 26-27, 30-31, 30-31, 30-31, 37-38, 37-38, 62] II (1927—Jan. 1, 16; Feb. 1, 16 [37-38, 36-38, 36-38, 36-38]).

---. *The Scarlet Letter* (Facsimile of the First Edition). Ed. Hyatt H. Waggoner and George Monteiro. San Francisco: Chandler, 1968.

Monteiro, George. "Introdução." *A Letra Encarnada*. Trans. Fernando Pessoa. Lisbon: Dom Quixote, 1988. 9-27.

---. "Pessoa and Hawthorne." *Estudos Anglo-Americanos* 12-13 (1988-1989): 68-77.

Pessoa, Fernando. *Obras em Prosa*. Ed. Cleonice Berardinelli. Rio de Janeiro: Aguilar, 1982.

---. *Oeuvres Complètes de Fernando Pessoa*. Ed. Joaquim Vital. 1 *Proses publiées (du vivant de l'auteur)*. Ed., annot., and intr. José Blanco. Trans. from the Portuguese by Simon Biberfeld, Dominique Touati and Joaquim Vital. Paris: Editions de la Différence, 1988.

---. "'Régie', Monopólio, Liberdade." *Revista de Comércio e Contabilidade* 2 (Feb. 25, 1926).

---. Translations of "Godiva" (Alfred Lord Tennyson), "Lucy" (William Wordsworth), "A Ultima Rosa do Verão" (Thomas Moore), "Barbara Frietchie" (John Greenleaf Whittier) and "Sobre Um Retrato de Dante por Giotto" (James Russell Lowell). *Folha de S. Paulo* 26 May 1990: F-4, F-5.

Rui de Sousa, João. *Fotobibliografia de Fernando Pessoa*. Preface by Eduardo Lourenço. Lisbon: Imprensa Nacional-Casa da Moeda/ Biblioteca Nacional, 1988.

Wagenknecht, Edward. *Nathaniel Hawthorne: Man and Writer*. New York: Oxford University Press, 1961.

Europe and the Invention of
Fernando Pessoa

Ronald W. Sousa

In terms of ultimate implications, the following pages have to do with the social functionality of literary criticism—that is, with the role criticism can play in formulating and promulgating social narratives. It is a functionality directly exercised through such activity as critical debate, literary historiography, and the educational process. At its root, however, it revolves around the very construction of literature as an object of one or another sort of reading and therefore as agent in the constitution of the social symbolic. While that entire dynamic will be alluded to in what follows, I shall be concentrating specifically on only one part of it, namely the creation of literary objects of study, along with the factors—and stakes—therein involved. Or, rather, I shall treat the creation—I shall henceforth use the term "invention"—of one such object, the Portuguese poet Fernando Pessoa (1888-1935). Moreover, the ensuing pages will approach even that issue in a partial manner. Grounded in a generalized historical discourse, some notions of critique of literary-critical modes, and a working metaphor from semiotics, they will set forth a preliminary analysis of but one set of factors involved in the "invention" of "Fernando Pessoa" as the key figure in Portuguese literary modernism.

Briefly stated, the premise underlying what follows is that the "Fernando Pessoa" with which we work today came into being in relation to specific historical necessities. In this sense, "Pessoa" is the product of a kind of semiosis: he has specific "characteristics" chosen and developed in a determinant relationship to the needs he is being formulated to fill. The set of such needs is, then, the locus of semiosis, and the often complex, frequently conflictive meaning-making activity at that locus seeks to define a literary object of study. To be sure, this particular invention is a complex one, for it involves the participation of elements from various areas of a Portuguese society undergoing symbolic and, to a lesser extent, material-structural remodeling after World War II, each area with its own socio-political interests. In short, "Pessoa's" "invention" was one caught up in socio-political conflict. The result: the invention of a number of "Pessoas" manifesting similar general characteristics and similarly located in Portuguese cultural history but within that general profile given different values according to divergent notions about that history.

One area upon which those divergent interpretations hinged involved evaluation of "Europe"—i. e., the "Europe" north of the Pyrenees—in relation to Portugal. The pages that follow set forth a close reading of key works from one set of "inventors" of Pessoa who position "Europe" in similar fashion.

In 1947 the publishing house Sá da Costa gave to the public a thin volume of literary criticism with the curious title *Três Poetas Europeus (Camões. Bocage. Pessoa.)*; the author appeared designated by the obvious pseudonym "Mar Talegre." The three poets are, of course, all Portuguese, and only the first, Camões, could at that time be said to have international renown. The word "European" in the title is, then, a discriminating adjective: for Mar Talegre there is a "Europeanness" in poetry that characterizes those three figures in some mode of contrast to other Portuguese writers. His volume is composed of four sections, an Introduction and a chapter on each "European" poet. The Introduction is a meditation on "Europeanness" from a viewpoint that seeks to substantiate the logic of the volume and thus goes some way toward grounding the discriminating adjective of the book's title.

For Mar Talegre, "Europe" is to be conceived as a set of "contributions" from all its constituent countries. Those "contributions" produce a "Europeanness" evaluated as follows:

> It is . . . diversity of elements, . . . struggle among contradictions, . . . multiplication of doubts and questions that give the European spirit its vitality. And the desire to reach a balance among the opposites and to elevate itself to the harmonizing of its disparate constitutive elements is not merely the point of polarization of its diversities; it is also a propulsive, conductive power, perhaps the greatest such power, of that spirit. It is, moreover, its ideal of effecting itself harmoniously, adjusting the forces of that spirit to the nature of humankind, and of communing with and integrating itself into the harmony of the universe. (24)[1]

That statement should be read in contrast to the precis of Portuguese poetry contained in the Introduction, for it sees poetry by Portuguese poets as by and large limited to the contours of the "Portuguese character" and therefore as restricted to

> immediate and momentary planes, to confidence in the anecdotal, the transitory mental state born of the casual encounter with a certain accident of the poet's being or of external reality. Only the great poets free themselves and transport themselves beyond emotion taken from the contingent, elevating themselves to the grand planes of thought and of timeless diction. (13-14)

To be sure, this analysis is couched in a distinctively Portuguese set of discursive holdovers from nineteenth-century notions of nationality, according to which cultural expression bears an indexical relationship to the state of the national culture. Camões, Bocage, and Pessoa are therefore being singled out as different from, and superior to, the norms of Portuguese poetry. The analysis also trades on a specifically Portuguese period sense of "European mission" (22). One must bear in mind that at this time Portugal was not only set on retaining its colonial possessions but in fact was consolidating its presence in Africa through planned urban expansion there. Mar Talegre's diction is in many respects of a piece with the language of Portuguese "mission" justificatory of that attitude. Indeed, it is noteworthy that, in his argument about "Europeanness," he at times defines that peculiar continental quality in opposition to the "Oriental" and the "American," but he never mentions the "African," thus by implication denying Africa a commensurate "culture."

What is of interest for present purposes, however, is not the direct political referentiality of the author's language but rather the sense it projects of Portuguese poetry in relation to "Europeanness." Mar Talegre speaks of a Portuguese "psychological complex" (17) in that regard. The features of that complex are reflected in the second of the two passages reproduced above— that is, Portuguese poetry is seen as not normally reaching the desired heights of "Europeanness." Indeed, Mar Talegre creates a hierarchy of Portuguese poets (cf. 16-17), with a very few transcending the immediate, the anecdotal, the sentimental, and the unredeemably personal to become "European." The ground of his argument for the "Europeanness" of Camões, Bocage, and Pessoa is to found in the claim that they express a degree of abstraction and engage in the practice of raising universal questions through a self-reflection in which they seek to balance opposites—particularly the specific and the universal—dialectically.

That precis of Portuguese poetry comes with a well-known historical narrative attached, of course. It is one that goes back to the seventeenth and eighteenth centuries, when, for Northern Europe, Iberia was the "barbarous South" beset by irrational behavior and medieval institutions. Indeed, elements of Iberian culture interiorized that evaluation as well. Early in the nineteenth century, however, the "South" saw its own version of Liberalism born and institutionalized, with constitutions modelled upon the French example and institution of a regime of modified free enterprise. In the decades of great European capital expansion, the 1840's, 1850's, and 1860's, liberalism developed greatly as a socio-political system, though, to be sure, nowhere in Iberia with the overall social power that obtained north of the Pyrenees. Especially during those decades, much of the stigma of the "barbarous South" was expunged by a sense of cultural value supposedly inherent in liberal institutional and infrastructural development. The *fin-de-siècle* European economic contraction, however, and the resulting Europe-wide weakening of faith in the explanatory power of the discourse of [applied] science, led to new thematization of the North-South split. Now, however, the language coming from Iberia takes up a new stance: the "South" represents the "North" as author and primary instigator of a dehumanizing scientificity in contrast to more "human" Iberian social practices. Miguel de Unamuno, in his argument for the presence of the "human" in what he saw as the peculiarly Spanish, "tragic" dialectical dualism of reason and faith, proclaims:

> And now to you, the younger generation, bachelor Carrascos of a Europeanizing regenerationism, you who are working after the best European fashion, with scientific method and criticism, to you I say: Create wealth, create nationality, create art, create science, create ethics, above all create—or rather, translate—*Kultur*, and thus kill in yourselves both life and death. Little will it all last you! . . .(Unamuno, 236; *Tragic Sense*, 329-330)

In the passage, Unamuno is reading Cervantes' *Don Quixote* as an allegory of Spanish culture. In that allegory, the character Don Quixote is a "ridiculous" (a term Unamuno gives very specific sense) and therefore "human" figure caught between reason and faith, while bachelor Carrasco, one of the characters who bring Don Quixote home to be "cured," represents dehumanizing reason alone. Hence his "Europeanness"—and his inability to create life-giving institutions for Spain.

Versions of that discourse so constituted would, of course, subsequently come to anchor the Iberian Fascist states of the 1930's to the 1970's. Within the logic of that justificatory discourse, "Europe" became the label for a liberalism that had failed Europewide but had never been fully implanted in Iberia anyway. In its "denaturalizing" of the Iberian nations in the recent past, as well as in its appearance as the guiding force of the "dehumanized" Europe (and United States) of the present, it could therefore figure as one of the two standing ideological opponents of the Iberian states and of the justificatory discourse of Franco and Salazar. The other opponent, even more clearly pinpointed, was, of course, "Communism" categorically conceived.

It is within that discourse of "traditionalist" Portuguese difference from "Europe" that Mar Talegre writes, and it is that language that enables him to link the concept of a "mission" and Portugal's intellectual (or at least poetic) non-"Europeanness." As regards what one sees of such discourse emerging from state sources, where "Portuguese mission" justifies anti-liberal and colonialist positions construed in opposition to "Europeanness," however, Mar Talegre has reversed the polarity of "non-Europeanness." For him "Europe" holds out the hope of a complexity of cultural expression that Portugal by and large lacks, and that complexity is desirable. Thus, while taking up much of the discourse of national tradition that state logic employed, he flies in the face of that logic.

Mar Talegre's approach to Pessoa is thus quite distinctive. Taking the poet's critical and poetic language as something like a transposed autobiography (the implications of the adjective will be apparent shortly), he engages in what amounts to a psychological/spiritual reading. To begin, he sees a kind of Platonism in Pessoa to which, using the poet's own diction, he refers to as a "religiosity":

> This religious concept of life gives his poetry its timeless cast, through a constant desire to try to capture the meaning of eternity, and it leaves it [that poetry] totally indifferent to present and immediate life. (80)

He argues that those qualities are expressed in an "algebraically precise" (97) poetry that manifests that preciseness through the presence of a working logic behind not only the diction of the individual poems but also Pessoa's famous self-division into poetic "heteronyms." He in effect sees that division as a part of a process of attempting to "capture the meaning of eternity" (ibid.) by what we might today call "role playing" in language— hence my invoking of the concept of transposition. He sees Pessoa as exploring some of the mental dispositions that bound his "own" but that, in Mar Talegre's words, the poet has excluded in order to delineate his "own" personality (86-89):

> What enables the coming-to-the-fore of these separate and individualized forms of Pessoa's personality is basically his desire for sincerity linked to a desire to live emotion fully, in all its possible contents and senses, "to feel everything excessively" [he is there quoting Pessoa] and the will to preserve the harmony of his personality. (86-87)

Thus, in Mar Talegre's analysis, is produced a poetry that is set in opposition to the "excess sentimentality" (98) of the Portuguese character, perhaps even one grounded in another sort of transposition: the translation of the "traditional sentimental melancholy" (94-95) of the Portuguese and of "traditional" Portuguese poetry into the self-reflexive mental dynamics that he sees as the hallmark of Pessoa's work.

He concludes by saying:

> Pessoa is, from the characteristics that I have described, a contributor of virgin poetic values that find no correspondence in modern European poetics. His unique poetic personality—unfortunately, an untranslatable one—gives that [European] poetics a new poetic experience that completes and enriches it. (99)

The last note is of special interest in that it pinpoints a dialectic that underlies the book's entire chapter on Pessoa. First of all, it holds that Pessoa is a *sui generis* case: Portuguese raised to "European," so to speak. In partial explanation of the assertion, Mar Talegre, like many Pessoa critics, points to Pessoa's English-language education in South Africa (other critics add his Jewish heritage to the mix). At the same time, precisely because of that unique combination, he represents a new element in "European" poetry itself. Here one should definitely see the notion of "mission" return: "Pessoa" represents a Portuguese "mission" to "Europe."[2] Mar Talegre has thus not only reversed the direction of the *fin-de-siècle* attitude exemplified in the Unamuno quote but has also doubly reinterpreted the formative interchange posited between Portugal and "Europe." For him "Portugueseness" can be raised to its highest level only through dialogue with "Europeanness" and, inversely, "Europe" benefits from what Portugal has to offer through the results of that process.

Mar Talegre was not the only post-war figure involved in such thinking about Pessoa. Jacinto do Prado Coelho, in his *Diversidade e Unidade em Fernando Pessoa* (1949), begins by calling Pessoa "cerebral and self-reflexive [retraído], enemy of ingenuous expansion," the last phrase being key since it forcefully invokes the presence of an opposing "ingenuous expansion," virtual analogue to Mar Talegre's syntagm about the "immediate and momentary" or his remark about the Portuguese tendency to "excess sentimentality" in poetry.

Prado Coelho, much more than Mar Talegre, was one of the small number of key figures who developed the "Europe"-oriented critical agenda around Pessoa. The reading set forth in *Diversidade e Unidade* is central to the development of "Fernando Pessoa," object of study. Indeed, it constitutes the single most important critical piece from Prado Coelho, though his editions of Pessoa's work and introductions to them may have had greater cumulative weight in promulgating his agenda.

Prado Coelho's work differs from Mar Talegre's in several important ways. It is the work of a professional academician whose career was dedicated to the promulgation of a specific brand of literary criticism within a literary-critical establishment by and large involved in romantic-positivist and biographical critical modes. Much of *Diversidade e Unidade* is dedicated to the careful reading of Pessoa's poetry and criticism from the viewpoint of what Prado Coelho would later identify, using what amounts to a translation from the German, as "immanent criticism."[3] What that mode of reading does, he says, is to enable an approach to "verbal expression" (3rd ed., xi) in itself. It is, to his mind, however, more than an approach to the materiality of language; it is instead an approach to language as the medium in which the mental dynamics of the poet display themselves. Thus, in Prado Coelho's hands, "immanent criticism" has an object of study that is linguistic-cognitive-psychological-biographical rather than unidimensionally "linguistic." In this sense he differs from Mar Talegre, who, involved in nationalistic premises, sees a national substratum showing through in Pessoa's work and also invokes critical terms generated from nationalist discourse in dealing with that work.

Indeed, Prado Coelho's "Preface" to *Diversidade e Unidade* speaks primarily in terms of critical methodology:

> In trying to clarify the genesis of the heteronyms I am of course carrying out an investigation of a psychological order; but that investigation leads me to something more important, the substance of Pessoa's poetry—that is, beyond states of mind the significance

of which he did not apprehend himself, a ceaseless
metaphysical anxiety, grave ontological concerns,
vibrant ideas about the situation of Mankind in the
World—and the melancholy of having nothing as
certain knowledge and of not being able to fall back on
the contentment of the common man. (10)

The claim there is that with a method free of "prejudices" (9) and
concentrating only on texts, the investigator can discover the "substance" of a
poetry, a "substance" unreachable even by the poet. Moreover, that "substance"
is basically "poetic" as opposed to psychological or biographical, even though
biography and psychology might have to be used for the critic to get to the
"substance." In the case of Pessoa, what is glimpsed is worthy of being set in
categorical terms: "the situation of Mankind in the World," or the relationship
between "metaphysical anguish" (9) and the knowledge that answers are not
forthcoming. Hence Pessoa's value as paradigm of "non-ingenuous" poetry
and the critic's centrality in understanding and elaborating the value and
implications of his "timelessness" (the same Portuguese word, "intemporal"
is used by Mar Talegre and Prado Coelho in the passages we have seen).
Indeed, Prado Coelho says as much in the second edition of *Diversidade e
Unidade*:

What can give value to the present essay is not so much
the thesis of unity as the fact that the method used to
discover it [that unity] has impelled me to seek out the
core of Pessoa's poetry. (3rd ed., xi)

Prado Coelho is, then, directly interested in modes of criticism and
the values that they propagate. There is an equation implicitly at work in his
"Preface": non-ingenuous poetry requires an exacting critical methodology,
one anchored in work with what he sees as "verbal expression" itself. And that
methodology, one developed in "Europe," can in turn reveal the great human
issues expressed in such literature. A reversal of the order of the equation's
terms is equally valid as well—and, for the present argument, more revealing:
"immanent criticism" and the values underpinning it, and in turn propagated
by it within institutions, require "non-ingenuous" poetry as their exemplar.
Fernando Pessoa is in effect "invented" by Prado Coelho's critical practice to
fill the bill.

That "invention" works in many ways, of course, among them to
stabilize Prado Coelho's critical posture itself. It is obvious that the claims he
makes about "immanent criticism" involve him in a set of assertions that

ultimately are paradoxical. The very notion that one can arrive at something called the "substance" of poetry in which all epistemological problems are resolved, in which, in Prado Coelho's own terms, "'matter' and 'form,' 'signified' and 'signifier' appear indissolubly linked" (3rd ed., xi), and which therefore precedes any value judgement on the part of the critic, is highly dubious. It is the illusion of a perfect science. Prado Coelho's "Pessoa," a figure whose multiplicity *Diversidade e Unidade* reduces to a series of what are presented as common underlying motifs and whose thematics are developed as speaking to universal issues that hold together psychology, biography, and various philosophical concerns while remaining apart from them, in fact acts as exemplar for the very argument for immanent criticism. In effect, Prado Coelho's formulation of that criticism foregrounds an *a priori* poetic "substance" that holds fundamental issues of human being, and then blithely sets out to discover that "poetic substance." Pessoa, as an object of co-construction along with "immanent criticism" so conceived provides that circular logic with a virtual mirror in which, through practical criticism, its circularity is occulted and the argument for its validity is simultaneously confirmed.

I should perhaps reiterate at this juncture—though it is suggested in my introductory remarks—that I am not claiming that the "Fernando Pessoas" of Mar Talegre or Jacinto do Prado Coelho are somehow fabrications. The point is simply that "Pessoa" is chosen and brought forth in relation to a set of historical-discursive needs, and those actions of choosing and bringing forth are carried out in such a way as to fill those needs. A corollary to that argument is that readings of "Pessoa" that conspicuously fail to fill those needs are explained away or suppressed. A case in point is to be seen in Prado Coelho's handling of Pessoa's authorship of the book of mystic-nationalist poems entitled *Mensagem*—in fact, the only book of poetry in the Portuguese language that Pessoa published in his lifetime. In *Diversidade e Unidade* Prado Coelho has to divide the heteronymic area "Fernando Pessoa himself" into two categories: one for the lyric poet, the second for the "author of *Mensagem*." Within the latter division, such phrases as "*sui generis* epic poet" (30), to designate something like an interiorized epic, and "the mental structure [of *Mensagem* poems]" (34), to indicate "points of contact" (ibid.) with the rest of Pessoa's work, are created to bring the "author of *Mensagem*" into some degree of commonality with the object of study presumed and elaborated through the rest of the book. Such terms are at best problematic in relation to the *Mensagem* text; the latter—namely, the "points of contact—is, in my view, outright indefensible. The point, however, is that a specific thematization of one aspect of Pessoa's work—one too well-known simply to be ignored— is necessary to maintain the contours of Prado Coelho's "Pessoa."

With Prado Coelho, then, the Europe-Portugal dialectic comes in relation to modes of poetic analysis. While he shares with Mar Talegre the analysis of Pessoa as a "non-ingenuous," "timeless" poet and many of the arguments that the two adduce to justify that analysis are compatible, Prado Coelho is not interested in imposing a local-versus-Europe map upon the poetic corpus itself. He is, rather, interested in implanting within Portuguese institutions both one of the dominant modes of literary criticism in post-War Europe and also the values potentially propagated by that critical mode, through development and promulgation of a figure readable according to that critical mode as he formulates it. His steadfast position in that regard and his presence as the Chair Professor of Portuguese Studies at the University of Lisbon in effect guaranteed the promulgation of a version of "scientific," "immanentist" criticism from the end of World War II into the early 1980's, with the curricular and other implications thereto linked.

A third figure in the development of Fernando Pessoa in such terms is Adolfo Casais Monteiro, prominent poet and essayist who left Portugal in the 1950's to become a university professor in Brazil and the United States. Casais Monteiro's work on Pessoa is quite diverse. Unlike the perspectives created by either Mar Talegre or Prado Coelho, he to a great extent sees Pessoa's poetry in relation to the craft of the poet. It is from that standpoint that the issue of "Europe" arises in a specific way in his work. I shall follow it out through examination of what is probably Casais Monteiro's best-known essay on Pessoa: "Teoria da Impersonalidade: Fernando Pessoa e T. S. Eliot" (1969).

The line of thought that culminates in that essay begins in the early 1950's.[4] Much of the work within that line of thought centers on the issue of Pessoa's "sincerity," an issue—and term—first promulgated by Pessoa himself. The issue is multifaceted and, to my mind, larger than the contours that Casais Monteiro gives it (see Sousa, 1981). It, however, does not constitute the issue at stake here. The point is that until "Teoria da Impersonalidade" Monteiro had approached the question of how a "poet" writing in many voices can be "sincere" almost solely in relation to the poet's craft. He had in effect posited a separate "poetic reality" created by the poet on the basis of daily reality. According to that outlook, the modern poet eschews any attempt to express his or her "own" emotions and instead explores ideas, mental states, emotionality, and so on which are not his or hers but which, in their impersonal nature, provide a means of seeing existence in ways more profound than simple expression of emotion allows. The parallels that that analysis holds with the work of Mar Talegre and Prado Coelho are clear.

With the 1969 essay, however, Casais Monteiro opens up his argument to new complexities, seeing Pessoa's "sincerity" and heteronymy as aspects of a language problem in general. His development of that problem—and simultaneously his solution for it as well—is effected through comparison with T. S. Eliot's remarks on "impersonal art." Casais Monteiro quite lucidly extends his discussion of "impersonal art" to include Kierkegaard's concept of romantic irony and in general links the entire question of Pessoa's "sincerity" to Northern European theorization about an "impersonal art in the 1930's and 1940's."[5]

Surprising, however, are the conclusions that Casais Monteiro draws from this North-South confrontation. He sets them forth in relation to Pessoa's famous poem "Autopsicografia":

> And how can we not call to mind the famous verses in which, after he seems to "affirm" that "the poet is a [pain-]feigner," he concludes by saying that he *feigns* the pain that he *really* feels? To feign what you do not feel, to feign what you do feel, to feign what you really feel: with this added factor, which we do not find in Eliot, the identification of the feeling of all men *amongst themselves* becomes visible; more than visible, it becomes necessary: for what does "sing the emotions that you do not have" and "feign" those that you do have mean except that the poet speaks for and to all men, that pain and joy are human emotions . . . (207)

With those words Casais Monteiro collapses the problem that Eliot, Kierkegaard—and Pessoa, rigorously read in relation to the former two figures—might have allowed to develop. The problems associated with the relationship between language and utterance are short-circuited for what amounts to a more sophisticated version of the solution Casais Monteiro had cultivated all along: in effect, comparison with such as Eliot enables Casais Monteiro to read Pessoa in relation to a polemic about poetry that rejects "sentimental romanticism" (208) for a more highly prized "impersonal expression." Its primary effect is to raise the stakes in interpretation of Pessoa as a poet. The result of that reading, however, is a rush to solution of the problem that Eliot's "impersonal art" suggests and Kierkegaard's "romantic irony" opens up and cultivates. That sudden resolution comes through invocation of a wide inter-subjectivity, which, in fact, would itself be crushed in the dialectical movement of irony as Kierkegaard develops it (see Kierkegaard). In effect, Casais Monteiro opts for a poet's version of Mar Talegre's "transposition" argument: for him, the poet, by writing poetry from various viewpoints, explores and communicates "humanity." He thus adds to

Mar Talegre's position the feature of an inter-subjective horizon in which
"transposition" works—and subtracts from that position its nationalist cast.
In the final analysis, then, Casais Monteiro appeals to a "European"
theorization about poetry that seems to provide an analogue to the problematics
that he sees in reading Pessoa. Eliot and Kierkegaard legitimize Monteiro's
"Pessoa" by presenting a theorization that seems to speak to, and to be
seconded by, Pessoa's theory and practice.

The three figures we have looked at briefly here all invoke some
notion of "Europe," seen in varying modes of distinction from Portuguese
tradition, in the development of Fernando Pessoa as an object of study—a
development in which they were pivotal figures. From presentation within
Portugal of "Fernando Pessoa" as a contributor of something "Portuguese" to
a generally superior European "poetics," to his use as anchor of a Europe-
oriented critical modality to be implanted as the bulwark of institutional
criticism, to a linking of him, taken as critical/poetic exemplar, to contemporary
European theorization about "impersonal" art, "Pessoa"—with all the diverse
stakes invested in him—was effected in considerable part through allusions to
a "Europe" toward which "Portugal" could profitably move. All three cases,
albeit variously, see "Europe" as a positive force, a source of cultural value
beyond Portuguese tradition.

This observation is important, for it in fact indicates a receptivity to
aspects of "European" culture in the late 1940's and early 1950's, in the face
of the official discourse which invoked a national tradition supposed to exist
precisely in opposition to "Europe." Portuguese allegiances during World War
II were divided at best, with a good deal of government-level cooperation with
the Axis powers. And, after the war's close, the country was run by a
government whose discourse of legitimation was still much of a piece with
that of the defeated Axis nations. It must also be recalled, however, that
Portugal's new alliances, the loose coalition of "Allied" forces that in early
1949—at, then, the very moment about which we are speaking—would be
formed into NATO, were perforce with the victorious Allies. It thus seems
fair to say that those Portuguese in a position to appreciate the ambiguities
therein involved—I am not necessarily speaking of conscious analysis here—
found themselves with some degree of maneuvering room for the discursive
grounding of their endeavors. What the foregoing precis suggest is that for a
significant number in the area of literary criticism, "Fernando Pessoa,"
available as a figure to be developed, provided a vehicle to exercise of some
of those options and had the basic contours of his "European" modality
"invented" in that struggle.

Notes

[1] This and all translations not otherwise indicated are my own.

[2] I should remark that there was a "traditionalist" "Pessoa" developed at this time as well and the notion of Pessoa as having a "mission" or bearing a "message" to the world at large is a central motif in that "invention." That line is followed by figures—António Quadros, Agostinho da Silva, and others—more thoroughly involved in traditionalist thought than is Mar Talegre and, moreover, figures who do not give positive consideration to "Europe." The issue is referred to in Sousa 1985.

[3] An explanation about the provenience of terms and nature of references is necessary here. The second edition (1963) of *Diversidade e Unidade* varies from the first in many ways, since one of the unspoken motivations of the reediting process was to keep the book (and bibliography) up to date with new criticism on the poet and his work. Thus in this case the very politics of editing represent a part of the "dynamics" at the "locus of semiosis": in effect, Prado Coelho intended to have "his" "Pessoa" continually updated and continually re-presented in relation to new formulations that arose over the years. One of the areas of change between the first and second editions is to be found in the prefatory material; the two-page "Prefácio" of 1949 is abandoned for a new, longer "Prefácio da Segunda Ediçao," and it is in the latter that the phrase "immanent criticism" is used. My reading here takes the preface of the 1949 edition as programatic and the 1963 replacement as to some extent a commentary upon that original preface. Thus I see the "immanent criticism" of 1963 as a label for the practice outlined and carried out in the 1949 volume. I therefore read back and forth between the two prefaces, though the 1949 text is my basis and I refer to it alone unless I indicate otherwise. I cite the 1963 second edition through the more accessible third edition (1969).

[4] See, e. g., Casais Monteiro 1954 and 1958.

[5] In Northern Europe, that theorization in fact came in correlation with what Prado Coelho calls "immanent criticism." The two issues come to us separately because of the particular mode of their cultivation in Portugal and because of the specific focusses of Prado Coelho, academic critic, and Monteiro, poet-essayist.

Works Cited

Casais Monteiro, Adolfo. *Estudos sobre a Poesia de Fernando Pessoa*. São Paulo: n. p., 1958.

---. *Fernando Pessoa, O Insincero Verídico.* Lisboa: Editorial Inquérito, 1954.
---. "Teoria da Impersonalidade: Fernando Pessoa e T. S. Eliot." *O Tempo e o Modo*:: 68 (1969): 204-209.

Kierkegaard, Søren. *The Concept of Irony, With Constant Reference to Socrates* (1841). Trans. Lee M. Capel. Bloomington: Indiana University Press, 1965.

Prado Coelho, Jacinto. *Diversidade e Unidade em Fernando Pessoa.* Lisboa: Edição da Revista 'Ocidente,' 1949.
---. *Diversidade e Unidade em Fernando Pessoa.* 3rd ed. Lisboa: Editorial Verbo, 1963.

Mar Talegre. *Três Poetas Europeus (Camões. Bocage. Pessoa.)* Lisboa: Sá da Costa, 1947.

Sousa, Ronald W. "Adolfo Casais Monteiro and Pessoa's 'Sincerity.'" *Selecta* 1 (1980): 71-74.
---. "Literature and Portuguese Fascism: The Face of the Salazarist State, Preceded by Two Pre-Faces." *Fascismo y Experiencia Literaria: Reflexiones Para una Recanonización.* Ed. Hernán Vidal. Monographic Series 2. Minneapolis: Society for the Study of Contemporary Hispanic and Lusophone Revolutionary Literature, 1985. 95-141.

Unamuno, Miguel de. *Del sentimiento trágico de la vida en los hombres y en los pueblos.* New York: Las Américas, 1965.
---. *Tragic Sense of Life.* Trans. J. E. Crawford Flitch. New York: Dover Publications, 1954. (English trans. of the preceding.)

Pepetela and the New Angolan Mythology

Mary L. Daniel

"Pepetela" is the literary pseudonym and former *nom de guerre* of Arthur Maurício Pestana dos Santos, born in Benguela, Angola, in 1941. His political and military involvement with the MPLA during the Colonial Wars and his subsequent role in the government of independent Angola lie outside the purview of this study but form the background for his fictional works. Pepetela is the Angolan novelist most concerned with a broad examination of national culture, past and present, with an eye to the construction of a coherent, multifaceted Angolan self-awareness and mythology. He has been called a "muralist" in the style of Latin American painters Siqueiros (Mexico) and Portinari (Brazil) though his painting is done with words rather than a brush. Students of Brazilian literature have likened him to Erico Veríssimo in the broad scope of his vision, the balance of his perspective, the sincerity and depth of his human commitment, and the accessiblity of his prose. It is too early to speak definitively of his literary accomplishments because he appears to be currently at the height of his career as a writer; nevertheless it is not too early to point out an aspect of his vision that may well be the key to the eventual interpretation of his work as a whole. During the ten-year period from 1980 to 1990, Pepetela published the three novels that form the basis of our analysis: *Mayombe* (1980), already in English translation; *Yaka* (1984); and *Lueji* (1990). Though unrelated to each other in terms of immediate thematic content, the three works form a kind of tripartite unfolding of a nascent national mythology; the presentation of such a mythology for a newly independent Angola is an enterprise to which Pepetela has dedicated himself with intentionality and vigor. Both Webster's definition of *myth* as "a story ... that ostensibly relates historical events, which are usually of such character as to serve to explain some practice, belief, institution, or natural phenomenon" (*New International Dictionary of the English Language*, 2nd ed.) and *The American College Dictionary*'s definition of sociological myth as "a collective belief that is built

77

up in response to the wishes of the group rather than an analysis of the basis of the wishes" are applicable to what Pepetela is about, though he may be seen as *creator* from one perspective and as *collector* from the other.

Mayombe, the first of the three novels under examination, is set in the forests of Cabinda during the early 1960s, near the onset of the Colonial War against Portuguese administration of the "Overseas Provinces." Its cast of characters is a group of guerrilla fighters from various regions of Angola who form a human nucleus working from a small base in the bosom of the rainforest. As their military activity proceeds throughout the novel, so do their attempts at coming to terms with their own ethnic and regional diversity and understanding the overall goals and administration of the independence movement. The group includes Kikongos, Kimbundos, Cabindas, a "detribalized" urban youth (Muatiânvua), a mulatto (Teoria), and sundry others caught in traditional inter-tribal tensions with a need to overcome these for the benefit of the greater cause. The predominantly masculine cast of characters includes European-educated Marxist theorists, pragmatic rural residents, and soldiers of varying degrees of politicization displaying a wide scope of personal and partisan commitment to the campaign for independence.

Mayombe takes on epic proportions, in addition to its immediate socio-political theme, from the initial epigraph preceding the text of the novel: "Aos guerrilheiros do Mayombe, que ousaram desafiar os deuses abrindo um caminho na floresta obscura, vou contar a história de Ogun, o Prometeu africano." The Classical Prometheus, stealer of fire for newly-created humanity, has been displaced by Ogun, the Nagô god of war. The Mayombe forest itself appears throughout the novel as a benevolent, though overpowering, matrix possessing both "masculine" and "feminine" qualities: the forest "gave birth" to the guerrilla base (70), nourishes the fighters by the edible fruits and pods falling from the trees (p. 71), and trembles at the mortar fire accompanying heavy fighting. Reversing the Eurocentric myth of Zeus punishing Prometheus for stealing fire to help humanity, Mayombe seeks to protect Ogun, now identified as the collectivity nestled under its canopy: "Zeus vergado a Prometeu, Zeus preocupado com a salvaguarda de Prometeu" (70). "Tal é o atributo do herói, o de levar os homens a desafiarem os deuses. Assim é Ogun, o Prometeu africano" (71). And as the guerrilla commander lies dying on the forest floor after being hit by enemy fire in a skirmish, he perceives the trunk and foliage of the jungle mulberry tree as symbolic of the hero-collective relationship: "O tronco destaca-se do sincretismo da mata, mas se eu percorrer com os olhos o tronco para cima, a folhagem dele mistura-se à folhagem geral e é de novo o sincretismo. Só o tronco se destaca, se individualiza. Tal é o Mayombe, os gigantes só o são em parte, ao nível do tronco, o resto confunde-se na massa. Tal o homem" (266). The commander's body is respectfully left to rest by his troops in the bosom of Mayombe, and the narrow human trails cut in the rainforest gradually begin to disappear: "O Mayombe recuperaria o que os homens ousaram tirar-lhe" (268). The apotheosis of Commander Sem-Medo at novel's end signals the multifaceted trajectory of reconciliation which Pepetela considers necessary: the merging of individual with group, of humanity with natural environment, of ethnic and linguistic groups with each other, to create the collective Angolan mythic hero of the future. The Africanized Prometheus is multiple and varied, and no single beaten track which all must tread may be discerned:

> "Sem Medo. . . insistia em que era um caminho no deserto. Por isso se ria dos que diziam que era um trilho cortando, nítido, o verde do Mayombe. Hoje sei que não há trilhos amarelos no meio do verde. Tal é o destino de Ogun, o Prometeu africano" (270).

Four years after the publication of *Mayombe*, Pepetela broadened his focus in the field of historical fiction to incorporate the southern region of Benguela over an eighty-five year period crucial to Angola's economic and political evolution; *Yaka* (1984) is the saga of a predominantly white Angolan family from 1890 through 1975 as it develops its generational branches in the context of the indigenous Cuvale and Bailundo cultures and the close proximity of South Africa. The resulting panoramic view of regional and national events, including the birth and activity of the three main Angolan independence movements (MPLA, FNLA, and Unita), makes use of two strands of mythological tradition—the African and the Greek. Almost all the given names of the nuclear Semedo family evoke Classical heroes, heroines, or writers; Alexandre, Aquiles, Aristóteles, Sócrates, Orestes, Eurídice, Helena, Heitor, Ulisses, and Demóstenes carry on the family respect for European antiquity, and patriarch Alexandre "[a]creditava mais em Afrodite e Atena que no Cristo" (ll3). His latent syncretism extends to other religious practices as well: "No fundo, ainda não tinha descoberto quais os deuses que o protegiam e os que o perseguiam. Pensou mesmo em ir ao grupo espírita" (113). This same man treasures a large wooden statue from the Lunda region of northeastern Angola which has worked its way south to Benguela and come into his family's possession. The tribal interaction of ancient Angola is saluted at the novel's beginning as the *yaka* statue is designated by the author as a symbol of cultural transmission from *within*:

> Yaka, Mbayaka, jaga, imbangala?
> Foram uma mesma formação social (?), Nação (?) —

aos antropólogos de esclarecer. Certo é que agitaram a
já tremeluzente História de Angola, com as suas incursões
no Reino do Congo... Foi o princípio do que se sabe.
Na Matamba, deram força à legendária Rainha Njinga
(ou Nzinga), que empurrou o exército português até no
mar. Talvez Njinga fosse yaka? A hipótese ainda não
morreu. Os ditos guerreiros, que por comodidade chamo
de yaka, desceram para o sul... Tiveram influência certa
no dito Reino de Benguela, formaram chefias nas terras
dos Muila, Gambo, já lá bem no Sul, irrequietamente
voltaram a subir, formaram chefias no Planalto Central,
em Caconda, Huambo, Bailundo, Bié...
        E o círculo yaka ficou fechado nesses séculos antigos.
        Criadores de chefias, assimiladores de culturas,
formadores de exércitos com jovens de outras populações
que iam integrando na sua caminhada, parecem apenas
uma idéia errante, cazumbi antecipado da nacionalidad.
        Mas não é deles que trata este livro, só duma estátua.
(6)

        As to the statue itself, "é pura ficção... [e]la poderia ter existido. Mas
não. Por acaso. Daí a necessidade de a criar, como mito recriado. Até porque
só os mitos têm realidade. E como nos mitos, os mitos criam a si próprios,
falando" (Ibid.). Throughout the novel, Alexandre Semedo uses the statue as
his "narratee" and sounding-board, but since he dies just when the factionalism
of the independence movements begins to assert itself, it is the statue itself
which has the "last word" in the novel. Foreseeing the future of a sovereign
Angola as the fulfillment of its own cultural "mission," Yaka ponders the
timing of political events and wonders if it is still premature to hope. Will the
future bring centripetal or centrifugal socio-cultural development? Will the
independent nation scatter or gather? Yaka's existence has thus far served as
a symbol of potential interregional unity and cultural continuity, but the time
has come for reality to replace symbol . . . or has it? The novel ends on an
uncertain note:

        Minha criação está aí em torrentes de esperança, a
        anunciada chegou.
                Posso então me desequilibrar do soco e ficar em
        cacos pelo chão, a boca para um lado, os olhos pelo mar,
        o coração embaixo da terra, o sexo para o Norte e as
        pernas para o Sul? Ou será melhor aguardar ainda?
        (302).

Yaka's ambiguous facial features had led family observers to identify her as both a parody of Europeans and a symbol of atavistic forces. The ambivalence as to who are the heroes and who the villains of Angola's past and future remains to the novel's end. The mythic monsters of the South, *oma-kisi*, are evoked as the equivalent of vampires because of the folk belief that they have sharp teeth and eat people every day, yet at the same time these awesome creatures represent in hydra-headed fashion the resurgent will of the people to be free of colonial oppression:

> Os colonos diziam tinha muitas revoltas. Não tinha nada, era só uma. Como os oma-kisi, monstros comedores de gente, renasciam de cada vez lhes cortavam uma cabeça. Sempre. Porque a fonte de oma-kisi não secava, estava nos olhos. Os olhos apontavam a lonjura da minha criação (96).

The Semedo family is a microcosm of multiple political factions and value systems emerging on the eve of Angolan independence, and serves to incorporate both southern Angola and an intellectual white/mulatto family into Pepetela's fictional "scheme of things." The third and (to date) definitive step in this broadening of ethnic, regional, and historical scope comes in the author's latest novel, *Lueji* (published late in 1990). This "double novel" simultaneously traces parallel lines of development between the career of Queen Lueji in sixteenth century Lunda and the mulatta ballerina Lu in the Luanda of 1999 as she attempts to create an authentically national ballet; in short, Pepetela intertwines the historical and thematic background and the future artistic realization of the subject of the founding of an Angolan empire. Replete with aesthetic and political artifacts and symbols, this quintessential example of what the novel itself calls "realismo animista" (451) is a *tour de force* of thorough ethno-historical research of northeastern and central Angola and multifaceted awareness of national and international trends and problems at the end of the twentieth century. The novel masterfully intertwines multiple threads into an incipient mythological tapestry of modern Angola, but avoids facile polarization by leaving hard questions for the reader (whether Angolan or foreign) to ponder: Should traditions be *kept* or *created*? If by definition ethnic versions of origins and heroes are ideological, should later versions of the same stories be stripped of their religious-ideological content in order to be contextualized in a wider scale? What constitutes cultural adulteration? What are the parameters of authenticity in the modern world? What is the role of the "cultural elite" (e.g., ballet troupes, artistic workshops, scholars of history) in the formation of a coherent national cultural awareness among the masses? Are myths "doomed" to continuous evolution without ever achieving a definitive form?

The sixteenth century strand of *Lueji* traces the development of the Lunda-Luba alliance, the breakdown of the traditional Lunda politico-social structures, and the expansion of empire in geographic scope and innovative practice as various factions interpret and develop the same ethnic traditions in diverse and sometimes conflictive ways. Simultaneously (the two novelistic strands intertwine within the same paragraphs and sentences), four hundred years later a Luandan ballet corps struggles to achieve an authentically national art form and preservation of a mythic past by rejecting the Marxist plot and Slavic musical patterns suggested by a visiting European choreographer in favor of the recreation of the story of Lueji and her empire danced to the music of African instruments such as the marimba and the kissanje. The stylization of the traditional and the aesthetic recreation of once-powerful beliefs lead to frequent debates among the dancers involved, who hail from all areas and several ethnic sub-groups of Angola; the result is a microcosm of the intellectual and cultural training experienced by a cross-section of Angolan creative artists, doctors, and business interests during the last quarter of the twentieth century. The invention of electronic kissanjes and the incorporation of lasers into the staging of the ballet are juxtaposed with the wearing of tribal amulets by dancers and the invocation by head ballerina Lu of the spirit of Queen Lueji to neutralize production problems as the ballet progresses. Lu herself synthesizes multi-ethnic differences as she draws inspiration from both the black and white sides of her family and attempts to neutralize value- and ethnic-based frictions among other members of her troupe.

In both the sixteenth century and contemporary strands of *Lueji*, strong female protagonists dominate the scene and face choices that affect not only their own professional careers (the queenship of Lunda and choice of husband-consort in the case of Lueji and the creation of ballet score and selection of head dance partner in the case of Lu) but also the long-term future of their enterprise: empire-building for the former and recuperation of an Angolan cultural patrimony for the latter. Both women stand at crossroads in their careers and know that their decisions will redound to their honor or dishonor in days to come; both are looked to as leaders of others and agonize over the implications of their responsibilities.

Though in this novel the equivalency of European and African mythical entities plays a lesser role than in the two previously mentioned works, the female gender of Tchyanza Ngombe — serpent-progenitor of the Lundas—is fundamental to the text. The *oma-kisi* change their role from symbol of grassroots opposition to colonialism (in *Yaka*) to menacing symbol of aerial military aggression originating in South Africa and interpreted in two parallel yet divergent ways in competing versions of the national ballet being created in *Lueji*. In the disastrous Marxist version propounded by the imported Czech choreographer, the invaders are repelled by Angolan soldiers determined to save their newly-won turf from further incursions, while in the version commonly understood among the national dancers themselves there is a magical element which the Eurocentric mind is incapable of comprehending:

> Ele mudou a estória, não é? A luta principal no "Cahama" é a dos soldados angolanos contra os oma-kisi, os monstros míticos do Sul, os quais se vencem pela coragem e sobretudo pela esperteza. Os oma-kisi vêm vomitando fogo pela boca, arrasam tudo, tentam tudo engolir. Se sentem donos e senhores, na sua superioridade branca de espectros. E pela frente encontram os soldados, quais miúdos espertos e teimosos que se não deixam engolir. Defendendo a sua onganda até ao fim... O espanto faz descomandar as engrenagens dos computadores que estão nas cabeças dos oma-kisi, as respostas ilógicas dos nossos queimam os circuitos lógicos deles, e os oma-kisi ardem em curto-circuitos electrónicos. Esta é a estória verdadeira do que passou na Cahama. Do que passou todos os dias no nosso Sul, mítico-verdadeiro. Vem um gajo, resolve mudar tudo. Claro, aconteceu o que tinha de acontecer. Os espíritos que com os nossos estavam na Cahama se revoltaram, sabotaram tudo e adeus espetáculo. Se ao menos o checo tivesse feito oferendas aos espíritos... (75)

The solution, from Lu's point of view, is the creation of an entirely different ballet which will emphasize not the bellicose images of the recent political past in southern Angola (note similarity with *Yaka*) but rather the broadly sweeping history of cultural diversity and integration incorporating all regions of the nation. It is to be an epic in which the principal culture hero will be a woman — Queen Lueji (Njinga) — and the continuing symbols of identity will be of a more peaceful nature: the sovereign's *lukano* bracelet, the sacred *mulemba* trees, and the *rosas de porcelana* which grow wild on the shore of Lueji's favorite lake.

Diverse opinions reign within the ballet troupe itself as the nature of heroism and mythic qualities is debated by the dancers who perform in the new ballet created by Lu. Cândido, a Cuvale of rural upbringing and Marxist training, maintains that mythic and ancient cultural heroes are somehow remote from current reality and should be discarded in favor of more relevant subject matter, while Lu seeks the middle ground of integration of the traditional and the innovative:

> —Da próxima vez que conceberes um bailado, deixa de lado os Tchinguris, Ilungas e outros e trata os camponeses, os pescadores, os escravos. . .
> —Aproveitei o que conta a tradição, Cândido, e a tradição não trata desses, só dos grandes. Os mitos não se interessam por gente comum. E da gente comum os mitos fazem heróis. A culpa não é minha.
> —Não podias deformar o mito?
> —Até deformei. Mas não a esse ponto. Deixa de ser mito. (478-479)

Three stages of cultural awareness and application emerge in the theoretical discussions among artists that make *Lueji* a work of metafiction. Cândido exemplifies a large rural population, part of which retains in relatively pristine form its belief in traditional gods and supernatural forces who determine the course of human existence while another segment (including the dancer himself) has rejected all such beliefs in favor of the alternative determinism of materialistic Marxism. Lu and others of the company have chosen the third, more reconciliatory position, which seeks out cultural foundations and artifacts with an eye to recreating and staging them in stylized and selective artistic fashion for a modern, largely urban public:

> O poder tradicionalista baseia-se nisso. Dos velhos sobre os novos, dos homens sobre as mulheres, das ideias velhas sobre as ideias novas. E a submissão do homem à Natureza. O homem se torna incapaz de iniciativas para mudanças benéficas, pois tudo gira segundo a vontade dos ventos ou do oma-kisi. O homem acaba por não contar, é um joguete das forças superiores. . . Devemos aproveitar os cânticos, as danças, as outras artes tradicionais. Mas depurando-as das crendices obscurantistas.
> — O que significa adulterar a cultura, pois esta é um todo.
> — Qualquer aperfeiçoamento é uma adulteração. E nenhuma cultura se mantém parada. (456)

Pepetela's latest novel combines theory and practice regarding the creation (or recreation) of a national Angolan mythology for the future. His conclusion that independent Angola must draw inspiration from all sources and achieve its own unique "mix" by consensus is suggested early in the work as he ponders the end of a millenium: "Os velhos mitos renasciam com a aproximação do ano 2000. Medos. Esperanças. Arritimias. Fim do Mundo. Julgamento Final? Bem procurávamos nos afastar desses temores, pensando isso são mitos da Europa, lendas criadas a partir dos semitas e do Novo Testamento, que temos nós, bantos, a ver com isso, os nossos mitos são outros, de nascimento e formação, não de mortes e catástrofes escritas em livros antigos. Mas o Mundo deixara de ser o somatório de mundos fechados, era um só, cada vez mais mestiço" (26-27). The ballet troupe itself becomes a metaphor for the reconciliation of ethnic, regional, and cultural differences as these become factors of enrichment rather than conflict.

From the recent past and far north of Cabinda, represented in *Mayombe*, through the panoramic view of the southern Benguela region and its unique drama, traced in *Yaka*, to the imperial history of the Lunda-Luba dynasty of northeastern Angola and its later proliferation throughout the national territory in both political and cultural terms, as viewed in *Lueji*, Pepetela has gathered the raw material and suggested a creative methodology for the formation of a national mythology for modern Angola, both inclusive and authentic, dynamic and lyric, problematic and promising, and having an increasingly decisive feminine component. At no point does he offer a set scheme or closed symbolic system, preferring rather to follow several alternative routes of investigation and suggest diverse thematic threads. It remains to be seen whether he will develop this focus further in future novels and whether other Angolan writers will also take up the tools of the New Historicism *and* of traditional African oral literature to pursue a similar epic enterprise.

Works Cited

Pepetela. *Lueji*. Lisbon: Dom Quixote, 1990.
---. *Mayombe*. (first Brazilian edition). São Paulo: Atica, 1982.
---. *Yaka*. São Paulo: Atica, 1984.

LINGUSITICS AND LANGUAGE

O Impacto da Reforma Ortográfica no Mundo Lusófono

Richard A. Preto-Rodas

O meu tema reflete uma constante da cultura portuguesa que remonta a vários séculos. Em pleno Renascimento, em 1540 para ser mais preciso, João de Barros na sua *Gramática da Língua Portuguesa*, observou com respeito á ortografia "... quem curiosidades quiser... achará tantas que pode gastar um par de vidas" (Barros, 40). No que segue eu pretendo focalizar umas quantas dessas curiosidades sobretudo as que se referem ao Acordo Ortográfico de 1986 e que são decorrentes desta tentativa mais recente para codificar o português escrito.

"Acordo ortográfico" como tema cultural constitui em si uma curiosidade da língua portuguesa, pois são poucas as línguas que oferecem tantas experiências gráficas como a nossa. A partir da *Gramática* de Fernão de Oliveira em 1536 e até os nossos dias têm - se vertido rios de tinta sobre esse assunto tão espinhoso que é a ortografia. Haja vista a pequena bibliografia que aparece ao fim deste trabalho. Depois das gramáticas renascentistas apareceu no século dezessete o tratado de João Franco Barreto, *Ortografia da Gramática Portuguesa* seguido no século dezoito pelo estudo de João de Morais, *Ortografia ou Arte de Escrever a Língua Portuguesa* (1739). No século dezenove temos o *Ensaio sobre A Ortografia* de Carlos Augusto de Figueiredo Vieira (1844). Outros trabalhos parecidos chegam a exemplificar as "curiosidades" de João de Barros. Na *Gramática Portuguesa* de Joaquim da Costa Rubim (1880), por exemplo, as regras ortográficas são versejadas por Feliciano de Castilho. No nosso século o afã para codificar a ortografia tem-se intensificado em vista da alfabetização crescente tanto em Portugal quanto no Brasil. O intuito sempre visa a simplificação da ortografia, aproximando a língua escrita à oral. Porém, esse propósito de simplificar, tão digno de louvor em teoria, contém as sementes duma controvérsia que ameaça a integridada da própria língua; i.é., se uma ortografia simplificada deve refletir a maneira de falar, então como se pode respeitar as várias maneiras de falar que caraterizam as modalidades brasileiras, europeias, e africanas dos países onde se emprega o português? Já em 1875 escrevia Macedo Soares na primeira página do seu *Dicionário Brasileiro da Língua Portuguesa*: "Já é tempo de os brasileiros escreverem como se fala no Brasil, e não como se escreve em Portugal" (Prestes). Como já foi indicado, o século vinte tem sido um período especialmente fértil no que se refere ao esforço para sistematizar o português escrito. E cada tentativa realça cada vez mais a divergência crescente entre o ideal e a realidade. O malogro do Acordo de 1907, quase universalmente ignorado, levou ao Acordo de 1931 que acabou com as grandes complicações gráficas, como os ph's e os y's de raíz clássica. Mas os defensores da essência latina da língua decretaram em 1934 a restauração da ortografia tradicional, ou seja a "clássica". Em 1938 se impôs o retorno à simplificação decretada em 1931. E o vaivém continua com reformas e acordos em 1940, 1943, 1945, e 1954.

Em maio de 1967 o primeiro Simposio Luso-Brasileiro sobre A Língua Portuguesa Contemporânea propôs a unificação definitiva. O propósito era acabar com as pequenas diferenças nos livros dos dois países. Para alcançar tal desiderato, o Simpòsio recomendou, primeiro, a eliminação das consoantes mudas, prática, aliàs, adotada havia muito no Brasil. O que não se pronuncia devia ser abolido na escrita. A segunda reforma afetava certas palavras proparoxítonas que levam acento agudo em Portugal e circunflexo no Brasil. A meta era neutralizar na língua escrita uma diferença notada na pronúncia. Portanto, se os portugueses dizem "económico" e os brasileiros "econômico", a supressão dos acentos agudos e circunflexos assim teria como resultado positivo a unidade ortográfica tão desejada sem falsear a realidade linguística dos dois países.

Mal terminou o Simpósio e já ardia o debate. Em Portugal opuseram-se os defensores da etimologia que lamentavam o desaparecimento das consoantes mudas. Sem dois c's em "secção" ou um p em "baptizado" a tendência dos portugueses para reduzirem as vogais átonas seria ainda mais agravada. Os que apelavam à retenção das consoantes mudas avisavam que sem as consoantes ameaçadas pela reforma, em conformidade com 'scada e 'spelho e m'nino se passaria a dizer "'s' ção" e "b'tizado." Para eles as consoantes mudas eram precisas para "abrirem" as vogais anteriores. De parte dos brasileiros houve também vozes contestatórias contra as recomendaçõs do Simpósio. A objeção principal se referia às proparoxítonas onde as vogais eram fechadas no Brasil e abertas em Portugal. Guimarães Rosa foi peremptório: "A proposta tira-nos bastante. . . somos por sua rejeição." Também em contra estava Adonias Filho. E Aurélio Buarque de Holanda achou que mesmo sendo possível a reforma, não deixava de ser "perigosa" por aumentar "a sensação de insegurança que experimentamos em face das successivas reformas." Só uns poucos, Josué Montelo entre eles, apoiaram a simplificação gráfica.[1] Porém, o desejo de muitos para neutralizar todas as diferenças ganhou força nos anos seguintes, em parte devido às instâncias de órgaos internacionais como a UNESCO que solicitavam uma ortografia oficial aprovada por Portugal e o Brasil. Outro acordo em 1971 entre a Academia Brasileira de Letras e a Academia das Ciências de Lisboa aprovou certas medidas que efetivamente aproximavam as duas grafias ao mesmo tempo que as simplificavam. Os representantes dos dois países recomendaram a abolição do circunflexo diferencial exeção feita de "por" e "pôr" e "pode" e "pôde". Assim é que acabaram-se os subtantivos das formas verbais homógrafas como "almoço" e "almôço." Como ainda está de vigor o Acordo de 1971, a codificação resultante se vê em qualquer livro ou jornal atual. Mas o mesmo jornal ou livro continua a oferecer certas irregularidades que persistem conforme o país de origem. Assim é que permanece a famosa questão das consoantes mudas. O "jornal atual" no Brasil é o "jornal actual" em Portugal. E as esdrúxulas ou proparoxítonas continuam a criar uma cisão que é polêmica no Brasil e polémica em Portugal. Além disso, as antigas discórdias entre familiares agora são causa de dissensão nos foros internacionais onde apareceram a partir dos anos setenta cinco países africanos que adotaram o português como língua oficial. Qual deve ser a grafia dos livros de texto e dos jornais angolanos e moçambicanos? É lógico que a antiga metrópole queira manter a sua ascendência cultural sobretudo no lucrativo mercado do livro. Agravando a situação é o fato que a ortografia de Lisboa nem sempre convém às editoras de Luanda e Maputo. Como amostra cito o famosa argumento luso para conservar as consoantes mudas (i.é., para "abrirem" as vogais pretônicas) que pouco peso tem entre os lusófonos dos países africanos onde a tendência é como no Brasil, para articular todas as vogais átonas. Nesse contexto imposto por considerações que transcendem as preferências nacionais, realizou-se no Rio de Janeiro em maio de 1986 mais um congresso onde esta vez participaram representantes de todos os sete países onde o português é a língua oficial. Os congressistas aprovaram a supressão das famosas consoantes mudas como também a eliminação de todos os acentos nas palavras proparoxítonas. Também reduziram a maioria dos hífens. As três reformas deveriam ser adotadas universalmente a partir do primeiro de janeiro de1989. Como se venceu o prazo há tempos e continuamos na mesma, é evidente que o Acordo de 1986 marcou mais um passo em falso. Agora vamos ver as causas e as implicações desse mais recente tropeço ortográfico.

Com respeito à eliminação das famigeradas consoantes mudas estamos diante dum caso de *déjà vu*. Para os portugueses que as conservam, abrir mão dos c's e p's é o mesmo que ceder à grafia brasileira onde a língua escrita acompanha mais de perto a língua oral há muitos anos. E por quê não ceder? pode-se perguntar. Há quem de fato ache que tal concessão por parte dos portugueses seria, nas palavras do lisboeta Ivo Castro, um exemplo "de lógica e de coerência."[2] Contudo, ele representa uma minoria. Invocando a dignidade nacional a maioria reclama contra a recomendação da sua própria Academia das Ciências. Assim é que a escritora Inês Duarte indaga "Por quê é que se reconhece a legitimidade da grafia brasileira?" Para ela como para muitos outros o que vale é menos o ortografia do que a política, já que resistem uma modificação por lhes parecer uma capitulação ao uso brasileiro.

Às vezes a oposição à reforma assume um ar de verdadeira causa jurídica. Assim é que Vasco Graça Moura vale-se do estatuto legislativo que reconhece a ortografia já em vigor para rejeitar tanto a linguística quanto a cordialidade internacional. Para ele a reforma é "inconstitucional por lesão do patrimônio cultural português. . . nos termos do artículo 71 da constituição da República." A mera suposição que Portugal possa vir a imitar o Brasil provoca Luisa Costa Gomes a vociferar "Antes o exílio. . . estamos dispostos a usar do nosso direito de resistência, promovendo um apelo à desobediência cívica generalizada." Assim é que uma questão como a das consoantes mudas desaparece por trás duma retórica descrita pelo brasileiro Moacir Werneck de Castro como "uma estranha explosão de zanga envenenada. . . como sequela do trauma da descolonização, do luto pelo império perdido. . . laivos rançosos de xenofobia, de sebastianismo, de salazarismo." Para alguns parece que a eliminação das consoantes mudas implica uma crise de identidade, se vamos a tomar em sério um escritor luso que observa: "Escrevendo acto sinto-me eu. Escrevendo ato, quem serei?" E sua patrícia Maria Lúcia Garcia Marques vê a supressão do c mudo em cores verdadeiramente trágicas quando ela parafraseia o famoso dilema de Hamlet: "C ou não C, eis a questão!"

Quanto à supressão dos acentos nas palavras esdrúxulas, o segundo ponto que há de levar à unidade tão desejada, o fervor oposionista é menos ardente. O brasileiro Celso Cunha aplaude a reforma como medida econômica achando que a proposta seria "um grande benefício, que cada acento que se escreve é como se escrevesse uma letra. . . é tinta que se gasta a mais, mais esforço." Porém, existe certa resistência nos meios escolares em geral já que sem acento muitos alunos não poderiam saber onde recai a tônica das palavras que lêem pela primeira vez. Celso Cunha rejeita essa objeção em nome da teoria gestaltista segundo a qual a criança "passa do signo escrito ao signo oral imediatamente." É evidente que ele supõe que os alunos tenham todos o português como a língua materna. Mas o que se pode esperar no caso do aluno que nunca ouviu a palavra? O problema seria bem mais sério fora de Portugal e do Brasil, naqueles paises onde a vasta maioria da população escolar aprende o português como língua escrita e não como língua materna. Em quase toda a Africa onde o português é a língua oficial a suposta simplificação que elimina o acento sobre a sílaba tônica pode ter a consequência de dificultar a aprendizagem. A reserva é muito notavel entre os moçambicanos que declaram que "sem acentos tudo vai ser mais difícil." O poeta Gulamo Khan chega a profetizar, de certo com exageração, "Não havendo acentos, será a catástrofe."

O terceiro ponto do acordo, a quase abolição do hífen, tem provocado relativamente pouca discussão. O crítico português Herculano de Carvalho até chega a classificá-lo "de somenos importância," o que não significa que haja pleno acordo. Pelo menos uma voz contrária levanta o problema do gênero das palavras compostas, sobretudo quando passam ao plural. Por examplo, se "escola-modelo" é evidentemente feminina (uma escola-modelo) e navio-escola é masculina (um navio-escola), os gêneros seriam menos evidentes no plural sem hífen. Como resistir à tendência para "os escolamodelos" e "as navioescolas"? Assim é que a supressão do hifen poderia afetar a morfologia em certos casos. A vacilação entre gêneros seria ainda mais séria nos países africanos onde abundam os termos compostos. Se pau-canela passasse a escrever-se como uma palavra sem hífen, seria fatal a tendência a mudar o gênero (o pau-canela) para o feminino (a paucanela).

Espero ter esboçado os três pontos principais em que se fundamenta a malograda reforma de 1986. Não obstante o consenso inicial a favor da unificação, o acordo das duas academias começou a desintegrar-se assim que entraram em cena o brio nacionalista de uns e as realidades pedagógicas de outros. Mesmo assim, os cinco paises africanos não se opuseram, e o malogro se deve principalmente à resistência da opinião pública portuguesa.

Como declarou o jornalista moçambicano Miguel Ouana: "Com material publicado pela imprensa portuguesa é possivel editar uma coletânea intitulada "O Desacordo Ortográfico." É dificil escapar à conclusão de que para muitos os portugueses querem ser os donos da língua. Que mais se pode deduzir duma opinião como esta de Freitas do Amaral: "A língua portuguesa é de todos os que a escrevem e falam, sem dúvida, mas começa por ser a língua *portuguesa* (em letras itálicas no original).

Como forjar um acordo quando a política predomina sobre a linguística e ânimos exaltados pouco caso fazem de espíritos imparciais como o português Fernando Cristóvão que aconselha que "Os problemas científicos não são sujeitos a plebiscito." O rancor luso contra um acordo que havia de aproximar a ortografia portuguesa ao uso brasileiro não é simplesmente um produto de vaidades imperiais. O jornalista luso Vasco Graça Moura é muito franco quando ele avisa que a Reforma de 1986 pode facilitar "a conquista do mercado cultural" a favor do Brasil nos países africanos. Contra ele se levanta Fernando Cristóvão que procura lembrar a seus conterrâneos a importância demográfica do Brasil. Como Portugal conta apenas 6,5% da população lusófona no mundo, a aderência portuguesa ao acordo seria aconselhável. Vai sem dizer que o prestígio da própria língua está "com o Brasil e com estas grandes potências que estão a nascer. . . Se alguém precisa dos outros somos nós. . . Isto não é inferioridade para ninguém, isto é pura e simplesmente um ato de inteligência." Outra voz que aconselha mais prudência é a do embaixador de Portugal em Maputo que prevê que o Brasil pode avançar sozinho independentemente de Lisboa. É óbvio que se o Brasil afirmasse o acordo, os países africanos aceitariam como deles a reforma e Portugal ficaria isolado. A consequência seria que a ortografia portuguesa seria reconhecida em toda a parte menos em Portugal. Como nos tempos de Salazar, o país que deu o nome à lingua ficaria "orgulhosamente só." O futuro há de dizer. . .

Ao rever a questão do Acordo de 1986 e a controvérsia desencadeada acabei por simpatizar com um poeta mocambicano que exclama, "O que me admira é que uma coisa tão simples gere tanta polêmica." Claro, para os moçambicanos sobretudo que vivem há anos em estado de guerra, discutir a supressão de consoantes mudas é, como observa o romancista Luis Bernardo Honwana, "como discutir o sexo dos anjos." Eles como os outros povos africanos vão seguir a aprovação decretada definitivamente, seja por Portugal e o Brasil seja pelo Brasil só numa ação unilateral. Entretanto, Moçambique, Angola, Cabo Verde, Guiné-Bissau, e São Tome e Principe têm outros problemas mais urgentes para debaterem.

Talvez essa atitude deva ser a nossa também: ficar na expetativa duma decisão tomada seja por quem for.

Afinal, a ortografia é uma convenção que permite certa flexibilidade, e mesmo um gênio da lingua como Eça de Queirós chegou a mandar um bilhete a seu editor para avisar: "Os acentos, deixo-os à composição, que os ponha onde quiser. " O autor de *Os Maias* estaria de acordo com um jornalista brasileiro anônimo que respondeu a uma sondagem sobre a Reforma de 1986 com o seguinte: "No Brasil já ninguém liga para quem põe ou quem tira acento. Isso é problema de epiderme."

Como ficou indicado no começo deste ensaio, o problema de epiderme que é a ortografia remonta a muitos anos. No nosso século manifesta-se na sucessão de reformas e acordos onde sempre paira a sombra acadêmica dos povos latinos e a sua mania com a correção linguística como dever patriótico. Contudo, o Acordo de 1986 tem revelado mal entendidos e casos de má vontade evitáveis. É realmente escandaloso a meu ver comprovar que eminências da nossa cultura como Celso Cunha, Óscar Lopes, e Herculano de Carvalho acreditem que só o mundo lusófono carece duma ortografia universalmente aceita. Como podem afirmar que "O Portugues é a única língua de cultura com uma dupla ortografia," quando a verdade é que "entre as ortografias oficiais do Reino Unido e dos Estados Unidos da América são maiores as diferenças do que entre as ortografias de Portugal e do Brasil"?[3]

É igualmente lamentável ver a ortografia confundida constantemente nesta controvérsia com a pronúncia. Também confunde-se a cada passo a pronúncia com a estrutura essencial da lingua. De tanta confusão não admira surgirem disparates como o desafio duma Luisa Costa Gomes que escreve: "Se os brasileiros quiserem falar brasileiro, estamos de acordo." E não menos disparatado é aceitar o desafio como faz Afrânio Coutinho ao declarar, "Realmente a língua portuguesa é deles. A nossa é a língua brasileira." Para nós, professores de Português no estrangeiro, opiniões como essas apresentam problemas bem mais graves do que questões sobre consoantes mudas e circunflexos nas proparoxítonas.

No meio de tanta algazarra acho significante que tenha sido a revista galega *Nós* que apoiou o acordo para unificar a ortografia portuguesa.[4] Há certa lógica nesta decisão dos Galegos, pois se há donos ou patriarcas da lingua, são eles. Como já não se interessam por questões de prestígio nacional, podem lamentar que os herdeiros briguem entre si, chegando a ameaçar a integridade da familia lusófona. Sem dúvida os Galegos apreciam o sentimento expresso numa quadra de Manuel Bandeira:

Deus deu a palavra ao homem
E o diabo a ortografia,
Por isso os homens se comem
Nesta orto-antropofagia.[5]

(1989)

Post-Scriptum (1992)

Desde os comentários expressos acima sobre a reforma ortográfica proposta para 1989 pouco de novo tem surgido sobre a questão. Tanto os partidários como os adversários ainda advogam pela sua causa respectiva apelando para princípios e argumentos que misturam considerações linguísticas, econômicas, políticas, e até psicológicas. Os que acham escandaloso que uma língua abranja duas grafias continuam a ignorar o caso semelhante no que se refere ao inglês. Outros parecem dispostos a aceitar a distinção estabelecida pelos tradutores franceses que descrevem um romance de José Saramago como "traduit du portugais" ao passo que outro de Jorge Amado é "traduit du brésilien." Pelo menôs os editores franceses são mais consistentes já que distinguem também entre :"l'anglais" e "l'américain." (Seria interessante saber em que língua editam os livros de autores *québecois*. . .). No meio de tanta confusão os professores de português no estrangeiro que pretendem forjar laços entre os povos ficam confrangidos por uma controvérsia que só pode criar divisões nocivas além de ofender contra a tolerância com respeito à coexistência de vários sotaques, léxicos, e variantes sintácticas.

A meu ver a situação que permite *atual* num país e *actual* noutro não diminui o prazer que se sente quando se lê um livro publicado em São Paulo e outro editado em Lisboa. Tambêm não me parece radical modificar a grafia a favor de *atual* se for aprovada uma só ortografia em benefício das culturas do mundo lusófono (afinal, já tem havido várias sem justificação tão válida. . .) O que não me convence é invocar graves consequências para o português se houver (ou não houver. . .) uma uniformização. Numa visita que fiz a São Paulo em 1990 e noutra a Portugal em 1992 achei razão suficiente para ficar algo preocupado com respeito à saúde do português sem ter que invocar a questão ortográfica. Como se deve encarar uma conjuntura em que as literaturas nacionais são preteridas a favor de traduções nem sempre boas, uma conjuntura em que pouca gente escreve nem que seja uma cartinha para os tios agradecendo o presente de Natal? Ao mesmo tempo por todo o lado parece imperar um jargão tecnocrático pejado de americanismos. Em Lisboa cheguei a perguntar-me se os intelectuais obcecados de consoantes mudas e esdrúxulas sem acento já assistiram a programas de televisão como os jogos olímpicos quando em vez de português preferia-se falar um inglês que seria curioso tanto em Londres como em Chicago. Quem mudava de canal podia consolar-se com um antiquíssimo programa americano dublado em italiano (!). E ainda pode haver quem tema uma crise de identidade provocada pela supressão de um 'c' mudo..? "Mísera sorte! Estranha condição!"

Notas

[1] A controvérsia em 1967 vem resumida no artigo de Prestes.

[2] Quanto a todas as citações que aqui aparecem veja o dossier especial, "Ortografia" publicado pelo jornal, *Letras e Letras* (Porto: Janeiro de 1988), pp. 11-18.

[3] Como exemplo da existência de mais duma ortografia com respeito á língua inglesa, veja D. W. Cummings, *American English Spelling, An Informal Description* (Johns Hopkins University Press, 1988).

[4] Na página 17 do dossier citado cita-se o seguinte que apareceu no numero de Maio/Agosto, 1986 da revista *Nós - Revista Galaicoportuguesa de Cultura:* "A ortografia simplificada. . . é muito mais adequada. . . sem. . . deixar de respeitar a unidade estrutural do Sistema Linguístico Comum e o gênio da língua."

[5] Citado no artigo de Prestes.

Brevíssima Bibliographia Sobre

A Ortografia Portuguesa

João de Barros, *Gramática da Língua Portuguesa* (1540), edição facsimilada da Faculdade de Letras de Lisboa, 1971.

Duarte Nunes de Leão, *Ortografia da Língua Portuguesa* (1576).

João Franco Barreto, *Ortografia da Língua Portuguesa* (1671).

João de Moraes, *Ortografia ou Arte de Escrever A Língua Portuguesa* (1739).

Carlos Augusto de Figueiredo Vieira, *Ensaio sobre A Ortografia Portuguesa* (1844)

Joaquim da Costa Rubim, *Nóvo Metodo da Gramática Portuguesa* (1880).
    V. Regras Ortográficas em versos de Feliciano de Castilho.

Ivo Castro, et al. *A Demanda da Ortografia Portuguesa* (1987).
Comentários sobre o Acordo Ortografico de 1986. O título sugere que o
    tema -uma ortografia oficial universalmente aceita- é mais ou menos
    tão alcançável quanto o Santo Graal.

Bernadete Prestes, "Os Abalos da Língua Portuguesa" no *Jornal do Brasil*
    (10 de setembro de 1967).

Vernacular Speech as a Social Marker in Alvaro Cardoso Gomes' *O Sonho da Terra*

Milton M. Azevedo

The analysis of the representation of vernacular speech in literature furthers our understanding of the ways in which nonstandard language can convey stylistic nuances, cultural connotations, or personality features that reflect character traits such as ethnic or territorial origin, social status, sex, age, or profession.[1] Such nonstandard language includes restricted codes such as regional or social speech varieties which, as Page (1988:94) points out, "however partially and imperfectly represented, enormously widen the range of fictional dialog [in a way] that could not easily be supplied by other means." While the literary depiction of nonstandard talk is not intended as a faithful rendering of its real life counterpart (anymore than a dialog in standard speech is an accurate portrayal of the way people talk), a literary dialect [2] imparts a touch of verisimilitude to characters' speech by capitalizing on the connotations a given regional or social dialect holds for readers.

The significant dichotomy of standard vs. vernacular in Brazilian Portuguese [3] cuts across geographical as well as social boundaries.[4] The scant prestige of the vernacular, with its negative connotations of low social status and scant educational achievement, have traditionally militated against its use as a significant literary medium in its own right. Nevertheless, salient vernacular features have long been utilized, particularly in regionalist fiction, to portray rural or lower-class characters. [5]

Such is the case with the representation of vernacular speech as a stylistic device in Alvaro Cardoso Gomes' prize-winning novel, *O Sonho da Terra*. [6] Its forty-eight chapters, supposedly written by a semi-literate character, narrate events that took place in a mine dubbed Rego Fundo ('Deep Ditch') [7] located somewhere in Brazil's industrialized south. The

99

action climaxes when the narrator and five companions, having survived the collapse of the mine (Chapter 39), go through a series of adventures underground (Chapters 40-47) and ultimately reach the surface somewhere in the state of Alagoas in northeast Brazil (Chapter 48). Such specific locales notwithstanding, Rego Fundo is clearly intended to represent a timeless anti-utopia that might occur anywhere.

The events in Rego Fundo span twenty-one chapters, which embed another twenty-seven containing stories told by individual workers or by characters in the workers' own stories. This story-telling process captures the essence of the rural tradition known in Brazil as *contar casos*, the kind of yarn-spinning that for generations has been a favored entertainment as well as a means of preserving and transmitting the beliefs and traditions of popular culture. Through astute manipulation of vernacular features and a colloquial, the narrators' discourse maintains a degree of verisimilitude thanks to which the scenario of the novel as whole, though anachronistic, remains fictionally plausible.

Several onomastic features underscore popular pratice. One is the use of conspicuously popular nicknames that both enhance in-group solidarity and symbolize some definitory trait of each individual's personality. For example, the supposed narrator's own sobriquet, *Quatroio*, derived from the vernacular pronunciation of *quatro olhos* [kwatróju] 'four eyes', is a common nickname for someone who wears eye glasses. Recalling the old saw that people with glasses are smart (as if metaphorically they could see more than others), this nickname alludes to Quatroio's role as eyewitness and chronicler of events in : "Mesmo Quatroio que é sabido não sabe" (13). The list of workers' nicknames include:

Cão 'hound' (a traditional euphemism for *Devil*): "o ruim do apelido era por causa de tanta ruindade." (15)
Chaminé 'chimney': "Chaminé era negro cabeçudo, mão e braço de pilão, metro e tanto de altura." (17)
Frege 'brawl': "também era esquentado. Não de soberba: é que não gostava de ver o mundo de quatro." (18)
Jegue 'donkey': "Jegue era danado de ignorante." (88)
Risadinha 'little laugh': "... por causa do gênio bom." (18)
Salcinha [standard (st) Salsinha] 'parsley' and *Goiaba* 'guava', slang (sl) terms for 'homosexual': "Não foi o caso de Salcinha, cara de homem, mas fazendo coisa ruim com Goiaba no escuro?" (16)
Zoião 'big eye', from vernacular *zóio*[8] 'eye' + the augmentative suffix -ão: "um sergipano de pêlo no olho" (18)

Fedegoso'stinky' (cf. *feder* 'to stink'): "um paraense fedido, porco."
(18)
Marmeleiro 'swindler, cheat' (cf. sl. *marmelada* 'a swindle'): "um outro, que acho nem raça tinha . . . logo fazendo amizade com os Seguranças . . . mais amigo dos de riba que da gente." (18)

In contrast with the workers, their nameless bosses are known by depersonalized role-titles: the technocrat who runs the mine is *Doutor Engenheiro* 'Doctor Engineer', the company's officials are *Graúdos* 'Big Ones', and the security guards are simply *Seguranças*.

Vernacular vs. Standard

Consistent with the presentation of *O Sonho da Terra* not as oral literature but rather as the transcription of a manuscript written by an uneducated author who retells what he saw and heard, Cardoso Gomes relies primarily on a combination of lexical and morphosyntactic vernacular elements to suggest, rather than reproduce popular speech faithfully.
An example of this discreet handling of vernacular traits is the limited use of such a widespread feature as lack of agreement between a noun and accompanying determiners or adjectives, or between a verb and its subject. Although non-agreement, which occurs regularly in the colloquial speech of educated speakers (Azevedo 1989), has been extensively exploited in literature to signal popular speech,[9] standard agreement is the rule rather than the exception throughout the novel. This choice is compatible with the putative editor's warning that: "chegamos a corrigir erros de ortografia e de sintaxe, mas nos permitimos respeitar impropriedades lingüísticas, que, a nosso ver, dariam mais naturalidades ao relato, de sabor eminentemente oral."(11)
Prominent among the elements that create an oral flavor is the use of *a gente* (literally 'people in general') as an indefinite pronoun ('one') with a first person referent that includes the speaker and optionally other persons of the discourse as well. Although morphologically singular, *a gente* may have a collective referent and so it may cooccur in popular speech with the corresponding first person plural verb form. The alternation of standard singular or nonstandard plural verb forms recreates the performance of vernacular speakers, for whom choice between a singular or plural verb depends on a variable rule.[10] The vernacular tone is thus set in the opening paragraph by two instances of the nonstandard *a gente* + plural verb, soon followed by one of standard *a gente* + singular verb: *A gente conhecemos Frege na primeira leva de "Rego Fundo". Era novato em dois anos. A*

*gente foi que inaugur*amos . . . . *A gente cata porque tem de catar.* (13)
The alternation of standard and vernacular verb agreement with *a gente* is apparent in a total of 50 occurrences, 35 of which have the verb in the plural while 15 have it in the singular, as shown in these examples:

a gente + 3rd sg verb (standard agreement):
>*a gente* ... *não devia de ver o sol* (16); *a gente se arruma*(43)

a gente + 1st pl verb (nonstandard agreement):
>*a gente olha*mos *e acha*mos *demais* (17)
>*a gente se fo*mos (212)
>*a gente se despedi*mos *de lágrima no olho* (215)

There are hybrid cases of *a gente* cooccurring with both a plural and a singular verb, as in the first example below, as well as in occurrences of singular *a gente* with a plural predicate adjective, and a singular verb as in the second example:

>*A gente como não te*mos *se maravilha com o alheio.* (156)
>*A gente, precisad*os, era, *bicho.* (155)

Pronouns

Regarding pronominal usage, in which standard and vernacular contrasts abound, systematic use of the archaic non-intimate pronoun *vosmecê* imparts an old-fashioned quality to dialogues:

>- *Mano* vosmecê *desce e cresce na vida.* (51)
>- Vosmecês *estão querendo ir pra riba.* (210)
>- *Fez bem* vosmecê. (53)

A similar effect is obtained from the obsolescent use of *um/uma* as a kind of indefinite subject or complement pronoun meaning 'someone':

>Uma, *ouvindo maus conselhos* ... *não ficara mal falada?* (97)
>Um *não pode consertar desajuste de destino* (69)

Other salient vernacular pronominal features include:

(a) Lexical pronouns used as direct objects:[11]
>*[Isaltina] Amava* eu (46)
>*levei* ela *pro pasto* (82)

estava eu de riba, sujigando [st. subjugando] ele (47)
(b) Lexical pronouns used as prepositional
complements:
   mas quem podia com nós? (30)
(c) *Lhe*, an indirect object clitic in the standard, used
as direct object:[12]
   É moço de futuro. E lhe *quer, Isaltina* (42)
   Tem gente lhe *esperando* (210)
   Foi Deus . . . quem lhe *pôs em minhas
   mãos* (154)
(d) Clitics in sentence-initial position:
   Me *alembrando hoje* (38)
   Te *capou os possuidos*? (86)
   Se *meta na vida sua* (55)
(e) The stressed pronoun *si*, reflexive in the standard
used as a non-reflexive prepositional complement:[13]
   Vosmecê não ama ela, nem ela a si. (47)
   Gosto só de si. (40)
   Te tirei da vidinha, Leonor. Matei por si. (199)

Alternation of intimate and non-intimate pronouns in direct address
signals a shift in relationships of power and/or solidarity (Brown and
Gilman 1960, Fasold 1990). For example, Vitoriano and Licurgo, two
cattlemen, normally address each other as *vosmecê*, but in a fight, when all
pretense of respect has been dropped, Vitoriano angrily uses intimate *te* as
he threatens Licurgo: *Mais um pio que* te *acabo, Cão do Inferno!* (47)

Likewise, the Engineer addresses the workers formally as *os
senhores* in a tense confrontation, and informally as *vocês* in a more relaxed
moment: *Os senhores não sabem o que querem. . . . Os senhores assinaram
contrato, não assinaram*? (57) *O Dr. Engenheiro deu gargalhada: - Coisa
muito melhor.* Vocês *vão ver.* (104)

Other features

Other vernacular constructions include:
(a) comparisons with *que nem, feito + noun*, or *de + demonstrative:*
   Zoião tremia, feito de terçã (68)
   Fugi que nem condenado (53)
   Homem daquele não era homem (116)
(b) infinitives introduced by a preposition:
   na cabina ninguém não podia de entrar (104)

104   Milton M. Azevedo

Homem deve é de bater (199)
Laudemino começou de tremer (200)
(c) double negatives:
Ninguém não *saía de lá sem satisfação* (89)
De nada não *sabia* (102)
Nunca não *podia sair* (102)

(d) idiomatic prepositional forms and phrases, such as *mais* for *com*
or *pra mode de*:
Morava, mais a mãe velhinha, em Xexém (32);
Pra mode de *convencer o Coronel* (154);
(e) the collective suffix *-aiada*, as in *bodaiada* (21), *cabraiada*
(26), *merdaiada* (184), as well as several instances of nonstandard suffixal
productivity with *-oso/a*: *humildosa* (32), *dinheiroso* (51), *iroso* (47),
lagrimosa (47).[14]

Lexicon

        The vernacular lexicon used includes archaisms still found in rural
speech: *cacunda* (st. *costas*) (14), *prenha* (st. *grávida*) (24), *dianhos* (st.
diabos) (102), *bucho* (st. *ventre*) used with a human referent as in *pensando
na criança no bucho* (51), *carecer* (st. *precisar*) as in *carecia de explicar*
(51), *de riba* (st. *em/de cima*) (47). Other archaic terms involve
morphophonemic variation, such as, for example:

        /v/ for /b/:*avantesma* [st. *abantesma*] (36), *lavaredas*
        [st. *labaredas*] (103)
        /g/ for /v/: *gômito* [st. *vômito*] (23)
        /r/ for /l/: *aluguer* [st. *aluguel*] (51)
        prefixal /a/:*arrespeitou* (17), *alevantar* (37),*apercebeu* (115),
        arresistiria (99)
        diphtongization: *escuitando* [st. *escutando*] (23)

        Vernacular euphemisms are also frequent, such as *os possuídos*
'testicles' (86), *as partes* 'genitals' (200), *as vergonhas* 'genitals' (209),*xibiu*
(188) and *o de entrepernas* 'female genitals' (198). Uninhibited use of
scatological terms, a stamp of Brazilian popular humor, defies purism,
linguistic or otherwise:

> Fedegoso ficou de tanto medo, que começou de peidar algo feito foguete. E deu caganeira nele tremenda, se borrando na calça. . . . Merda começou de escorrer e desceu no chão. . . . E vi coisa muito porca. O povinho juntava merda de Fedegoso e guardava no bolso. Tinha outros que ficavam só adorando a merdaiada. Virei a cara de anojado. Ora, onde se viu modos assim! (184)

Sentence structure

Reflecting Quatroio's limited literacy, constructions typical of oral language pervade the novel, blurring the distinction between written medium and speech. Duplication, used as an iterative mechanism is typical of the spoken mode:

> *Licurgo gritou iroso e* veio que veio. (47)
> ... *se puseram de joelho*, chorando que chorando ... (178)
> queria porque queria *me pôr pra fora* (101)

Quite naturally, the illusion of orality is strongest in dialogs like the following (with extraneous narrator's comments deleted):

> *-Não interessa. A gente não pode parar. Atrasa serviço.*
> *-Assim vosmecê estrupia a máquina!*
> *-Óia, que ainda despenca!*
> *-Despenca nada, alimária. Pois havia-de despencar?*
> *Foi o doutor que disse.*
> *-Deixa o Dr. Engenheiro decidir, homem. Não custa.*
> *-Pois, vosmecê acha que eu não sei das coisas?*
> *Ainda dou jeito.* (122)

Short or fragmented sentences strengthen the illusion of fast speech:

> *Pois. Assim, já nascido errado. Em barriga malina fui gerado. Satanice.* (69)
> *Fugia a gente. Ele, de sangue preto no chão. De tanto escarrado. Mal do pulmão.* (14)
> *A barriga começou de doer no outro dia. Desde cedo. Coisa de muito gás. Zoião filho da puta!* (77)

> *Criança berrando de fome, carecida de leite? Que viesse*
> *escravidão.* (49)

Clipped sentences with no articles, few prepositions or conjunctions, and limited embedding, are particularly effective in endowing Teju and Anhê, two Indians found hiding in a tunnel, with pidgin-like speech:

> Camunhá vivia alto da terra. Em cima, Pai Pedi,
> embaixo, Mãe Cedi. Caça, peixe, mandioca, milho,
> Camunhá fazia festa. Comia inimigo. Terra boa,
> mulher plantação. . . Caça corria, peixe no rio. . . .
> Teju disse: "Anhangá vem. Anhangá zangado".
> Camunhá dançando. Pai Pedi brabo, Mãe Cedi braba.
> Anhangá zangado, Anhangá descia." (137)

In the description of Quatroio and his companions' underground sojourn, old-fashioned narrative formulas and archaic word order arrangements combine with vernacular speech to create an anachronistic ambiance:

> Hei nome *Rosaflor* (190)
> Sonhado não tinha *donzela a quem servir*? (206)
> Comida tenho e pousada *para vosmecês.* (207)
> De pequenina nascida (190)
> Pai meu, *sendo padre, no podia* de *ser pai* (190)
> Havia-de eu ser *rainha* (201)

Style variation

The contrast between vernacular and standard speech plays a crucial role in differentiating the workers from their bosses. For example, the consultative style (Joos 1961) used by the Engineer to address the workers signals the language of power and functions as a counterpoint to their powerless vernacular:

> Senhores, o salitre é colocado em pequena
> quantidade. É receituário medicinal. Recomendado
> contra moléstias. Não altera o metabolismo do
> indivíduo. (57)

As formal language identifies the opressor, it is not surprising that the instructions for the *máquina-de-prazer*, a token-operated appliance that dispenses sexual favors to the workers, thus dehumanizing them to the level of objects, are written in a "parodical stylization" (Bakhtine 1978:132) of the frozen style (Joos 1961) typical of technical manuals and bureaucratic language in general:

> A "máquina-de-prazer" é aparelho de alta precisão, projetado segundo as técnicas mais modernas, veloz e seguro. Consta de um corpo principal, de látex, napa e estrutura metálica, onde, acima, se localizam os comandos, as luzes de advertência e, embaixo, a fenda operatória, de dimensões variáveis .... Na traseira, abaixo, há um conjunto de 2 (duas) polpas, de material elástico (espuma de polietireno) e, do mesmo material, acima, 2 (dois) suportes de mão, de forma cônica e bojuda, providos de bico. (108-109)

As if to enhance the outlandishness of the pleasure machine, a company official inaugurates it with a bombastic speech that satirizes the verbosity of political discourse:

> Neste momento solene, tenho a honra de lhes comunicar que a Companhia resolveu atender a seus anseios . . . premiando aos que, com esforço, trabalharam em prol do crescimento da Companhia e da Nação! (105)

Rhetorical pomposity reaches full identification with mendacity in the sermons of Padre Angelo, a midget priest who is lowered into the mine in a glass elevator equipped with special-effect mirrors that make him look like a giant, to preach humility and obedience to the workers. Representing organized religion as a means of domination, his stilted sermons include rhetorical features such as the obsolete pronoun *vós* and overuse of the inflected infinitive:

> Vós não ouvistes a Palavra de Deus. Fechastes vossos ouvidos sujos pela Voz da Luxúria, pela voz do pecado! Ao invés de pensardes nos intuitos puros,

> ao invés de vos entregardes ao honesto labor,
> intentastes servir à Corte de Satanás! . . . Sede
> humildes. Respeitai vossa condição. (61-65)

There is a clear symbolism in the contrast between the workers' genuine vernacular and their exploiters' overcorrect speech: like the pleasure machine that kills one of the workers (Chapter 26), or the excavator that crushes several others (Chapter 27), formal language is exposed as an instrument of deceit and oppression. The workers, however, are aware of this:

> Arrazoado, coisa boa em boca de Graúdo, do Dr.
> Engenheiro, de Pe. Angelo, a gente escuitando sem
> atinar. Mas bicho não atina, não adianta, nem precisa
> de atino. . . . É o que Frege dizia: "Os de lá de cima
> eram conversados". Pobre da gente se ficasse na
> escuita deles. Como de música de baião ou de xaxado.
> Deixa a gente enrolado. (156)

Cardoso Gomes' skillful deployment of vernacular features creates a literary dialect which, though not isomorphic with the speech of any specific region or social group, retains the essence of the popular language of Brazil. This literary dialect transcends the stylistic function of adding realism to the narrator's speech, for the very decision to set up the vernacular as an alternative to established practice summons readers to ponder on the multiple implications of this linguistic choice. Furthermoe, by creating a series of hurdles for the readers, the literary dialect imposes on them an interpretative effort of variable magnitude (depending on factors such as familarity with the vernacular, acceptance of its use in a literary context, and so on). Finally, while the vernacular can be amusing and entertaining, its sustained use also serves as a reminder of the otherness that sets readers -by definition literate persons in a largely illiterate society- apart from those who must endure opressive situations such as Rego Fundo symbolizes.

The interaction of the vernacular with other variants, such as formal or technological styles, creates a dialogical confrontation (Bakhtine 1978:135) that underscores the novel's satirical intention. The vernacular is not only indicative of the characters' working class status, but also symbolic of the author's decision to hold up their socially stigmatized speech as a valid subcode of discourse that readers must decipher at three levels at least: that of the *parole*, where they must have recourse to morphosyntactic, lexical, and semantic information on the dialect in question; that of the *langue*, where an interpretative relationship creates a nexus between that linguistic information and the standard language of the readers; and the level of *intentionality*, where the purpose of using the vernacular is clarified both in terms of what it implies about the message and its originator, and for what it contributes to the understanding of this message in terms of complex correlations such as humor, paradox, irony, or tension. In a subtle metonymic relationship between the linguistic codes and the characters, the vernacular both legitimates Quatroio as the spokesman for the underdog and emerges as a flexible and eloquent medium of self-expression that challenges the dominant -linguistic as well as social- viewpoint.

Notes

[1] This article is part of a project on the literary representation of vernacular speech. Portions were included in the paper "Language levels in Alvaro Cardoso Gomes' *O Sonho da Terra*," given at the 1991 meeting of the American Association of Teachers of Spanish and Portuguese. I thank Jerry Craddock for his comments on an earlier version. My research was partly made possible by a one-semester sabbatical from the University of California.

[2] In the sense of Ives' definition (1971:146): "A literary dialect is an author's attempt to represent in writing a speech that is restricted regionally, socially, or both." On literary dialect, see also Cole 1986. For an overview of the application of linguistics to literary texts see Traugott and Pratt 1980.

[3] The working definition of vernacular adopted here is that of Bell 1976:147-152. The essential works on vernacular Brazilian Portuguese include Amaral 1920, Bortoni-Ricardo 1985, Guy 1981, Head 1973, Holm 1987, Istre 1971, Nascentes 1922, Rodrigues, 1974. Other items of varying interest are listed in Dietrich 1980, Magalhes 1983, Magalhes and San-Martin 1983, and Reinecke et al. 1975.

[4] This was noted by Cunha (1968), who argued cogently for the study of the vernacular on its own merits.

[5] Examples of texts and authors' statements are found in Pinto 1978, 1981. On the use of popular language in João Guimares Rosa's novels, see Daniel 1968 and Ward 1984.

[6] *O Sonho da Terra* (São Paulo: L R Editores, 1983) received the 1982 Nestlé Biennial Award for Brazilian Literature, 3rd place in the novel category. Contemporary short reviews include Brat 1983, Cruz 1983, and Paes 1983.

[7] Since the novel was written in São Paulo between July and December of 1978 (216), it is safe to think of the construction of a subway in the seventies and the polemics regarding the treatment of its workers as a likely source of inspiration for the plot.

[8] The vernacular *zóio* 'eye' is a backformation based on the pronunciation of the plural *os olhos* [uʒɔju] (the palatal [l], ortographically *lh*, is reduced to the front glide [j] in the vernacular).

[9] Two remarkable instances of this usage are Pires 1924 and Guarnieri 1987.

[10] See Guy 1981 and Bortoni-Ricardo on variable agreement rules in non-standard Brazilian Portuguese.

[11] On contemporary pronominal usage in Brazil, see Duarte 1989.

[12] Câmara (1972:85) points out that "in the Brazilian colloquial language, even that of the educated classes, the third-person subsystem . . . *lhe* and . . . *lhes* have become adverbial forms indicating the hearer addressed in the third person and thus are now identical to *te* in function." Silveira (1952:391) suggests that direct object *lhe/lhes* "parece também sobrevivência de arcaísmos portugueses", while Câmara considers this usage "an autonomous structural fact that is to be explained by process of remodeling" (1972:85, n. 15). Ward (1984:65) documented that the 2nd person direct object "*lhe* . . . reflete a língua oral, principalmente o dialeto rural." See also Duarte 1989.

[13] Non-reflexive *si*, however, is current in standard European Portuguese.

[14] Compare with *lacrimosa*, a learned derivative from Lat. *lacrima* + -*osa*).

Works Cited

Amaral, Amadeu. *O Dialecto Caipira*. São Paulo: Casa Editora "O Livro", 1920.

Azevedo, Milton M. "Vernacular features in Educated Speech in Brazilian Portuguese." *Hispania* 72.4 (1989): 862-872.

Bakhtine, Mikhail. *Esthétique et théorie du roman*. Translated by Daria Olivier. Paris: Éditions Gallimard, 1978.

Bell, Roger T. *Sociolinguistics. Goals, Approaches and Problems*. London: B. T. Batsford Ltd., 1976.

Bortoni-Ricardo, Stella Maris. *The Urbanization of Rural Dialect Speakers. A Sociolinguistic Study in Brazil.* Cambridge: Cambridge University Press, 1985.

Brait, Beth. "Bom. Mas poderia ser melhor, sem algumas inutilidades." *Jornal da Tarde,* Caderno de Programas e Leituras. 23 April 1983: 4.

Brown, Roger, and Albert Gilman. "The Pronouns of Power and Solidarity." *Style in Language.* Ed. Thomas A. Sebeok, Cambridge, MA: MIT Press, 1960. 253-276.

Câmara, Joaquim Mattoso, Jr. *The Portuguese Language.* Trans. Anthony Naro. Chicago: The University of Chicago Press, 1972.

Cole, Roger W. "Literary representation of dialect: A theoretical approach to the artistic problem." *The USF Language Quarterly,* 24:3-4 (Spring-Summer 1986): 3-8, 48.

Coutinho, Eduardo de Faria. *The Process of Revitalization of the Language and Narrative Structure in the Fiction of João Guimarães Rosa and Julio Cortázar.* Valencia: Albatros Hispaniofila Ediciones, 1980.

Cruz, Ulysses. "Estórias de quem trabalha nas minas." *Diário do Comércio* 1983, Caderno A:14.

Cunha, Celso. *Língua Portuguesa e Realidade Brasileira.* Rio de Janeiro: Edições Tempo Brasileiro, 1968.

Daniel, Mary L. *João Guimarães Rosa: Travessia Literária.* Rio de Janeiro: José Olympio Editora, 1968.

Dietrich, Wolf. *Bibliografia da Língua Portuguesa do Brasil.* Tübingen: Gunter Narr Verlag, 1980.

Duarte, Maria E. L. "Clítico acusativo, pronome lexical e categoria vazia no português do Brasil." *Fotografias sociolingüísticas.* Ed. Fernando Tarallo. Campinas: Editora da Universidade de São Paulo. Editora Pontes, 1989. 19-34.

Fasold, Ralph. "Address Forms." *The Sociolinguistics of Language.* Cambridge, MA: Basil Blackwell Inc., 1990.

Guarnieri, Gianfrancesco. *Eles não Usam Black-Tie*. Rio de Janeiro: Civilização Brasileira, [First published 1955] 1987.

Guy, Gregory R. *Linguistic Variation in Brazilian Portuguese: Aspects of the Phonology, Syntax, and Language History*. Diss. University of Pennsylvania, 1981.

Head, Brian F. "O estudo do 'r-caipira' no contexto social". *Revista Vozes* 67.8 (1973): 43-49.

Holm, John. "Creole Influence on Popular Brazilian Portuguese." *Essays in Memory of John E. Reinecke*. Ed. Glenn G. Gilbert. Honolulu: University of Hawaii Press, 1987. 406-429.

Istre, Giles L. *A Phonological Analysis of a Brazilian Portuguese Interior Dialect*. Diss. Louisiana State University and Agricultural and Mechanical College, 1971.

Ives, Sumner. "A Theory of Literary Dialect." *A Various Language: Perspectives on American Dialects*. Juanita Williamson and Virginia M. Burke, Eds. New York: Holt, Rinehart and Winston, Inc., 1971. An earlier version appeared in *Tulane Studies in English* 2 (1950): 137-182.

Joos, Martin. *The Five Clocks*. New York: Harcourt, Brace and World, 1961.

Magalhães, Erasmo D'Almeida. "Notas aos estudos sobre o português falado no Brasil". *III Encontro de Professores de Língua Portuguesa. O Português falado no Brasil. Contribuição para seu estudo*. Taubaté: Universidade de Taubaté, 1983. 5-42.

Magalhães, Erasmo D'Almeida, and Maria Resende San-Martin. "Seleção bibliográfica e comentários sobre o português falado no Brasil". *III Encontro de Professores de Língua Portuguesa*. 1983. 43-105.

Medeiros Mongelli, Lênia Márcia de. "Alvaro Cardoso Gomes: Ambiguidades em 'O Sonho da Terra'." *Colóquio/Letras 86*, 1985.

Naro, Anthony J., and Miriam Lemle. "Syntactic diffusion." *Papers from the Parasession on Diachronic Syntax.* Chicago: Chicago Linguistic Society, 1976. 221-240.

Nascentes, Antenor. *O linguajar carioca.* Rio de Janeiro: Sussekind de Mendonça. 2nd edition 1953. Rio: Organização Simões, 1922.

Paes, José Paulo. "À Macunaíma." *Veja* 11 May 1983: 117.

Page, Norman. *Speech in the English Novel.* 2nd Edition. London: The Macmillan Press Ltd., 1988.

Pinto, Edith Pimentel. *O Português do Brasil. Textos Críticos e Teóricos.* São Paulo: Editora da Universidade de São Paulo, 1978 [vol. 1], 1981 [vol. 2].

Pires, Cornélio. *As Estrambóticas Aventuras do Joaquim Bentinho (O Queima Campo).* São Paulo: Imprensa Metodista, 1924.

Reinecke, John E. et al., Eds. "Brazilian Portuguese: The Question of Creolization." *A Bibliography of Pidgin and Creole Languages.* Honolulu: The University Press of Hawaii, 1975: 110-118.

Rodrigues, Ada Natal. *O Dialeto Caipira na Região de Piracicaba.* São Paulo: Editorial Atica S. A., 1974.

Silveira [Alvaro] Sousa da. *Lições de Português.* 4th ed. Coimbra: Atlântida, 1952.

Traugott, Elizabeth C., and Mary L. Pratt. *Linguistics for Students of Literature.* San Diego: Harcourt Brace Jovanovich, 1980.

Ward, Teresinha Souto. *O Discurso Oral em Grande Sertão: Veredas.* São Paulo: Livraria Duas Cidades, 1984.

Helvecian Portuguese:
Vernacular Dialect or True Creole?

William W. Megenney

1.0. Introduction.
As equally intriguing as the question of the existence of a pan-Caribbean creole Spanish is the question regarding the existence of a creole Portuguese in Brazil which may be a small example of the proto-language of present-day Popular Brazilian Portuguese (PBP). The existence of Palenquero, of the Cuban Bozal language, of the Panamanian Congo language (*lengua de los congos de Panamá*), and perhaps of the dialect spoken among the people of the Choc on Colombia's Pacific coast, point to the possibility of either some kind of wide-spread Spanish-based creole prevalent in the Caribbean basin or of pockets of structurally similar semi-creoles (cf. Holm 1989, Vol. II: 308) having formed there due to typological similarities among the substratum languages. Portuguese America could not boast of such pockets of creole-like language until the recent discovery of Helvécia in 1961 by a Brazilian student of linguistics, Carlota da Silveira Ferreira, who published the results of her inquiries in 1985. According to her analysis, certain anomalies in the language spoken here point to "vestígios de um falar crioulo" (traces of a creole language). Based on these preliminary findings, Alan N. Baxter of La Trobe University, Australia, conducted field research in several small communities around the area of Helvécia and presented his own findings in a paper read at the *Colquio Internacional sobre Crioulos de Base Lexical Portuguesa* (Lisbon, June 25-28, 1991). After careful examination of the data collected by these authors, I should like to offer some comments relating to the existence of Helvecian Portuguese (HP) with regard to its status as a creole. The existence or absence of isomorphic creole structures in HP when compared to other Iberian-based creole languages should enable us to classify it or not as a creole or semi-creole language (cf. Green and Michel 1991), even though this type of evidence

may not always be totally conclusive when attempting to identify creoles versus popular or non-standard varieties of a language.

One interesting base-line clue to the discovery of HP as a creole language rests on the somewhat subjective description of the dialect as told by people living in the area: "..que naquela cidade havia muita gente que falava diferente, engraçado, principalmente os mais velhos, e .. muitas vezes era difícil, para eles mesmos, filhos da terra, entenderem." It was for very similar reasons that Aquiles Escalante began his study of Palenquero in Colombia (personal communication). Such linguistic anomalies were also responsible in part for the investigative work done by Lorenzo Turner among the Gullah of South Carolina and Georgia, and therefore represent important catalytic forces which help to broaden and deepen our understanding of certain aspects of the Atlantic slave trade and its impacts on linguistic change.

2.0. Phonology.

Guided by the information found in Silveira Ferreira (1985), let us proceed with the linguistic analysis of HP's unique features.

2.1 Variable vowel reduction to simple nasal vowel from nasal diphthong, word-final: /ãw̃/ > /õ/. Some of the examples given are:

(1) /krasõ/ *coração*,
(2) /latõ/ *latão*,
(3) /maró fakõ/ *amarrou o facão* (here non nasal -ou becomes -ó),
(4) /nõ/ *não*.

Examples of the use of /ãw̃/ are also given in the Helvecian data, e.g., *fraturão, pirão, não*, etc.

Holm (1988:120) informs us that "European diphthongs were often replaced by single vowels without glides in the early creoles." Examples here are given from São Tomé Creole Portuguese, Surinamese Creoles, Krio (Sierra Leone), Miskito Coast Creole English, and American Black English. My own examination of Gullah has shown that there is also a limited amount of diphthong reduction here too, i.e., [oᵘ] > [o], [eⁱ] > [e] and also of the combination of [o] plus the English retroflex [r] to a back, low vowel. This phenomenon may be due to matching typological profiles of the sub-Saharan languages involved in the contact situations since in these languages vowel sequences which may seem to be diphthongs are actually distinct segments, each being set apart as such by the presence of a tone as part of the pitch pattern. Another possible explanation would be the absence of similar diphthongs in the substrate languages, thus limiting their use by the creole speakers in the TL. This would seem to be the case,

116   William W. Megenney

for example, in Annobonese Creole Portuguese (cf. Granda 1986:120-1), where we note that all falling diphthongs found in Portuguese are reduced to pure vowels in the creole variety (e.g., *barbeiro* > [baßɛlu] *céu* > [o se]). 2.2 The categorical use of the tap [r] intervocalically in place of the voiceless velar or pharingeal fricative [x] usually heard:
(5) /baríga/ *barriga*,
(6) /arói/ *arroz*,
(7) /koréu/ *correu*.

Such a phenomenon is highly suggestive of the possible former use of the voiced alveolar trill [r] in the Portuguese spoken by the inhabitants of this area in southern Bahia State, the conversion of which to a single tap would have been simple and expected, given the phonetic similarity between [r] and [r̄] and the fact that [r̄] is virtually non-existent in most of the Niger-Congo languages spoken by the slaves taken to Brazil. One wonders, however, whether the German, the Swiss German, the Swiss French, and the French who helped found Helvécia, used a velar/pharingeal fricative or an alveolar trill in their own respective languages, and whether, indeed, the Portuguese being spoken here employed the [x] or the [r̄] for word-initial and double "rr". Three possibilities come to mind: (1) that the European masters used [r̄] in their speech (either German, French, or Portuguese) which was then reduced to [r] by the black slaves, (2) that the European masters used [r] for [r̄] when speaking Portuguese, which was then imitated by their slaves, or, (3) that the Portuguese spoken in the 18th and 19th centuries in this part of Brazil (and in which other parts of Brazil??) employed the [r̄] according to the European manner, which was then reduced to a single tap by the black slaves. This last possibility obviously raises many questions concerning the Brazilian conversion of Portuguese [r̄] to [x], i.e., when, where, why?[1]

The categorical use of the tap [r] for the trill [r̄] is obviously limited to those creole languages which were formed with languages having the tap, which overshadowed the trill due to the precedence of one facet of analogous articulatory bases over another (in this case, the isomorphic phonetic bases of the substrata languages against the phonetic base of a superstrate language). In terms of a time scale with regard to language acquisition, it is perhaps true that children learn to pronounce the tap [r] before mastering the trilled [r̄], therefore suggesting some kind of universal phonetic advancement along a scale of articulatory realizations. If language acquisition processes in children parallel those in language contact situations, then the presence of tapped [r] in pidgin and creole languages and the concomitant absence of [r̄] would be partially explained by this phenomenon.[2]

Another explanation, however, would be based on the simple non-existence of trilled [r̄] in the African substrate languages supposedly present in the formation of the creole variety spoken in the southern part of Bahia State. This interpretation is confirmed through specific examples recorded in the Spanish of Equatorial Guinea (cf. Granda 1986-87, 1985, Lipski 1985:44-7), of Colombian Palenquero (cf. Friedemann and Patiño Rosselli 1983:96, Megenney 1986:110), and of Papiamentu (cf. Lipski 1985:48). This reduction, in turn, is probably related to the variable neutralization of liquid consonants and alveolar/dental stops (i.e., r, rr, l, d, n) found in many of the Atlantic creole languages (cf. Holm 1988:135, where he discusses apicals in creole languages). Lipski (1985:50) has pointed to this possibility while speaking of the liquid consonants, the neutralization of which among Latin American populations with a history of slavery is probably due to the Bantu substratum languages, as is seen in Guinean Spanish. A further bit of support for its having been generated in an interlanguage due to substratum influence is the testimony by Pichardo (1862:vii) who describes the Spanish of Cuba's *bozales* (African-born slaves) as having no "strong" (i.e., trilled) r.

2.3. A tendency toward CV structure:

(8) /kiláru/ *claro*. It should be noted here that although Brazilian Portuguese does not display epenthetic vowels between consonant clusters such as the one noted here (i.e., [kl]), it does in words like *objeto*, typically pronounced at all diastratic levels as [obiʒɛtu] (cf. Lipski 1992:32).

The tendency towards a CV structure is quite common in the Atlantic creoles. Once again, Holm (1988:110-11) provides some examples of epenthesis and paragoge from Príncipe Creole Portuguese, Negerhollands Creole Dutch, Cameroonian Creole English, Bahamian Creole English, Papiamentu, Saramaccan Creole English, and Krio. The epenthetic vowels present in HP could easily reflect a creole structural pattern.

2.4. Reduction of voiced alveopalatal fricative with secondary lip protrusion to an alveolar fricative with partially spread lips:

(9) /zanɛla/ *janela*

(10) /za/ *já*.

The [ʒ]> [z] occurrence is also found in the Gulf of Guinea creoles in environments except before high front vowels, a rule which parallels one in the kiKongo dialects (cf. Ferraz 1983:125).[3] Therefore, this feature of HP would also seem to support an African sub-stratum theory of origin.

2.5. Denasalization of *minha*:

(11) /famía di bánda da mía mãe/ *família de banda da minha mãe*.

Given the nasal phonemes present in both Portuguese and many of the sub-Saharan languages which were instrumental in the formation of a creole-type Portuguese in Brazil, one would not expect to find de-nasalization in HP. However, it does exist in some creole forms, i.e, Bahamian Creole English (cf. Holm 1988:124), Haitian Creole French, and, according to the data gathered during some interviews I held on the island of Bonaire, in Papiamentu. Perhaps this is part of what Gilman calls *form selection* (1985), although even this would seem to go against the grain of linguistic accomodation which continues the use of structures as closely as possible to the ones of the native languages of those forming the creole. Normally, in pidginization or abrupt creolization, the grammar should contain only the marked features that are widely shared among the source languages. The de-nasalization in HP seems to contradict this basic principle. Since there is, however, some degree of arbitrariness or randomness in form selection, this particular phonological feature of HP could be categorized as entropy within the linguistic valence of the creole.

3.0. Morpho-syntax.
(a) the noun phrase (NP):
3.1.0. The variable absence of the article:
(12) /kwándo abrí zanela/   *Quando abri a janela*
(13) /io sábi día do ánu/   *Eu sei o dia do ano*
(14) /io koẽīsé pái di úgu/   *Eu conheço o pai de Hugo*
(15) /depói ki zatĩã fíu feiistasō/   *Depois que Zatinha foi à Feistação*

The elimination of the article has been cited by Perl (1982:429-30) as a typical creole morphosyntactic feature, while showing that the same kind of ellipsis occurs in Cape Verde, São Tomé, Príncipe, and Annobón Creole Portuguese, as well as in Colombian Palenquero. Refining this a bit, we might say that this reflects the creole usage of a singular noun without the article to express a general category (cf. Holm 1988:192; Bickerton 1981:56), although at least two of the four examples cited without the article have specific referents, and would therefore counter this creole praxis as expressed by Perl. In fact, articles are quite common in creole languages, having a rather wide variety of uses and meanings (cf. Holm 1988:190-2). I feel, therefore, that we would be somewhat hard pressed to assign article deletion in HP to a creole structural pattern. Rather, it seems to be a type of sub-categorical *hapax legomenon* occurring in HP outside of the most common syntactic-semantic pattern of determiner usage in creole languages.

3.1.1. Variable interchange of gender in articles:
(16) /io nõ pódi rũmá u káza/   *Eu não posso arrumar a casa*
(17) /ségu duma λu/   *cego de um olho.*

The variable lack of gender agreement within the NP, occurring in the articles, adjectives, and possessive adjectives, is quite common in many creole languages, and is no doubt a reflection of the relative lack of grammatical gender in the Niger-Congo languages (cf. Holm 1988:195).

3.1.2. The variable use of *ūna*:

(18) /si **ūna rapás vem pidí ūna mósa**/ *Se um rapaz vem pedir uma moça.*

The variable use of **ūna** with an [n] as in Spanish rather than an [m], as in Portuguese, is somewhat baffling. The only possible source that comes to mind is the Old Portuguese form **ūa**, which had no intervening nasal consonant. Having been separated, then, from standard Portuguese, HP may have independently developed an intervening alveolar [n] instead of the standard bilabial [m], which would have been a totally logical outcome of such a vocalic combination with a nasal overtone. It is highly doubtful that the [n] is a result of Spanish influence, especially since there were no Spaniards among the Europeans who settled the southern part of Bahia State.

3.1.3. Variable lack of gender agreement within the NP:

(19) /**tra meu m ʲádu**/ *terra minha molhada*
(20) /**ese istasõ**/ *essa estação*
(21) /**me avó é lavadéru** *minha avó é lavadeira*

3.1.4. Invariable gender form of the possessive pronoun used variably:

(22) /**me**/ *minha, meu* (See example in number 21 above.)

3.2. The Verb Phrase (VP):

3.2.1. Variable but preferred use of the 3rd person singular verb form with 1st person singular pronoun:

(a) present indicative:

(23) /**io fas**/ *eu faço*
(24) /**io kõmi**/ *eu como*
(25) /**io sábi**/ *eu sei*
(26) /**io vai**/ *eu vou.*

(b) past indicative:

(27) /**io eskeséu**/ *eu esqueci*
(28) /**io foi**/ *eu fui*
(29) /**io coréu**/ *eu corri*
(30) **io paró** *eu parei.*

Non-agreement between subject pronoun and verbal desinence may have its origin in an early pidgin/creole construction **ta** plus **infinitive (INF)**, examples of which we find in Caribbean bozal Spanish (cf. Lipski 1987; Alvarez Nazario 1974; Mason and Espinosa 1927). From such a construction (e.g., Palenquero **ele ta cogé mangombe** = "él coge el ganado"), one could expect a development in some stage of apparent time during the de-creolization process which would reflect a movement toward the TL, in which **ta** (a tense/aspect marker) would have vanished and the INF would have been replaced by one inflected form (possibly two) which would remain invariable throughout the conjugation. An example from HP (also occurring in PBP) is:

(31) /n nũ krió na r sa, n krió ẽ káza/ *Nós não [nos] criamos na roça, nós [nos] criamos em casa.*

Here, the third person singular verb form is used with the first person plural personal subject pronoun. In Barlovento (Venezuela) Spanish, a possible creolized form (cf. Megenney, in press), we find examples such as **Nohotro le decíãŋ**, in which the first person plural subject pronoun is linked with the third person plural verbal desinence.

As part of his attempt to discover a creole-like history for PBP, Guy (1989:234) draws attention to the lack of any such phenomenon in the development of either Portuguese or Spanish, and suggests that the variable use of subject-verb non-agreement, which is based on a saliency scale[4], is a natural product of the decreolization process. This seems quite logical, and fits well with the preceding paragraph, in which I allude to decreolization as the process responsible for the present state of subject-verb non-agreement in Caribbean Spanish-based creole or semi-creole languages, which of course, in turn, accepts the creole status of these languages, notwithstanding their having been original pidgins or abrupt creolized varieties (cf. Thomason and Kaufman 1988). At the same time, if such non-agreement constructions could be found in dialects in the Portuguese- or Spanish-speaking worlds where no Sprachbund-type contacts existed, or even shift-induced interference from one language on another, our case for substratum interference would be considerably weakened. Since, to my knowledge, there are no such cases of non-agreement produced through internal drift in either Spanish or Portuguese dialects, one could conclude at this point in time that the subject-verb non-agreement present in HP, PBP, and Barlovento Spanish, may be a reflection of a former creole existence.

3.2.2. Three instances of the infinitive (without final r̄) used for the finite:

(32) /io koñecé/ *eu conheço*
(33) /éle moré/ *ele morre*
(34) /io andá / *eu ando.*

As stated above, infinitive forms used in place of finite ones could reveal an older **ta + INF(without r̄)** construction, which may post-date or be coeval with a simple form of the verb used without any pre- or post-verbal markers, a phenomenon quite common in creole languages and in many West African languages (cf. Holm 1988:150). Since there is no apparent ta present in any of the HP examples, however, we may only have before us some examples of a very early simple verb form which depended on context for time frame reference and which may have been used *passim* in the first developmental stages of HP. The construction **ta + INF** may not have existed at all in HP, as it did in some Spanish-based Caribbean creoles. The three examples of the construction **PRON + INF** from HP do, however, point to a definite creole-like unmarked verbal pattern, notwithstanding the presence or absence of similar VP constructions with tense/aspect verbal markers.

    3.2.3. Instances of verbal enallage (i.e., present tense used for imperfect) were also noted by Silveira Ferreira, but I choose not to discuss them at this time since sufficient context was not given with the examples.

    3.2.4. Untypically high frequency use of the 1st person singular pronoun *eu*, which occurs as *io* (stress on first vowel).

    The untypically high frequency usage of the 1st person singular pronoun in HP is directly linked to two specific verbal patterns (i.e., the INF without -r, or the exclusive use of the 3rd person singular). Since HP is apparently not a **PRO-drop** language in part, the verb is not morphologically distinguished in the category of person, and hence requires a surface manifestation of a pronoun to avoid ambiguity. Perl (1982:426-8) includes examples of this from the Cuban *habla bozal*, as well as from the creoles spoken in São Tomé, Annobón, Palenque de San Basilio, and in the Zamboangueño dialect of Philippine Spanish. It seems logical to assume from this that a high frequency usage of personal pronouns would indicate a former creole language.

    3.2.5. One example of what appears to be the use of a prepositional pronoun without the preposition:

(35) /**kulpádu mi**/   *culpa de mim (?)*.

    The single example of what appears to be a prepositional pronoun could stem from a similar type of analytical construction found in the Spanish and Portuguese of the sixteenth century (cf. Keniston 1937), during which time many Peninsular authors showed a definite preference for constructions such as *de nosotros* over *nuestro ~ nuestra*. There is also a very slight possibility that it reflects some kind of creole-like construction similar to the ones found in Papiamentu and Colombian Palenquero. In the former, constructions such as "**Unda di bo bai?**" ("Where is yours going?"), in which the possessive pronoun follows the preposition **di**. In Palenquero, the possessive pronoun follows the noun as if to suggest a former prepositional construction: "**i a ten casa mi**" ("yo tengo mi casa"). Perhaps a combination of the two analytic-type constructions can account for its somewhat cryptic appearance in HP, with a proto-form based on the XVIth century tendency towards prepositional phrases to denote possession apparently prevalent in the Iberian Peninsula. The Papiamentu and Palenquero constructions may also have originated from this tendency rather than having followed some putative universal penchant typical of creole languages (cf. Holm 1988:195-7).

4.0. It would be tempting to conclude (provisionally) from the above that HP represents a more conservative rendition of PBP which has been preserved in its microcosm due to isolation from the society at large. In his article, Guy (1989) argues in favor of the creole or creole-like status of PBP, supporting his claim with historical, social, and linguistic information, much of which does point toward the possible former existence of a Sprachbund-type creole language (made up of Portuguese and several sub-Saharan languages) having a rather wide diatopic spread in Brazil. However, some of the linguistic phenomena included in Guy's study as part of a possible African-influenced creole language (e.g., reduction in the use of pronominal clitics) also exist in areas of Brazil where very few black slaves lived (e.g., the *caipira* dialect of the southeast must have very little, if any, African-language contact, let alone influence). At the same time, some of the linguistic deviations found in Silveira Ferreira's data as well as some included in Guy's article are also present in some dialects of Spanish which had no sub-Saharan contacts in any part of their histories. For example, the phonotactic processes of aphaeresis, syncope, apocope, and metathesis, which are listed in Silveira Ferreira (1985:27) as part of PBP and HP, are quite common in dialects throughout the Spanish-speaking world, usually occurring due to drift within the language. Vowel heightening, the simplification of diphthongs, the vocalization of the palatal "l" (i.e., "lh" > "ei", λ> [e^i]), the [b] ~ [v] alternation, and the deletion of word-final lexical -s (e.g., *tres* > *tre*), also occur with relative frequency in dialects of both Portuguese and Spanish as forms of drift, and so do not strike us as being changes brought about through language contact. A more detailed examination of these features may lead to a better understanding of HP in Brazil as well as of its place among American Spanish-based creole languages.

On the level of morphosyntax, we may note that the agglutination of article and noun occurring in PBP is also found in the *fala de preto* in the works of the Portuguese Renaissance author Gil Vicente, which may or may not be an indication of a unique linguistic feature expressed only by the blacks in Portugal and Portuguese Africa (cf. Lipski 1986; Megenney 1985, 1990; Granda 1988). If it is, it is paralleled by like phenomena in

Philippine Spanish which has no links with sub-Saharan Africa, thus proving that contact with African languages is not a requisite for its appearance.

5.0. Conclusions.

For all intents and purposes, it seems logical to conclude that HP may very well have been a former creole, spawned by virtue of the accumulation of African slaves in the southern part of Bahia State, beginning in the XVIIIth century and growing in the XIXth. Although the phonological evidence may seem questionable as having originated in a creole, the morphosyntactic examples appear as stronger evidence to help solve the apparent conundrum.

Some of the features found in the Helvecian dialect may be identifiable as having arisen as a result of multilingual slave communities not having had access to a TL, so that the features will be notably sub-Saharan within an Indo-European linguistic context. The presence of such features in addition to the all-important aspect of knowing the social situation in which the suspicious dialect came about should provide sufficient proof for the existence of a creole language. Can we identify such features in HP?

5.1. Features.

5.1.0. There is no absolute proof that the change from a diphthong to a pure vowel was triggered by substrate languages in HP. However, upon examining the typological profiles of the sub-Saharan languages presumably responsible for the formation of HP, we note that none have word-final /-aw/ or /-ãw̃/; in fact, words end in simple vowels. Also, those segments which appear to be diphthongs are actually two distinct segments, each containing one vowel, since most of these African languages are of the register tone kind, exhibiting separate segmental units composed of one pure vowel and one tone (cf. Welmers 1973, Ladefoged 1968). A logical transition, then, among the substrate speakers, would be precisely that of shifting a Portuguese diphthong to a simple vowel, to conform to the phonological patterns of their own articulatory bases. The variable presence of the word-final diphthong in HP can be attributed to the process of decreolization in which the creole language speakers attempt to approximate the TL.

5.1.1. Regarding the categorical use of the tapped [r], the possibility of the superstrate languages having influenced the nascent creole should not be discarded. Here, an important missing link is the social situation which existed in southern Bahia State during the 18th and 19th centuries, which, if known, would no doubt shed much light on the origin of this phenomenon, pointing to a superstrate influence in a close social contact situation between plantation slave and owner, and suggesting a substrate cause in the case of the plantation workers having been isolated from their European masters. Given the usual social pattern of the latter which obtained throughout the Americas, it is reasonable to assume that the slaves did not share any social interchange with their owners since generally only house servants partook of this privilege. Based on such a socio-historical assumption, one would have to conclude that the tapped [r] in HP had its origin in the substrate African languages.

5.1.2. The tendency toward CV structure in HP is a rather well documented phenomenon in creole languages. Holm (1988:108-11) makes a special point of this while discussing phonotactic rules. He points out the "abundant evidence of this phonotactic rule [adhering to CV structure] having been carried over into a number of Atlantic creoles, particularly those whose structure is least influenced by that of their European lexical-source language such as the Portuguese-based creoles of the Gulf of Guinea or the English-based creoles of interior Suriname" (cf. Granda 1986).

5.1.3. Since palatalization is a feature of many African languages, it is difficult to determine the cause of the [ž] > [z] de-palatalization found in HP. The voiceless alveopalatal fricative [š] occurs in the HP data, yet the palatalization of [t, d] before the high front vowel [i], which occurs in many dialects of Brazilian Portuguese, is not found here (e.g., *Zatinha* transcribed *[za'ťã]* and *pode* as [pɔdi]) . According to the limited data available on HP, it appears that [š] is the only palatal sound occurring in the dialect. This fact would seem to counter an argument in favor of HP having originated from the Portuguese-based Gulf of Guinea creoles (i.e., São Tomé, Príncipe, Annobón), since here we find generalized palatalization of the alveolar stops before the high front vowel [i] (cf. Ferraz 1975:153-64, 1979:22-4, 51-3, and 1987:342; Green 1988:432-3; Granda 1988:233, note 83). Moreover, there is evidence from Palenquero (**cho/cha**) and Curazoleño (**cha**) that this feature did originate in an early Afro-Portuguese pidgin/ creole (cf. Schwegler 1991- to appear).[5] The lack of palatalization in HP, though, could indicate one of two things: (1) that today's HP underwent de-palatalization through contact with the surrounding PBP which was a de-palatalized variety, or (2) that HP never had palatalization, which would be an indication of its totally independent development (i.e., not related to the Gulf of Guinea creoles or to any other Portuguese-based creole) within an isolated area. Supposedly, the second possibility would raise serious questions regarding the palatalization process as an African-caused feature in language contact situations, unless none of the sub-Saharan languages involved in the formation of Helvecian Portuguese had palatalized sound patterns-- something which seems highly unlikely, given the fact of its presence in many African languages.

5.1.4. The process of denasalization in creole languages is difficult to explain. Holm (1988:124) lists two examples of denasalized forms which were hypercorrected during decreolization due to a misinterpretation of the original forms which had /V/ + /-N/ (vowel plus syllable-final nasal consonant; N = n, ŋ, m). This is obviously not the case with the denasalization of HP **minha** > **mía**. Until such time as a better explanation can be formalized, drift will have to suffice as a reason for the occurrence of denasalization in HP, which is also the only rationale available at this time to explain the same phenomenon in Bonaire Papiamentu, as mentioned above.[6] Closer examination of the HP example, though, may reveal a process quite similar to the one at work in New Mexican Spanish, where palatal sounds are deleted (e.*g*., *ella* > *ea; villa* > *vía*). HP **minha** has a palatal nasal (more precisely, a palatalized nasal approximate). If the palatalized sound, which is also nasal, should be deleted, it would be logical to expect concurrent or subsequent deletion of the anticipatory nasal component present in the preceding vowel. This may be our answer, pure and simple, especially since we have an isomorphic process occurring in the very same example (i.e., **família [famíλa]** > **famía**), which is the deletion of the palatalized lateral.

5.1.5. As stated previously, the variable absence of the article in HP seems to follow a general creole-type pattern of having been generated by forces in the substrate languages as well as those in the lexical-source language, so that African influences per se would not be directly responsible for this trait.

5.1.6. It seems logical to assign both lack of gender agreement and gender interchange to African substrate influence for the reasons discussed above (i.e., this kind of gender agreement is virtually non-existent in African languages).

5.1.7. The unusually high frequency of subject pronoun usage coupled with the variable non-agreement of subject pronoun and verbal desinence (preferred use of 3rd person singular for most persons) probably has its origin in the African substrate languages since the latter are for the most part non-pro-drop languages with invariable verb forms throughout the conjugation (cf. Welmers 1973).

5.1.8. Even though I chose not to discuss the few examples of verbal enallage present in the HP data due to lack of context, I should say that if these are, indeed, true cases of tense interchange, they may very well have stemmed from sub-Saharan patterns, since many African languages render time references via context rather than morphosyntax. At any rate, this point needs further study.

Based on the six cases of probable sub-Saharan influence in HP given above (5.1.0 - 5.1.2, 5.1.6 - 5.1.8) and on the socio-historical context of its formation, I would have to conclude, albeit provisionally, that HP is, indeed, an example of a Portuguese-based *Sprachbund*-type creole language with sub-Saharan substrate-induced components, which no doubt had a wider diatopic extension in the State of Bahia during the XVIIIth and XIXth centuries. As such, its relationship to PBP still needs further study, for even though the African contribution to Brazilian language and culture may be quite extensive (cf. Guy 1981, Schneider 1991, Megenney 1978, Dos Santos and Juana Elbein 1967), it may not be as pervasive nor as endemic to Brazil as some might suppose. For example, some of the linguistic features of PBP, such as the decrease in copying of the {-s} for plurality in the NP based on position, and the "great reduction in the use of pronominal clitics" (cf. Guy 1981), are probably a result of simple drift (the first happens in areas throughout Latin America, many of which had never been affected by the slave industry, and the second is common in virtually all dialects of vernacular Brazilian Portuguese). The relatively large percentage of African lexical items present in PBP does not, by itself, constitute proof of a former creole language either, since we know that lexical borrowing occurs without structural borrowing (cf. Thomason and Kaufman 1988). However, the African lexicon in conjunction with the integration in HP (and perhaps the few tentatively identified as such in PBP) of African structural borrowings identified in this study, do point to the existence of a creole language in Brazil diastratically separate from the normative language. Hopefully, further investigations with ample field work and careful historical research will uncover many of the uncertainties still in need of clarification.

Notes

[1] The author of the article on Helvecian Portuguese states the following regarding the history of the area: "O primeiro núcleo foi formado por alemães, suíços (francófonos e germanófonos) que desde o século XVIII espalhavam-se pelo sul do Estado. O interesse principal desses europeus era a cultura do café e para isso compravam escravos em número cada vez maior, adquiridos no próprio Estado da Bahia." She goes on to cite a publication by Dr. Carl August Toelsner, which "refere-se àquele núcleo como uma região, muito próspera onde já existiam (by 1858) 40

fazendas, 200 brancos (na maioria alemães, suíços, alguns franceses e brasileiros) e 2000 negros; os últimos, na maior parte, já nascidos na futura Helvécia."

[2] This third possibility certainly deserves more attention, which it cannot receive in this study. Its etiology, as that of the same phenomenon in Puerto Rican Spanish, needs more exploration and it is hoped that future studies will reveal many interesting facts about the development and spread of such an intriguing sound change.

[3] In his study *Child Language, Aphasia, and Phonological Universals*, Roman Jacobson states that segments which are *marked* for phonological features occur less frequently in a given language than do their *unmarked* counterparts, and that these are the same segments that are acquired later and used with less frequency in first language acquisition and which appear less frequently in languages universally. According to this study, fricatives presuppose the existence of stops, affricates presuppose the existence of fricatives, and palatals presuppose the existence of front consonants.

[4] A formal negative constraint rule for this particular phnomenon would look like this:

$$
\begin{bmatrix} +\text{coronal} \\ +\text{voice} \\ +\text{strident} \\ -\text{anterior} \end{bmatrix} \rightarrow \begin{bmatrix} +\text{coronal} \\ +\text{voice} \\ +\text{strident} \\ +\text{anterior} \end{bmatrix} / \underline{\quad} \sim \begin{bmatrix} V \\ +\text{hi} \\ -\text{bk} \end{bmatrix}
$$

[5] According to Guy (1989:234), the variable non-agreement between subject and verb happens through a *continuum* based on *saliency* or "distinctiveness of the morphological opposition between the singluar form and the plural form, so that verbs whose plural forms are maximally different from the singulars have the highest rate of agreement, while those with a minimal singluar/plural opposition are very unlikely to agree."

[6] According to Schwegler, Palenquero **cho/cha**, hypocoristic terms used for older persons, stem from Portuguese *tio/tia*, "uncle, aunt", which were palatalized under the influence of African substrata. Over time, these terms became void of meaning and did not relexify toward Spanish, thus remaining fosilized within the Palenquero lexicon. This makes sense for Palenquero and helps to establish a link between it and the Gulf of Guinea Portuguese-based creoles, but it does not enable us to understand the process of de-palatalization present in HP.

[7] For a thorough discussion of nasalization, see the study by John M. Lipski, "Spontaneous nasalization in Afro-Hispanic language [preliminary

version, October 26, 1990}. Paper presented at the 47th International Congress of Americanists, held at Tulane University, New Orleans, LA in April of 1991. Herein, the author briefly discusses the counter-process of denasalization in the following terms:

That Afro-Hispanic speech was characterized by occasional vowel nasalization, but not by an overwhelming introduction of new nasal consonants, is also suggested by the frequent apparent *loss* of nasal consonants in word-final position. Unlike apparent cases of spontaneous word-final nasalization, word-final denasalization did occur phrase-finally, as well as word- and phrase-internally (e.g. atención > atesión/atesió, enredador > eredadó [Alvarez Nazario 1974:150]). Since many of the West African languages presumed to have come into contact with Spanish during the *bozal* Spanish period had either word-final nasal consonants or nasal vowels, there is no reason to suppose total loss of the nasal consonant in *bozal* Spanish. A more likely hypothesis is absorption of the nasal consonant by the preceding vowel (following the general tendencies to reduce syllable-final consonants), whose nasality might not be perceived by a Spanish speaker unaccustomed to nasal vowels." Denasalization might be expected in Afro-Hispanic speech for the reasons given here, whereas in Afro-Portuguese speech it would be highly unlikely given the presence of nasal consonants and nasal vowels in both the substrate languages and in Portuguese. None of the speakers involved in the creation and maintenance of the creole (HP) language would be unaccustomed to nasal sounds of any kind. According to expected occurrences, then, there should be no denasalization in HP.

Bibliography

Alvarez Nazario, Manuel. 1974. *El elemento afronegroide en el español de Puerto Rico*. San Juan: Instituto de Cultura Puertorriqueña.

Dos Santos, Deoscredes M. and Juana Elbein. 1967. *West African Sacred Art and Rituals in Brazil*. Ibadan:Institute of African Studies.

Ferraz, Luiz Ivens. 1975. "African Influences on Principense Creole." In *Misceláea luso-africana*, ed. Mário F. Valkhoff. Lisboa: Silvas. 153-64.
---.   1979. *The Creole of São Tomé*. Johannesburg: Witwatersrand University Press.

---. 1983. "The origin and development of four creoles in the Gulf of Guinea." In Ellen Woolford and William Washabaugh, eds., *The Social Context of Creolization.* Ann Arbor: Karoma: 120-5.

Friedemann, Nina S. de, and Carlos Patiño Rosselli. 1983. *Lengua y sociedad en el Palenque de San Basilio.* Bogotá : Instituto Caro y Cuervo.

Gilman, Charles. 1985. *Form selection or simplification.* Indiana University: Linguistics Club Publication.

Granda, Germán de. 1985. "Fenómenos de interferencia fonética del fang sobre el español de Guinea Ecuatorial. Consonantismo." In *Anuario de lingüística hispánica.* I: 95-114.
---. 1986. "Retenciones africanas en la fonética del criollo portugués de Annobón." In *Revista de filología románica.* IV: 111-23.
---. 1986-7. "La lengua española en el Africa subsahariana. Estudio histórico-lingüístico." In *Cuadernos del Sur.* Bahia Blanca, Argentina: Universidad Nacional del Sur.
---. 1988. "Posibles vías directas de introducción de africanismos en el 'habla de negro' literaria castellana." In *Lingüística e historia: temas afro-hispánicos.* Valladolid: Imprenta KADMOS.
---. 1991. "Sobre un fenómeno sintáctico del español de Guinea Ecuatorial: la marcación en superficie de los pronombres personales sujeto." In *El español en tres mundos: retenciones y contactos lingüísticos en América y Africa.* Valladolid: Universidad de Valladolid.

Green, John N. 1988. "Romance Creoles." In *The Romance Languages*, eds. Martin B. Harris and Nigel Vincent. New York:Oxford University Press. 420-73.

Green, Kate, and Abigail Michel. 1991. "Semi-Creolization and the Emergence of Nonstandard Caribbean Spanish." MS: CUNY Graduate School.

Guy, Gregory. 1981. "Linguistic variation in Brazilian Portuguese: aspects of the phonology, syntax and language history." Diss. University of Pennsylvania.
---. 1989. "On the nature and origins of popular Brazilian Portuguese." In *Etudios sobre español de América y lingüística afroamericana.* Bogotá : Instituto Caro y Cuervo.

Huttar, George L. 1989. "The Portuguese contribution to the ndjuka lexicon." In *Estudios sobre español de América y lingüística afroamericana.* Bogotá : Instituto Caro y Cuervo.

Jakobson, Roman. 1968. *Child Language, Aphasia, and Phonological Universals.* The Hague: Mouton.

Keniston, Hayward. 1937. *The Syntax of Castilian Prose: The Sixteenth Century.* Chicago: University of Chicago Press.

Ladefoged, Peter. 1968. *A Phonetic Study of West African Languages.* Cambridge: Cambridge University Press.

Lipski, John M. 1985. *The Spanish of Equatorial Guinea: the dialect of Malabo and its implications for Spanish dialectology.* Tübingen: Max Niemeyer Verlag.
---. 1986. "The Golden Age 'Black Spanish': Existence and Coexistence." In *Afro-Hispanic Review.* V: 1,2,3 (January, May, September): 7-12.
---. 1987. "On the Construction ta + Infinitive in Caribbean Bozal Spanish." In *Romance Philology.* XL, 4:431-50.
---. 1992. "Literary 'Africanized' Spanish as a research tool: dating consonant reduction." Department of Romance Languages, University of Florida, Gainesville. M.S.

Martinus, Frank. 1989. "The Influence of the Afro-Portuguese on the Papiamentu of Curaçao." In *Estudios sobre español de América y lingüística afroamericana.* Bogotá : Instituto Caro y Cuervo.

Mason, J. Alden, and Aurelio Espinosa. 1927. "Porto-Rican Folklore: Folk-tales." In *Journal of American Folklore.* 40: 313-414.

Megenney, William W. 1978. *A Bahian Heritage.* Chapel Hill: University of North Carolina Press.
---. 1985. "La influencia criollo-portuguesa en el español caribeño." In *Anuario de lingüística hispánica.* I. 1. 157-79.
---. 1986. *El Palenquero: un lenguaje post-criollo de Colombia.* Bogotá : Instituto Caro y Cuervo.
---. 1990. "Fenómenos criollos secundarios en textos portugueses del Renacimiento." In *Anuario de lingüística hispánica.* VI: 335-82.
---. In press (Academia Venezolana de la Lengua). 1992. "Aspectos del lenguaje afronegroide en Venezuela."

Perl, Matthias. 1982. "Creole morphosyntax in the Cuban 'Habla Bozal'." In *Studii si Cercetari Lingvistice*. Vol. XXXII, Nº 5: 424-33.

Pichardo, E. 1862. *Diccionario provincial casi razonado de voces cubanas.* La Habana: Imprenta la Antilla.

Schneider, John T. 1991. *Dictionary of African Borrowings in Brazilian Portuguese*. Hamburg: Helmut Buske Verlag.

Schwegler, Armin. 1991. "El Palenque de San Basilio (Colombia): Persistencia africana y problemas de (auto)identificación de elementos lingüísticos subsaháricos." To appear in *Persistencia africana en el Caribe*.

Thomason, Sarah Grey, and Terrence Kaufman. 1988. *Language Contact, Creolization and Genetic Linguistics*. Berkeley: University of California Press.

Welmers, William E. 1973. *African Language Structures*. Berkeley/Los Angeles: University of California Press.

BRAZILIAN LITERATURE

Traços do Discurso Épico em
Iracema de José de Alencar

M. Elizabeth Ginway

Machado de Assis estabeleceu o valor literário de *Iracema* já em 1866, um ano depois da publicação do romance indianista, quando declarou: "Poema lhe chamamos a este, sem curar de saber se é antes uma lenda, se um romance: o futuro chamar-lhe-á obra-prima" (27). Um dos objetivos deste presente estudo é sondar as possíveis razões pelo contínuo interesse por este romance de Alencar, entre elas, o "discurso épico" que Alencar evoca no estilo e na temática da obra. Quando Machado de Assis denominou *Iracema* "poema em prosa" (15) já distinguiu o romance alencariano das epopéias brasileiras do século anterior: *O Uraguai* (1769) de Basílio da Gama, e *Caramuru* (1781) de Santa Rita Durão, obras que seguem o modelo épico europeu e celebram a conquista das terras brasileiras. Para Machado, o romance de Alencar, portanto, "não é destinado a cantar lutas heróicas, nem cabos-de-guerra; se há aí algum episódio, nesse sentido, se alguma vez troa nos vales do Ceará a pocema de guerra, nem por isso o livro deixa de ser exclusivamente votado à história tocante de uma virgem indiana, dos seus amores e dos seus infortúnios" (15). Entretanto, Machado de Assis, ao chamar *Iracema* um "poema em prosa," reconhece a carga poética do romance, um eco, talvez, do modelo épico. A base ou a intenção épica da parte de Alencar pode explicar um dos atrativos subjacentes do romance e a razão pela qual é considerado um dos "clássicos" brasileiros.

Num ensaio introdutório a uma edição para celebrar o centenário de *Iracema*, Alceu Amoroso Lima comenta sobre o encanto da obra, notando que, "é tanto um livro nitidamente *universal* como produto mais típico da *nacionalidade* e da autonomia de nossa literatura" (60). O discurso épico de *Iracema*, isto é, a transformação alencariana dos temas e das convenções da epopéia, contribui para a dimensão "universal" do romance, enquanto a história em si oferece uma visão complexa da nacionalidade brasileira. Ao nível da trama, *Iracema* capta o espírito épico porque se baseia num episódio extraído da história brasileira, incorporando eventos de significado nacional no estilo elevado do "poema em prosa." A importância da temática nacional de *Iracema* é indiscutível e por isso a obra representa também o espírito épico, porque oferece, como Alencar bem quis, "o berço da nossa nacionalidade" (Haberly 54).

O tema principal de *Iracema* representa, sem dúvida, a formação de uma identidade nacional dentro do romantismo brasileiro, um movimento que afirmava a independência histórica e cultural do país. Como resume Antônio Cândido: "Com efeito, a literatura foi considerada parcela dum esforço construtivo mais amplo, denotando o intuito de contribuir para a grandeza da nação. Manteve-se durante todo o Romantismo este senso de dever patriótico, que levava os escritores não apenas a cantar a sua terra, mas a considerar as suas obras como contribuição ao progresso. Construir uma 'literatura nacional' é afã, quase divisa, proclamada nos documentos do tempo até tornar enfadonha" (10). Alencar segue esta linha patriótica no romance *Iracema*, como declara na carta ao Dr. Jaguaribe, que serve de posfácio à primeira edição: "Verá realizadas nele minhas idéias a respeito da literatura nacional; e achará aí poesia inteiramente brasileira, haurida na língua dos selvagens" (230). Enquanto Alencar ressalta a novidade da linguagem como fonte do seu espírito nacionalista, os críticos contemporâneos enfatizam a importância da estrutura mítica de *Iracema* que sustenta a legitimidade da formação nacional (Lemaire 66; Haberly 47; Wasserman 818; Zilberman 145). A base mítica da obra, porém, encaixa bem no estabelecimento do discurso épico, o qual retoma personagens míticas e eventos históricos para celebrar e comemorar o heroísmo do passado como cerne do caráter nacional. Embora *Iracema*, como uma lenda, focalize duas personagens principais e não várias como uma epopéia tradicional, Alencar realiza uma transformação das convenções tradicionais do épico a fim de estabelecer uma obra de importância nacional em forma acessível para seu público: o romance.

Tradicionalmente escreve-se a epopéia em poesia como já fizeram Camões, Basílio da Gama, e da geração de Alencar, Gonçalves de Magalhães na *Confederação dos Tamoios* (1856), obra que Alencar criticara por não ser representativa da poesia "americana." Na carta ao Dr. Jaguaribe, Alencar confessa sua imprudência por criticar obra alheia sem poder oferecer um "grande poema" da sua própria mão (226). Enquanto Alencar diz na mesma carta que admira o poema épico inacabado *Os Timbiras* de Gonçalves Dias, o seu próprio poema épico, *Os filhos de Tupã* (1863) nunca o satisfez (227-229). Por isso, resolveu tentar outro caminho com *Iracema*, confessando:

"Em um desses volveres do espírito à obra começada, lembrou-me de fazer uma experiência em prosa. O verso pela sua dignidade e nobreza não comporta certa flexibilidade de expressão, que entretanto não vai mal à prosa a mais elevada. A elasticidade da frase permitiria então que se empregassem com mais clareza as imagens indígenas, de modo a não passarem desapercebidas. Por outro lado conhecer-se-ia o efeito que havia de ter o verso pelo efeito que tivesse a prosa" ("Carta" 230). Alencar também ressalta seu desejo de criar uma obra acessível que pudesse captar a imaginação do público leitor em vez de "dar leitura dela a um círculo escolhido, que emitisse juízo ilustrado" ("Carta" 229). Assim, Alencar, ao justificar seu uso de prosa, sentiu a necessidade de mencionar outras epopéias da sua geração, revelando sua própria intenção épica. O estilo da obra, segundo Wasserman, "strives for the poetry of the primitive, for the mode of the great romantic epics" (821); embora não elabore este comentário, esta observação clama uma indagação mais profunda do discurso épico de *Iracema*.

Dir-se-ia que uma função do épico consiste em transformar eventos históricos em narrativa. No primeiro épico literário (não folclórico), *A Eneida* de Virgílio, recria-se todo um passado heróico para estabelecer a origem da grandeza do império romano. Virgílio combina eventos históricos com figuras míticas, e intercala uma história amorosa entre a rainha de Cartago e Enéias, criando assim um dos episódios mais bem sucedidos da obra. O próprio Alencar menciona sua admiração pela epopéia virgiliana como seu "livro predileto" ("Cartas sobre *A Conferação dos Tamoios*" 882), e não é surpreendente que ele proceda da mesma maneira que Virgílio, combinando mito e história. Alencar baseia sua obra nas crônicas históricas com que trabalhava para escrever a biografia de Antônio Filipe Camarão, o modelo da personagem Poti ("Carta" 230). Foi nessa fonte histórica que Alencar descobriu a matéria para sua obra de ficção; na vida de Camarão, "sua mocidade, a heróica amizade que o ligava a Soares Moreno, a bravura e lealdade de Jacaúna, aliado dos portugueses, e suas guerras contra o célebre Mel Redondo: aí estava o tema. Faltava-lhe o perfume que derrama sobre as paixões do homem a alma da mulher" ("Carta" 230). Tal qual Virgílio, Alencar resolve acrescentar uma história amorosa para completar sua visão épica. Entretanto, Alencar, ao seguir a lógica do discurso épico, foi acusado de falso historiador, ou falsificador de história: "The tale itself is loosely based on historical events. A series of footnotes that anchor the poetic text to a reality of archives, annals, chronicles and anthropological observations recount and document events, figures and information about the Indian population of the region. But with the same movement that ties fiction to truth, Alencar chooses the part of the truth he will use to butress

important points of his story (Wasserman 822); e "*Iracema*, despite its
subtitled description as a legend, purports to be a fact; a large number of
detailed scholarly footnotes serve as one frame of the text, presenting it as
a historically accurate account of the first European settlement of Ceará
and explaining the etymologies and meanings of dozens of Indian words
and names which appear in the text" (Haberly 54). Por um lado, o épico tem
a intenção de "mitificar" o passado, ou, nas palavras de Fernando Pessoa,
estabelecer o mito, "...o nada que é tudo" (25). Por outro lado, as etimologias
e as notas podem servir a função "enciclopédica" do épico, isto é, registrar
os costumes, os hábitos de outros povos e também catalogar os heróis do
passado. Há listas de guerreiros e navios nas epopéias da antigüidade que
comemoram os antepassados heróicos. Talvez as notas e etimologias de
Alencar sirvam ao mesmo propósito: resgatar a memória de uma língua e
uma cultura heróica indígena já desvanecidas. Assim, Alencar consegue
incluir uma base histórica e uma visão abrangente de uma cultura do
passado como na epopéia, mesmo numa obra de menor extensão como
Iracema.

　　　Além de estabelecer a historicidade de *Iracema*, Alencar também
cria a atmosfera mítica da epopéia. Normalmente o épico ocorre numa
época remota e num lugar distante ou exótico, e retrata eventos importantes
na formação de uma nação ou raça. Em seu estudo "Myth and Brazilian
Literature," Zilberman estabelece definitivamente os elementos míticos em
Iracema, a saber: os eventos ocorrem antes do estabelecimento das
instituições coloniais; Iracema e Martim se encontram num lugar sagrado,
o bosque onde se preserva o mistério da jurema, o segredo do sono; o pajé
Araquém, pai de Iracema, possui poderes mágicos; o tema estabelece a
formação da primeira família brasileira, representada pela família nuclear
(145). Zilberman também chama atenção à semelhança entre a trama de
Iracema e o mito da fundação de Roma, no qual uma virgem vestal, como
Iracema, é seduzida e dá a luz perto de um rio. Após a morte da mãe, uma
loba cuida dos filhos, os futuros fundadores da capital romana (145).
Zilberman também assinala a intervenção divina nos eventos humanos
(146), outro elemento típico das epopéias, ao citar o seguinte trecho de
Iracema: "Nunca tão disputada vitória e tão renhida pugna se pelejou nos
campos que regam o Acaracu e o Camucim; o valor era igual de parte a
parte e nenhum dos dois povos fora vencido, se o deus da guerra, o torvo
Arequesi, não tivesse decidido dar estas plagas à raça do guerreiro branco,
aliada dos pitiguaras" (*Iracema* 190).[1] Neste parágrafo, Alencar emprega a
fórmula épica na qual os deuses decidem o desfecho da batalha. Assim, o
estudo de Zilberman fortalece o discurso épico de *Iracema*, mostrando
algumas das fontes clássicas da lenda cearense.

Em *Iracema*, então, Alencar consegue combinar história e mito e também contrastar gestos heróicos e sofrimento humano, igual aos poetas da epopéia clássica. Além dessas semelhanças temáticas, a obra de Alencar contém convenções épicas tão óbvias que não foram reconhecidas como tais; por exemplo: a invocação da musa, a pergunta retórica inicial, o começo *in medias res*, e o uso de símiles extendidos, e finalmente, a repetição de epítetos para denotar as personagens. *Iracema* também inclui dois episódios chaves, parecidos com os da *Eneida*, que estabelecem o desenvolvimento do caráter do herói: uma descida aos infernos que motiva o herói a agir, e a descrição da "armadura" heróica, que justifica a vitória final da conquista. Escondidas sob a linguagem e as tradições indígenas, as convenções épicas quase passaram despercebidas, embora Araripe Júnior comentasse de passagem, "Na *Iracema* é fácil distinguir o que vem de Homero, o que vem de Ossiam, o que vem dos poemas judaicos, o que vem de Chateaubriand" (Lima 60). Ao mesmo tempo, porém, *Iracema* é uma epopéia moderna e única porque, debaixo da vocação nacionalista do Romantismo, existe uma visão problemática do nacionalismo e da nacionalidade. O contraste entre o heroísmo do romance e o desfecho negativo dá ao discurso épico alencariano seu teor peculiar e original. Depois de estabelecer as convenções épicas presentes em *Iracema*, examinar-se-á a contribuição da leitura épica à interpretação do romance.

A epopéia tradicional sempre abre com a invocação da musa, uma das deusas de inspiração artística. Alencar transforma esta invocação de modo romântico, incarnando a deusa na forma da Natureza quando invoca os "Verdes mares da minha terra natal" para inspirar-lhe a contar sua história. Sua terra natal, Ceará, cujo nome é de origem indígena, contém a idéia do canto, como explica o autor na primeira nota: "Ceará é nome composto de *cemo*, cantar forte, clamar, e *ara*, pequena arara ou periquito. Essa é a etimologia verdadeira, não só é conforme à tradição, como às regras da língua tupi" (215). Assim ao invocar a inspiração de sua terra natal, Alencar consegue desdobrar o canto poético e o canto do pássaro na natureza. Enquanto a etimologia fortalece a idéia de inspiração poética da musa da Natureza, fonte da espiritualidade para os românticos, a disposição das primeiras linhas da obra lembram até versos poéticos:

Verdes mares bravios de minha terra natal onde
canta a jandaia nas frondes da carnaúba;

Verdes mares que brilhais como líquida esmeralda
aos raios do sol nascente, perlongando as alvas
praias ensombradas de coqueiros;

Serenai, verdes mares, e alisai docemente a vaga
impetuosa para que o barco aventureiro manso
resvale à flor das àguas. (83)

A personificação do mar também evoca a idéia da musa, que deve "serenar"
ou acalmar o mar para proteger o barco onde viajam "um jovem guerreiro
cuja tez branca não cora o sangue americano; uma criança e um rafeiro que
viram a luz no berço das florestas e brincam irmãos, filhos ambos da
mesma terra selvagem" (83). Portanto, Alencar começa a história *in medias
res* seguindo a ordem dos eventos da *Odisseia* e da *Eneida* que abrem "with
the hero far from his home and at the end of the quest, and then work
forward and backward to the end and beginning of the total action"
(*Harper's Handbook* 171). A obra de Alencar também se inicia com o herói
longe de sua terra natal, no fim da busca. Descobre-se ao final, que, depois
de enterrar o corpo de Iracema, a mãe de seu filho, o guerreiro volta para
Portugal, levando o filho "americano" para lá. No entanto, a trama de
Iracema é mais unida e simples do que a da epopéia tradicional, e por isso
não há tantos desvios ao nível da ação; a partir do segundo capítulo,
começa a ordem cronológica de eventos, o qual retoma a pergunta inicial
do romance e estabelece o pretexto da ação: "Que deixara ele na terra do
exílio?" (84). Esta frase é parecida à pergunta retórica do épico, depois da
qual inicia-se a ação. Na obra de Alencar, esta pergunta serve para abrir e
encerrar a história num movimento circular do mito. Quanto à forma, as
epopéias antigas contêm doze "livros" ou capítulos; Alencar, porém, divide
sua obra em 33 episódios, um número que lembra a trindade e a base cristã
da sociedade brasileira, e também a idade da morte de Cristo, e portanto, o
sofrimento e sacrifício que vão juntos na cataquese e na colonização.

Em geral, considera-se o romantismo como rebelião ou reação
contra os padrões do classicismo e talvez seja por isso que os elementos
épicos em *Iracema* não têm sido estudados em detalhe, senão mencionados
de passagem. Por exemplo, Haberly nota que Martim é chamado
freqüentemente pelo *epíteto* "o guerreiro do mar," e assim personifica o
povo português tal como Iracema, cujo nome é anagrama de "América,"
representa a terra e a raça a serem conquistadas pelos europeus (55).
Haberly não menciona os vários epítetos que se referem a Iracema, que
também ressaltam sua conexão com a natureza ou sua raça: "virgem dos
lábios de mel" (85); "virgem dos olhos negros" (109); "filha de Araquém"
(111, 143); "filha dos tabajaras" (130); "virgem das florestas" (130);
"virgem formosa do sertão" (140); "virgem de Tupã" (141); "filha das
florestas" (159); "filha dos sertões" (174). Esta variedade de epítetos para

uma só personagem destaca o valor poético da obra, e constitui uma espécie de homenagem à poesia épica (embora não se use os epítetos exatamente segundo a fórmula épica clássica, na qual cada personagem principal tem um ou dois epítetos usados repetidas vezes). Esta repetição de epítetos também contribui para o tom solene e elevado da obra, típico da epopéia.

Haberly também assinala o uso repetido do símile extendido em *Iracema*, outro recurso épico. Segundo Haberly, a função do símile faz parte da recriação de Alencar do mito da idade de ouro ao nível da linguagem; o autor, "places a comma as a form of equation, and then essentially translates his Portuguese statement, through simile, into a new language—not Tupi, although it contains Indian words still commonly used to refer to flora and fauna, but the present-tense language of the enduring reality of Brazil itself, of the land and its creatures and plants, unchanged despite the historical accidents of conquest and settlement....Thus, symbolically and linguistically, the Golden Age remains...(56). Entretanto, os símiles elaborados de Alencar também encaixam perfeitamente no projeto épico do romance. Mais uma vez, o estilo alencariano evoca o discurso épico, no qual as comparações costumam ser extensivas. Examinaremos dois exemplos que se referem à reação de Martim e Iracema a seus primeiros encontros:

> Volta a serenidade ao seio do guerreiro branco, mas todas as vezes que seu olhar pousa sobre a virgem tabajara, ele sente correr-lhe pelas veias uma onda ardente. Assim quando a criança imprudente revolve o brasido de intenso fogo saltam as faúlhas inflamadas que lhe queimam as faces. (104)

> A filha do Pajé estremeceu. Assim estremece a verde palma quando a haste frágil foi abalada; rorejam do espato as lágrimas de chuva, e os leques ciciam brandamente. (108)

Nesses exemplos, o símile funciona como registro da tensão que existe entre Iracema e Martim; podemos notar que no primeiro exemplo, o símile não se refere à natureza, mas à imprudência de uma criança na vida diária. Homero, na *Ilíada*, descreve em detalhe a vida diária que está retratada no escudo de Heitor; estas cenas de paz, ou, como Haberly notou em *Iracema*, da tranqüilidade da natureza, servem como contraponto à violência guerreira do épico e oferecem um sentido de continuidade e paz. Assim, Alencar consegue recriar o estilo épico no contexto americano, quase disfarçando suas fontes clássicas no exotismo da paisagem brasileira. Wasserman também observa certo classicismo na sintaxe da obra; Alencar inventou, "a highly stylized poetic idiom...short sentences, short paragraphs, great density of imagery and incantory rhythms that, within an *almost classical syntax*, allow language to carry out the combination of American and European elements" (824, grifo nosso). Assim já desvendamos o (neo)classicismo presente em *Iracema* através dos epítetos, símiles extendidos, e a sintaxe clássica, que constatam a intenção épica de Alencar.

A presença de convenções épicas ao nível poético chama atenção para os paralelos temáticos entre *Iracema* e as epopéias clássicas. O épico tradicional inclui personagens heróicas que representam os arquétipos de uma raça ou cultura. Como Zilberman apontou, Martim e Iracema formam a primeira família brasileira em forma mítica e também exemplificam qualidades admiráveis: coragem, fidelidade, e sacrifício. Tipicamente, os heróis realizam viagens e aventuras em terras novas, inclusive uma viagem aos infernos. Podemos comparar a trajetória heróica de Martim com a de Enéias; no processo de realizar seu destino e fundar uma nação, ambos ficam "presos" pelo amor de uma mulher. Ao início da sua história, Martim, como Enéias, está incapaz de agir; fica preso em terras alheias depois de uma longa viagem. Para escapar deste estado de cativeiro físico e mental, o herói precisa renovar sua força por uma descida aos infernos, que significa uma morte simbólica depois da qual renasce fortalecido. Alencar inclui esta idéia de descida quando Martim e Iracema escapam dos tabajaras, entrando nas "entranhas da terra" (133). Depois, "perdidos nas entranhas da terra, descem a gruta profunda" (135) onde se encontram com Poti, o "irmão" pitiguara de Martim. A partir deste momento, Martim recupera seu poder, enquanto Iracema perde o seu. Ela já não usa arco e flecha, nem os poderes mágicos que herdou do pai. Zilberman nota que "...Iracema vai assumindo gradualmente outra imagem: a de mulher submissa e mãe abnegada, ideal de esposa do guerreiro..." ("Natureza e Mulher" 56). É significativo também que Martim consiga derrotar os tabajaras na primeira batalha depois do escape, porque nisso vemos o herói branco renascido, que prenuncia a morte de Iracema e sua tribo.

Para enfatizar o heroísmo de Martim e justificar o abandono de Iracema, Alencar dedica todo um capítulo ao simbolismo da pintura guerreira que Martim usa no corpo. É interessante notar o paralelo entre este capítulo de *Iracema* e o oitavo livro da *Eneida* onde Virgílio descreve o escudo de Enéias. O escudo retrata as "futuras" vitórias do império romano e justifica, de certa forma, a importância da missão de Enéias, que, tendo abandonado sua amante, provoca seu desespero e suicídio. Alencar, ao descrever o significado da pintura de Martim, retrata-o como o herói perfeito: inteligente, forte, saudável, veloz e compassivo (179-181). Assim, Martim personifica a vitória da raça branca e, ao nível da trama, justifica sua subseqüente partida. Como Haberly comprova em seu estudo, as lendas literárias do Novo Mundo geralmente ressaltam a superioridade da cultura dominante que se funda nas ruínas da cultura conquistada (47). Assim, Alencar inclui um capítulo tal qual o da armadura de Enéias como antidoto ao comportamento anti-heróico de Martim, a deserção da esposa. Ainda que Martim não abandone Iracema completamente como faz o herói da *Eneida*, que parte sem dar explicação alguma à rainha de Cartago, as partidas Martim contribuem para a lenta morte da heroína. O sacrifício feminino, como mostraremos mais adiante, também constitui um tema recorrente no discurso épico. Iracema reconhece o sentido de dever de Martim quando ele começa a passear na praia em busca de seu povo: "Quanto tempo há que retiraste de Iracema seu espírito? Dantes teu passo te guiava para as frescas serras e alegres tabuleiros; teu pé gostava de pisar a terra da felicidade e seguir o rasto da esposa. Agora só buscas as praias ardentes, porque o mar lá murmura vem dos campos em que nasceste; e o morro das areias porque do alto se avista a igara que passa" (195). Com efeito, Martim e Poti partem logo para voltar à guerra e lutar para uma vitória definitiva contra os inimigos dos portugueses e seus aliados. A vitória de Martim parece ser dupla quando nasce seu filho no momento da celebração da derrota dos inimigos. Entretanto, estas vitórias coincidem com sacrifício de Iracema. Podemos notar dentro que, da tradição épica, muitas vezes há um sacrifício feminino que acompanha a fundação de uma nação. Virgílio exemplifica este sacrifício na rainha de Cartago; Camões o recria na história trágica de Inês de Castro; assim, até a morte de Iracema tem precedente na tradição épica.

A *Enéida* e *Os Lusíadas*, como epopéias literárias, (não originais ou folclóricas como as obras de Homero), mantêm certa visão crítica da sua própria sociedade; no caso de Virgílio, a grande compaixão que demonstra para a rainha de Cartago serve de contrapeso à severidade com que se retrata Enéias e sua missão de conquista. Na obra de Camões, o discurso do Velho de Restelo critica a empresa marítima portuguesa, que trouxe não só fama e riqueza mas também corrupção para Portugal. Como os mestres do discurso épico, Alencar se insere nesta tradição ao mesmo tempo heróica e crítica. A pergunta inicial, "Que deixara ele na terra do exílio?" é a memória da dor da conquista e da catequese, representada na morte de Iracema. Assim, a memória de morte acompanha o herói e não só a glória da conquista. O desfecho não é apenas simples ou fácil como argumenta Roberto Ventura em seu conceito de "exotismo sentimental" da síntese da cultura indígena e européia (38), nem consiste só na imposição do patriarcado em terras brasileiras como sustenta Lemaire (70). Se considerarmos a ambivalência do final de *Iracema*, podemos sondar uma visão crítica e complicada da identidade nacional. Como conclui Luiz Fernando Valente, em vez de "representar a identidade nacional como uma síntese harmônica entre o elemento português e o elemento nativo, este projeto pouco a pouco se desfaz na medida em que se configura uma insolúvel *diferença* entre os elementos que se queriam sintetizar. Desta forma o romance que pretendia contar a história de uma harmonização, começa a assinalar a presença de uma violação" (81). Isto não quer dizer que *Iracema* seja um épico falho, muito ao contrário, contribui para a complexidade da obra. Alencar já percebeu certas contradições raciais e sociais latentes na sociedade brasileira, que ele resolve ao nível da trama com a morte de Iracema, mas que continuam sendo "insolúveis" ao nível socio-filosófico.

A dedicatória de *Iracema*: "à terra natal/um filho ausente" retoma a idéia de um exílio interno ou espiritual. De certa forma, as palavras, ausência, exílio e morte abrem e encerram a história de *Iracema*. A obra capta o exílio espiritual da própria formação do país, como resume Wasserman: "...all Brazilians are strangers in their own country, the Indians made so by their contact with the Europeans, and the Europeans and Africans made so by their contact with the land" (817). Alceu Amoroso Lima também reconhece outro sentido de protesto e crítica implícita em *Iracema*, de base sociológica; "da passagem do Brasil da fase agrícola, dominada pela natureza, para a fase industrial, em que a natureza é dominada pela máquina" (59). Enquanto este protesto pode ser considerado como típico do passadismo do romantismo, é central para uma interpretação mais profunda de *Iracema*. Lima cita um trecho do poema épico de Alencar, *Os filhos de Tupã*, para ilustrar a crítica da parte do autor da nova invasão européia, a industrial:

O cavalo a vapor nitrindo espuma
Corcova escarva o chão: relinche e parte.
Come a terra, sorvendo o espaço, voa
Percorre o globo deste àquele pólo
Das áridas estepes do Cáucaso
Pastar nos Andes a virente grama.
Seu hálito abrasado já te escalda
Mesmo de longe a fronte. Em breve tempo
Aqui virá pisar com férrea pata
As flores mais mimosas de teus seios,
E o veludo de relvas te cobre
Calvaga a fera o gênio do progresso,
Espírito de luz, asas de chama,
Tem o corisco o vôo: o rasto é cinza.

Alencar personifica as terras do continente da América do Sul em forma de mulher, que sofre a violação de um novo invasor (a locomotiva), disfarçado como progresso e iluminação. O resultado final é o rasto de "cinza," uma imagem de morte e destruição que contrasta com a vitalidade e abundância da natureza primordial.

Então, nesses versos, Alencar reduplica a violação de terras brasileiras na re-colonização do país pela máquina e identifica-se com o sentido de perda e ausência que experimentam as personagens principais de *Iracema*. Ceará, terra remota, espécie de Paraíso perdido para Alencar, recebe a dedicatória do livro, do "filho ausente." Esta ausência não só se refere a presença física de Alencar, longe do Ceará, mas também à perda da inocência pré-industrial e da visão edênica de origem. Embora o programa patente dos românticos fosse, segundo Antônio Cândido, o "estabelecimento de uma genealogia literária, análise da capacidade criadora das raças autóctones, aspectos locais como estímulos da inspiração" (323), Alencar acaba retratando uma ausência irremediável numa genealogia falha, representada metaforicamente pela morte de Iracema, o exílio de Martim e a orfandade de Moacir.

Se considerarmos *Iracema* como primeiro exemplo da narrativa conscientemente nacional no Brasil, veremos um épico problemático que reflete a melancolia de perda do passado e uma incertidão sobre o futuro. Flora Süssekind emprega a metáfora da orfandade para descrever a genealogia peculiar do romance brasileiro em geral, que "já nasce sob o signo da descontinuidade, da falta e da culpa. 'Tu és Moacir, nascido de meu sofrimento'...morta a mãe, o filho é levado para a Europa, condenado a ver a própria terra de longe, com um olhar aculturado, semelhante ao do pai estrangeiro" (196). Portanto, *Iracema*, em vez de apresentar uma utopia do nacionalismo, das origens, reconhece-se como uma construção literária, o órfão da escritura: "What is the father?...Writing, the lost son, does not answer this question—it writes (itself): (that) the father *is not*, that is to say, not present" (Derrida 146). A partida de Martim e Moacir e a morte de Iracema deixam só rastos ou traços da origem, que implica já a *diferença* da escritura, e não da *presença* plena ou utópica da nacionalidade.

Assim, a orfandade de Moacir e o exílio de Martim deslocam o discurso épico, do Logos, da identidade, para desmentir a retórica nacionalista de "cataquese, progresso, desenvolvimento" (Reis 6), afirmando uma ansiedade de origens, e, ao mesmo tempo, a impossibilidade desta volta. O "filho ausente" tenta substituir ou suplementar esta falta de origem que se representa na ausência da mãe e no exílio do pai da "raça de cabelos do sol" pelos traços da pena. No desdobramento Moacir/Alencar (os filhos ausentes), vemos a pré-condição para o particular discurso épico de Alencar,

146   M. Elizabeth Ginway

em que a filiação substitui a noção da presença do Pai. Então, a obra de Alencar não é o mero portavoz do nacionalismo, mas vai além das oposições *mythos/logos* ou lenda/história para a *disseminação* de conceitos sobre as origens e a identidade brasileira. Eis a riqueza da visão alencariana, e a razão pela qual poder-se-ia considerar *Iracema* como épico nacional brasileiro, porque fornecerá uma contínua fonte de debate sobre a nacionalidade e o nacionalismo literário do Brasil.

Notes

[1] A páginas citadas de *Iracema* e as notas de Alencar são retiradas da Edição do Centenário, ed. Augusto Meyer, São Paulo: Instituto Nacional do Livro, 1965.

Works Cited

Alencar, José Martiniano de. *Iracema*. Ed. Augusto Meyer. São Paulo: Instituto Nacional do Livro, 1965.
---. "Cartas sobre *A Confederação dos Tamoios*." *Obra completa*. Vol. 4. São Paulo: Aguilar, 1965. 4 vols.
---. "Carta ao Dr. Jaguaribe." *Iracema* By José de Alencar. Ed. Augusto Meyer. São Paulo: Instituto Nacional do Livro, 1965. 225-230.

Camões, Luís Vaz de. *Os Lusíadas*. Porto: Porto Editora, 1982.

Cândido, Antônio. *Formação da literatura brasileira*. Vol. 2. 3rd ed. São Paulo: Martins, 1969. 2 vols.

Derrida, Jacques. *Dissemination*. Trans. Barbara Johnson. Chicago: University of Chicago Press, 1981.

Haberly, David T. "Form and Function in the New World Legend." *Do the Americas Have a Common Literature?* Ed. Gustavo Pérez-Firmat. Durham, North Carolina: Duke University Press, 1990. 42-61.
The Harper Handbook to Literature. Eds. Northrop Frye, Sheridan Baker, George Perkins. New York: Harper and Row, 1985.

Homer, *The Iliad*. Trans. Richard Lattimore. Chicago: University of Chicago Press, 1951.

Lemaire, Ria. "Re-reading *Iracema*: The Problem of the Representation of Women in the Construction of a National Brazilian Identity." *Luso-Brazilian Review* 26.2 (1989): 60-73.

Lima, Alceu Amoroso. "José de Alencar, esse desconhecido?" *Iracema* By José de Alencar. Ed. Augusto Meyer. São Paulo: Instituto Nacional do Livro, 1965. 35-72.

Machado de Assis, Joaquim Maria. "A tradição indígena na obra de Alencar." *Iracema* By José de Alencar. Ed. Augusto Meyer. São Paulo: Instituto Nacional do Livro, 1965. 13-27.

Pessoa, Fernando. *Mensagem. Obras Completas.* Vol. 5. Lisboa: Atica, 1970. 9 vols.

Reis, Zenir Campos. "Um novo mundo." *Iracema* By José de Alencar. São Paulo: Atica, 1982. 5-6.

Süssekind, Flora. *Tal Brasil, Qual Romance?* Rio de Janeiro: Achiamé, 1984.

Valente, Luiz Fernando. "Oswald/Alencar: a antropofagia revisitada." *Atlântida* 35 (1990): 75-86.

Ventura, Roberto. "Literature, Anthropology, and Popular Culture in Brazil: From José de Alencar to Darcy Ribeiro." *Komparatistische Hefte* 11 (1985): 35-47.

Virgil. *The Aeneid.* Trans. Rolfe Humphries. New York: Charles Scribner and Sons, 1951.

Wasserman, Renata R. Maunter. "The Red and the White: the Indian Novels of José de Alencar." *PMLA* 98 (1983): 815-827.

Zilberman, Regina. "Myth and Brazilian Literature." *Literary Anthropology: A New Interdisciplinary Approach to People, Signs and Literature.* Ed. Fernando Poyatos. Amsterdam: John Benjamin, 1988. 141-159.
---. "Natureza e Mulher—Uma Visão do Brasil no Romans Romântico." *Modern Language Studies* 19 (1989): 50-64.

Alencar's Flawed Blueprints

Luiz Fernando Valente

By the middle of the nineteenth century, Brazil had found at least temporary solutions to many of the problems that had marked the turbulent first thirty years following its independence from Portugal, and was about the enter what historian Richard Graham has called the country's "golden age," that is, two decades of political stability, internal peace and relative prosperity (160). National politics was dominated by a skillful accommodation between Liberals and Conservatives, known as "Conciliação," which made possible a government of national consensus. Unlike his impulsive father, Pedro II was a sober man, who, despite his propensity for authoritarianism, projected an image of benevolence and impartiality that was perfectly suited to the "moderating power" vested in the emperor. The rebellions that had threatened the unity of the country for most of the 1830s and the 1840s had been suppressed, coffee exports kept growing steadily, and the emergence of a national entrepreneurial spirit, best represented by the financial ventures of Irineu Evangelista de Souza, the baron and later viscount of Mauá, reflected a confidence in the economic future of Brazil. In sum, the Brazilian elites had been able to consolidate their hegemony and carry out what José Murilo de Carvalho has called their "construction of order."[1] By combining political conciliation with a system of clientelism and patronage left over from colonial days, the elites succeeded in minimizing tensions and exercising tight control over the rest of society.[2]

Nevertheless, the deceptive tranquility of these two decades concealed many insidious problems, which became increasingly more visible after 1870 and were to play a key role in the historical developments of the last quarter of the century. The continued presence of slavery exposed the extreme inequalities in Brazilian society, while leading to a skewed distribution of wealth that hampered lasting economic development (Graham 133). Slavery also posed a potential threat to social stability, of

148

which the 1835 insurrection of the Malês (African Muslims) in Bahia was a sobering reminder.[3] Furthermore, the memory of the recently-quelled rebellions called attention to the fragility of a political system that failed to incorporate large segments of society.[4] Finally, although national unity had been maintained, it was questionable whether a true sense of national identity had been forged.[5]

José de Alencar's most productive years, both as a public figure and as a man of letters, fall within this period. After graduating from the São Paulo Law School, one of the main training grounds for the Brazilian elites, Alencar returned to Rio de Janeiro in 1850 to begin a public life devoted to law, journalism and politics.[6] In 1860 Alencar was elected to the Parliament as a deputy from his home province of Ceará, and in 1868 he was appointed Minister of Justice in the Itaboraí cabinet. When his ill-fated candidacy for the Senate was rejected by Pedro II in 1870 on the grounds that Alencar was too young for this life-long post, Alencar developed a bitter animosity towards the emperor. After flirting for a brief period with the theater, Alencar focused his creative talents on the narrative. With the exception of *Senhora* and *O sertanejo*, which were published in 1875, most of Alencar's best novels were written in the late 1850s and during the 1860s: *O Guarani* was published in 1857, *Lucíola* in 1862, *Iracema* in 1865 and *As minas de prata* in 1866.

As a journalist and politician, Alencar generally identified with the elites, particularly concerning the polemical racial issues of the time. He subscribed to the self-image of Brazil as the product of three races,[7] a compensatory strategy devised by the elites against the evidence of a society sharply divided along racial lines, and, despite having shut down the infamous Valongo slave market in Rio de Janeiro during his tenure as Minister of Justice, had an ambiguous attitude towards abolition. As Brito Broca pointed out, although Alencar recognized the inhumanity of slavery, he regarded slavery as an economic necessity, without which Brazil, much like the United States, would not have developed (1042). As a member of Parliament, Alencar strongly opposed passage of the Law of the Free Womb, submitted by the Rio Branco cabinet in 1871. Arguing that slaves were unprepared for freedom and that premature abolition would throw Brazil into chaos, Alencar charged the abolitionists with skirting their responsibility to the country for the sake of immediate political gain.[8] In admitting the possibility that such a heinous and demoralizing institution could be saved by an infusion of humanitarianism, Alencar concurred with the prevailing position of powerful segments of the elite, particularly the coffee planters from Rio de Janeiro. It would be unfair, however, to dismiss Alencar as insensitive and reactionary. Contemporary research has demonstrated that many of his political ideas were surprisingly advanced for the time.[9] Moreover, his journalistic writings indicate that his thinking on matters of public policy was quite progressive. Alencar should not be viewed, therefore, as a mere spokesman for conservative ideology. Rather, the apparent inconsistencies in his positions make him the perfect embodiment of the conflicts and ambiguities that characterized Brazil in the second half of the nineteenth century.

Recent criticism has tended to interpret Alencar's fiction as expressing the ideals and values of the Brazilian elites at mid-century. For example, in "Liderança e hierarquia em Alencar" Silviano Santiago suggests that O Guarani is the literary counterpart to the model of social organization dominant in nineteenth-century Brazil, based on a strict social hierarchy and a lack of social mobility. In A permanência do círculo, Roberto Reis picks up where Santiago leaves off, arguing that despite his attempts to criticize Brazilian society, Alencar is unable to create characters that transcend traditional patriarchal values. More recently, Doris Sommer in Foundational Fictions establishes links between Alencar's "foundational novels" and Brazilian history of the nineteenth century, concluding that O Guarani can be read as an allegory of the "Conciliação" and interpreting Martim's "saudade" in Iracema as nostalgia for the missed promises of the "Conciliação" government. Although these readings have contributed to the rehabilitation of Alencar as an "adult" writer, they are too cautious about giving Alencar the full credit he deserves as one of the most perceptive interpreters of Brazilian society in the third quarter of the nineteenth century.

Timothy Brennan has called attention to the close ties between the novel as a genre and the concept of the nation. Relying on Benedict Anderson's definition of the nation as "an imagined community,"[10] Brennan has suggested that, unlike the epic, which reaffirms the existence of a people, the novel provides a "practical means of creating a people" (50). By utilizing a form that allows for the representation of multiplicity, the novel is capable of "objectifying the nation's composite nature" (51). The links between the novel and national formation are particularly important in Latin America. As Jean Franco has proposed, "it was in the novel that different and often conflicting programs for the nation were debated." Since the nineteenth century the intelligentsia has appropriated the novel to "work out imaginary solutions to the intractable problems of racial heterogeneity, social inequality, urban versus rural society" (204). Alencar's fiction participates in this interaction between nation and narration. This is especially true of O Guarani and Iracema, which are consummate examples of what Franco has named "blueprints of national formation" (203).

Undoubtedly, these two novels are part of the elites' project of imagining Brazil as a nation according to Anderson's definition, that is, as a sovereign community whose boundaries are clearly marked in terms of space and time. Nevertheless, they are not mere validations of the elites' project for Brazil. Behind the outward conformity to the official discourse of national formation stands a perceptive social observer who is acutely aware of the unresolved contradictions of his day.

Since the sixteenth century writers have focused on the lushness of Brazilian nature as one of the most important differentiating criteria between Brazil and Europe. This attitude is at the root of "ufanismo," that pride in all things Brazilian, which influenced the thinking of many Romantic writers, including Alencar, as they strove to carry out their twofold goal of defining Brazil's national identity and creating a Brazilian national literature. It should not be forgotten, however, that the view of Brazil as a natural paradise, which has become part and parcel of the Brazilian collective unconscious, is not a native construction, but an invention of sixteenth-century European travellers, one in which "nature" marks the non-European and supposedly uncivilized "other." Its origins can be traced back to the first written document about Brazil, Pero Vaz de Caminha's letter to the Portuguese king Dom Manuel announcing the "discovery" of Brazil in 1500, reaching the nineteenth century via transformations by such writers as Gândavo, Léry, More, Montaigne, Rousseau and others.[11] Although the practice of "ufanismo" by nineteenth-century writers is supposed to express national pride in what is uniquely Brazilian, it also reveals the impossibility for the Brazilian intelligentsia to separate itself completely from European attitudes towards Brazil. Therefore, romantic "ufanismo" should be considered as a manifestation of what Antônio Cândido has called the "genealogical tendency" in Brazilian literature, which consists in underscoring the native elements that most closely resemble European norms and ideals.[12] Furthermore, the Edenic view of Brazil proves insufficient for the construction of Brazilian national identity, for a nation is, by definition, not a geographical location, but a community of human beings who see themselves as different from members of other national communities and, at the same time, as bound to one another through their shared sense of nationality.[13]

The description of D. Antônio de Mariz's homestead in the first chapter of *O Guarani* reveals a narrator torn between extolling the natural beauty of Brazil and praising the industriousness of the country's new inhabitants. The passage begins by presenting Brazilian nature according to the rules of "ufanismo": "Tudo era grande e pomposo no cenário que a natureza, sublime artista, tinha decorado para os dramas majestosos dos elementos, em que o homem é apenas um simples comparsa" (27). Gradually, however, more importance is attached to the human intervention in the natural processes: "Aí, ainda, a indústria do homem tinha aproveitado habilmente a natureza para criar meios de segurança e defesa" (28). The passage concludes by lauding the human capacity to transform and tame nature: "Flores agrestes das nossas matas, pequenas árvores copadas, um estendal de relvas, um fio d'água fingindo um rio e formando uma pequena cascata, tudo isto a mão do homem tinha criado no pequeno espaço, com uma arte e graça admirável" (28). At first notice, this passage appears to depict the peaceful coexistence between the bountiful land and the material needs of human beings, which the men who have accompanied D. Antônio seem intent on preserving: ". . . aproveitavam os recursos dessa natureza tão rica, para proverem os seus habitantes de todo o necessário" (31). Nevertheless, the balance between nature and civilization is not perfect, for European technology must be introduced before the bountiful American land can begin fulfilling its promise as a human provider.

Equally noteworthy is the opening paragraph of the novel, in which nature functions as an allegory for the ambiguous situation of Brazil in the middle of the nineteenth century, that is, a peripheric country still deeply dependent on slave labor, but one that wishes to be seen, much like the other recently independent nations in the New World, as the heir to the French Revolution ideals of freedom, equality and brotherhood. In that paragraph the Paquequer river is described as "altivo" and as "o filho indômito desta pátria de liberdade," a paragon of the idealized view of Brazil in the post-independence period. Nevertheless, when the Paquequer meets the mightier Paraíba river, which is presented as a king ("rei das águas") and a lord ("suserano"), and whose course is described as majestic ("rola majestosamente em seu vasto leito"), the Paquequer becomes a vassal ("vassalo") and a slave ("escravo submisso"), by yielding to its master ("sofre o látego do senhor"). This description foreshadows the relationship between Peri and D. Antônio de Mariz, for although Peri is supposed to epitomize the love of freedom innate to the native of Brazil, he acknowledges the supremacy of the Portuguese nobleman. But more importantly, the insertion of images based on the master/servant dichotomy into a passage that starts as a celebration of Brazil's natural beauty and of native Brazilians' love of freedom mirrors the gap between the idealized self-image of Brazil as the land of the free and the brave, and the social and political reality of the country in the nineteenth century.

Iracema goes even further than *O Guarani*, starting with a hymn to Brazilian nature, written in melodious, poetic prose: "Verdes mares bravios de minha terra natal, onde canta a jandaia nas frondes da carnaúba" (11).

From the very beginning of the novel the comparisons of Iracema to the fauna and flora of Brazil suggest that she is intimately connected with the forces of nature:[14]

> Iracema, a virgem dos lábios de mel, que tinha os cabelos mais negros que a asa da graúna, e mais longos que seu talhe de palmeira. O favo da jati não era doce como seu sorriso; nem a baunilha recendia no bosque como seu hálito perfumado. Mais rápida que a ema selvagem, a morena corria o sertão e as matas do Ipu, onde campeava sua guerreira tribo, da grande nação tabajara. (12)

Like Peri, Iracema is "selvagem" in the literal sense, for she knows all the secrets of the forests, most notably the preparation of a magic potion from the leaves of the sacred "jurema" tree, which is used in the religious rituals of her tribe. Nature participates in every important moment of Iracema's life, including her union to Martim ("A floresta destilava suave fragância e exalava arpejos harmoniosos; os suspiros do coração se difundiram nos múrmuros do deserto. Foi a festa do amor e o canto do himeneu." 45) and her pregnancy with Moacir, who is to become "the first Brazilian" ("por cima da carioba trazia uma cintura de flores da maniva, que era o símbolo da fecundidade" 57). Nevertheless, the novel does not conclude with a celebration of Brazilian nature, epitomized by Iracema, but of the European, "civilized" values introduced by the Portuguese soldiers, who, under Martim's command, have landed on the beach (where Iracema had given birth to Moacir), to establish a permanent Portuguese settlement. Although the return to this site brings memories of Iracema back to a wistful Martim, the purpose of the trip is not to honor Iracema, but to found the "mairi dos cristãos," an outpost that will guarantee Portuguese control of this "savage" territory against incursions by adventurers from other nations: "A mairi que Martim erguera à margem do rio, nas praias do Ceará medrou, Germinou a palavra do *Deus verdadeiro* na *terra selvagem*, e o *bronze sagrado* ressoou nos vales onde rugia o *maracá*" [my emphases] (76). Furthermore, although the depiction of indigenous customs in the novel indicates Alencar's appreciation of native Brazilian culture, Alencar remains safely distant from it by always presenting it as exotic. To this effect Alencar uses his authorial control to its fullest, appending to the text more than one hundred explanatory notes, in which he comments on indigenous traditions and provides information about the etymology of Tupi words. Perhaps the most telling of these notes is the one in which he provides a rational explanation for the alleged power of the shaman Araquém (Iracema's father) to summon the thunder (which the Tabajaras believe to be the voice of Tupã), thereby insuring the absolute respect and obedience of the members of the tribe. Alencar explains in detail how Araquém is able to produce the loud roaring sound that frightens the Tabajaras by lifting a rock that has been deftly positioned over one end of a wind tunnel connecting the floor of his tepee with the outside. Alencar finishes the note by declaring authoritatively that "o fato é, pois, natural: a aparência, sim, é maravilhosa" (74). Despite being generally sympathetic, Alencar always assumes an ethnocentric position towards indigenous culture. The result it that he ends up perpetuating the image of the Brazilian native as childlike, which was created by such sixteenth-century texts as Caminha's *Carta* and Montaigne's "Des Cannibales," and persists in contemporary Brazilian legislation dealing with the citizenship rights of Indians: "Todo esse episódio do rugido da terra é uma astúcia, como usavam os pajés e os sacerdotes de toda a nação selvagem para fascinar a imaginação do povo" (74). It should be noted that while helping Martim escape the fury of the Tabajara chief Irapuã, Iracema does not hesitate to lead Martim through the sacred tunnel. As a civilized, rational European, Martim is, of course, expected to be above believing in Araquém's supernatural powers.

Seen in this light, Alencar's Indianism appears as a carefully-crafted strategy to mediate between Brazil as "natural" and Brazil as "civilized." As was suggested above, however, this strategy does not insure a perfect balance between the "natural" and "civilized" elements. Peri knows all the secrets of the forests and often acts in an instinctive, "natural" manner, but he is also capable of such "civilized" behavior that D. Antônio de Mariz describes him as a "cavalheiro português no corpo de um selvagem" (54). Iracema is inextricably linked to the forces of nature, but she and her family abide by the Portuguese code of hospitality. Peri, Iracema, Araquém, and Martim's loyal Indian companion Poti are seen as noble and deserving of admiration because they behave according to Portuguese rules. On the other hand, the Aimorés, enemies of the Portuguese in *O Guarani*, are viewed as brutish and despicable, and their customs are dismissed as barbaric: "esse povo bárbaro tinha seus costumes e suas leis; e uma delas era esse direito exclusivo do vencedor sobre o seu prisioneiro de guerra, essa conquista do fraco pelo forte" (212). Likewise, in *Iracema*, the Pitiguaras, allies of the Portuguese, are clearly "better" than the Tabajaras, enemies of the Portuguese. Irapuã is initially presented as a great chief ("o maior chefe da nação tabajara"), but he is later described as dishonorable ("Irapuã é vil e indigno de ser chefe de guerreiros valentes") when he decides to exact revenge on Martim, whom he believes to have violated the sacred Iracema, a suspicion that later becomes a reality. Peri's worth derives less from what is unique to him as a native of Brazil than from his moral resemblance to D. Antônio de Mariz: "o fidalgo com sua lealdade e cavalheirismo apreciava o caráter de Peri, e via nele, *embora* selvagem, um homem de sentimentos nobres e de alma grande" [my emphasis] (72). Poti plays a similar role in *Iracema*. His devotion to Martim is such that he forsakes the cultural heritage of his tribe for Martim's European values: "Deviam ter ambos um só Deus, como tinham um só coração. Ele recebeu com o batismo o nome do santo, cujo era o dia: e o do rei, a quem ia servir, e sobre os dous o seu, na língua dos novos irmãos. Sua fama cresceu e ainda hoje é o orgulho da terra, onde ele primeiro viu a luz" (p. 87). In spite of the efforts to present Peri as D. Antônio's equal, the relationship between Peri and D. Antônio mirrors the traditional system of patrons and clients. Similarly, despite being Martim's closest friend, Poti always defers to Martim, and Iracema refers to Martim as her "senhor," while calling herself his "escrava" (46). There is a homology between these relationships and the ambiguities that characterized Brazilian society in the middle of the nineteenth century, which serve as a reminder of the inability of Brazil to achieve a complete break with its colonial legacy.[15] For despite being officially an independent country, where all citizens are theoretically equal, Brazil is ruled by a royal family of Portuguese descent, populated by masses of slaves and other disenfranchised groups, and controlled by an elite whose interests are intimately tied to those of foreign nations, particularly England and Portugal.

Brazilian ethnic identity was a particularly vexing question in the nineteenth century. Historical evidence prevented Brazilians from completely identifying with the country's indigenous origins, yet it was necessary to establish a clear ethnic difference between Brazil and Europe, particularly Portugal. The solution found by the Brazilian elites and the Brazilian intelligentsia was to present the Brazilian people as a synthesis of native, European and African elements. As was said above, Alencar subscribed to "fable of the three races" and accepted miscegenation as an essential component of the Brazilian identity.[16] It is not surprising, then, that Isabel, a natural daughter of D. Antônio de Mariz and an Indian woman, personifies the Brazilian female, thus becoming one of the first in a long line of dark-skinned female characters, which includes Rita Baiana (in Aluísio Azevedo's *O cortiço*) and Gabriela (in Jorge Amado's *Gabriela, cravo e canela*) : "Era um tipo inteiramente diferente do de Cecília; era o tipo brasileiro em toda a sua graça e formosura, com o encantador contraste de languidez e malícia, de indolência e vivacidade" (43). Isabel's acceptance into D. Antônio's home appears to be intended to confirm D. Antônio's lack of racial prejudice, also suggested by D. Antônio's cordial relationship with

Peri, the mutual admiration and respect between D. Antônio and Peri, and D. Antônio's steadfast defense of Peri against attacks on Peri's character by D. Lauriana, D. Antônio's Brazilian-born wife. Since D. Antônio embodies the best in the Portuguese value system, his attitude towards Isabel and Peri is to be read as evidence of the proverbial absence of racial prejudice among the Portuguese, which is often adduced as the origin of Brazil's supposedly unique racial harmony. The epilogue of the novel points in a similar direction. Having survived the bloody confrontation between the Aimorés and the Portuguese, Peri and Ceci, so much alike that they address each other as brother and sister, stand for a new and more authentic beginning for a racially-mixed Brazil. Upon closer examination, however, this representation of racial harmony begins to unravel.

D. Lauriana considers non-whites to be inferior, does not hide her dislike for Isabel, and, for a good portion of the novel, displays haughty contempt for Peri. D. Lauriana's behavior calls into question the popularly-held theory that the Portuguese had no difficulty in transmitting their allegedly innate lack of racial prejudice to Brazilians. Isabel seems to be painfully aware of the curse of her skin: "Cuidas que não percebo o desdém com que me tratam" (44). Realizing that her own dark skin victimizes her, she admits wishing that her complexion were as fair as Cecília's: "E eu daria a minha vida para ter a tua alvura, Cecília" (46). She also makes the following comment about Peri: "Como queres que se trate um selvagem que tem a pele escura e o sangue vermelho" (44). It is significant, moreover, that Isabel lacks Ceci's immaculate purity and is capable of actions which have tragic results, much like Rita Baiana or Gabriela. Erroneously assuming that D. Álvaro de Sá, with whom she is deeply in love, is dead, Isabel, in a Brazilian adaptation of Romeo and Juliet, decides to poison herself and ends up causing both her death and D. Álvaro's, just as the Portuguese gentleman appears to be awakening from a stupor. It should be noted that Isabel had contemplated suicide before, when she felt rejected by D. Álvaro. Had Isabel carried out her suicide then, she would have been reenacting the fate of her mother, another indigenous woman doomed by an ill-fated love for a white man.[17] Thus, while ostensibly subscribing to the official image of racial harmony, Alencar records the grim truth of race relations in Brazil. The double death of Isabel and D. Álvaro can also be read as evidence of Alencar's awareness of the gap between the ideal and the reality of race relations. By giving Isabel and D. Álvaro a proper romantic death, Alencar complies with the romantic requirement that love be fulfilled (on an ideal plane), while he avoids dealing with the complications that such a union would pose on a real plane.

The canonical reading of *Iracema* considers the book as an unproblematical celebration of the founding of Brazil. Relying on Alencar's own statements,[18] Afrânio Peixoto was one of the first and most eloquent proponents of this interpretation:

> *Iracema* é o poema das origens brasileiras, noivado da Terra Virgem com o seu Colonizador Branco, pacto de duas raças na abençoada Terra da América. Não foi, pois, sem emoção que descobri nessa "Iracema," o anagrama de "América," símbolo secreto do romance de Alencar que, repito, é o poema épico definidor de nossas origens histórica, étnica e sociologicamente. (*Noções de história da literatura brasileira* 163).

According to this interpretation, Brazilians, represented by Moacir, the son of the Portuguese Martim and the Indian Iracema, who is born at the exact moment when the Pitiguaras, allies of the Portuguese, defeat the Guaraciabas, enemies of the Portuguese, would be the perfect synthesis of European and indigenous elements. But the novel is unable to sustain this ideal harmony. Most revealing in this respect is the passage in which the birth of Moacir is announced: "Nesta hora em que o canto guerreiro dos pitiguaras celebrava a derrota dos guaraciabas, o primeiro filho *que o sangue da raça branca, gerou nesta terra de liberdade,* via a luz nos campos da porangaba" [my emphasis] (69). The syntax of the relative clause highlighted above reflects an imbalance between the European and indigenous elements. The former, represented by the blood, with all the heroic associations of the word, is dominant, functioning as the subject of the clause, whereas the latter, equated with the land, merely functions as an adverb of place. A similar imbalance occurs in what at first glance would appear to be a perfect exchange of customs and traditions between Martim and Poti. The ceremony in which Martim is "indianized" by having his body painted and by being given the name Coatiabo turns out to be theatrical, for Martim never really converts to the indigenous religion nor does he permanently adopt his Indian name. In fact, only a few lines after the description of this ceremony, Martim is referred to as "o cristão" (60). On the contrary, at the end of the novel Poti renounces his indigenous heritage and becomes a true Christian: "Deviam ter ambos um só deus, como tinham um só coração" (76). From the moment Poti is baptized, his Christian name, Antônio Felipe Camarão, becomes the only one by which he is known, as in the history books about the seventeenth-century wars against the Dutch, in which he distinguished himself. This name reflects Poti's acceptance of the three pillars on which Portuguese culture rests: the Catholic religion (Antônio), the Portuguese monarchy (Felipe) and the Portuguese language (Camarão is the Portuguese translation of Poti): "Ele recebeu com o batismo o nome do santo, cujo era o dia: e o do rei, a quem ia servir, o sobre os dous o seu, na língua dos novos irmãos" (76).[19] It is important to remember, furthermore, that the red dye, with which Martim's body is painted, will eventually wash off, whereas Poti receives, with the sacrament of baptism, a mark which, according to the Catholic tradition, is indelible.[20]

Seen in this light, *Iracema* is an unsettling story of violation and destruction of indigenous culture, rather than an unproblematical celebration of the founding of Brazilian nationality. So that "the first Brazilian" can be born and live, Iracema must renege on her vow of chastity, abandon her original home, discard her culture, lose her happiness forever, and eventually die, while Martim, on the other hand, is able to retain his values and even take their son to Portugal. Indigenous people must surrender and adjust to Portuguese ways, as does Poti, or be mercilessly destroyed. The gap between the program for a foundational novel and the story of destruction that was told is not accidental, for Alencar seems to have been very much aware of the contradictions built into his project. Despite initially appearing as a celebration, the opening chapter turns out to be an elegy to Iracema, who has died and been forgotten. In this sense the beginning of the novel forecasts the woeful final sentence: "Tudo passa sobre a terra" (77). The name Iracema chooses for her child, "the first Brazilian," is Moacir, which is supposed to mean "born from my suffering." And even before Moacir's birth, Poti's grandfather, Baturité, predicts the destruction of his people by the Portuguese: "Tupi quis que estes olhos vissem antes de se apagarem o gavião branco junto da narceja" (55).[21] It is significant that the "negative" elements are much more obvious in *Iracema* than in *O Guarani*, suggesting Alencar's growing awareness of the contradictions between ideal and reality during the intervening eight years between the publication of the two novels.

The epilogues of the two novels are eloquent proof of the dilemmas faced by Alencar. Obviously Peri could not have kept his promise to D. Antônio de Mariz and accompanied Ceci to Rio de Janeiro. Much like Iracema, Peri is a child of the forests, and is only whole as a person while he is in direct contact with nature. Besides, since Portugal, and by extension Brazil, is at the time under Spanish rule, Rio represents the antithesis of the freedom indispensable for Peri's existence. Finally, the novel previously indicated that the color of one's skin is an important mark of social difference, and that, therefore, racially-mixed unions are doomed. There is simply no hope for Peri and Ceci to remain together in the "civilized" world, yet their union is essential for the portrayal of the origins of Brazilian nationality. Approaching such an impasse, Alencar chooses to have Peri and Ceci reenact the creation myth of Tamandaré, the indigenous Noah.[22] In *Iracema*, Alencar faces even thornier problems. It is obvious that the indigenous people of Brazil will only be able to survive if, like Poti, they adopt the values of Portuguese culture. Nevertheless, because Iracema is the embodiment of the American land, she can never be completely assimilated. Here the solution is to have Iracema die. Death makes it possible for Alencar to remove Iracema from the real world and to transform her into a symbol, which allows her to continue to exist on an idealized plane.

Commenting on anthropologist Bronislaw Malinowski's definition of myth, Peter Worsley has suggested that "myth acts as a charter for the present-day social order; it supplies a retrospective pattern of moral values, sociological order, and magical belief, the function of which is to strengthen tradition and endow it with a greater value and prestige by tracing it back to a higher, better, more supernatural reality of initial events" (5).[23] The connections between communal origins and social order proposed by Malinowski are particularly significant in nineteenth-century Brazil. As was indicated above, the Brazilian elites were deeply concerned with the question of order, for the consolidation of their political and economic hegemony had been an arduous and complex process, which, to the extent that social life continued to be characterized by a recalcitrant ambiguity, remained incomplete.[24] The elites were understandably worried about the potential threats posed by the segments of society that could not be co-opted by the pervasive system of patronage and clientelism. It is not surprising, then, that much of the plot of the two novels being discussed revolves around the opposing poles of order and disorder. From the very beginning of *O Guarani*, D. Antônio understands that he must assert his authority so that order can be preserved: "a severidade tinha apenas o efeito salutar de conservar a ordem, a disciplina e a hierarquia" (32). Yet order remains precarious, for it is constantly being assaulted from within (that is, by Loredano and his henchmen) and from without (by wild animals and, especially, by the Aimorés). The order achieved by D. Antônio is so fragile that it can be easily compromised, as evidenced by the accidental killing of an Aimoré woman by D. Antônio's son, D. Diogo, which precipitates a series of destructive events. The very setting suggests that precariousness. The novel takes place in a no-man's land, where the borders between "nature" and "civilization" are quite fuzzy; D. Antônio's homestead is perched on the edge of a precipice; and although the house is a kind of heaven, dominated by the presence of the pure Cecília (whom Peri likens to the Virgin Mary),[25] the ravine directly below, populated by snakes, is a kind of hell. As previously suggested, in *Iracema* Edenic images coexist with a depiction of violation, death and destruction. But Alencar is constantly seeking ways to minimize conflict and preserve order. Although the first meeting between Iracema and Martim is initially marked by an act of violence (she wounds him with an arrow), suggesting that the encounter between Europe and the New World was far from peaceful and cordial, as a good Christian male, who "aprendeu na religião de sua mãe, onde a mulher é símbolo de ternura e amor" (13), Martim does not react. At the same time Iracema immediately assumes the role of a prototypical motherly female. She expresses sorrow for what is to be excused as a reflex action, apologizes, and nurses Martim back to health. When Martim violates Iracema, he does so under the influence of the potion prepared by Iracema, which is supposed to exempt Martim from any blame, while transferring to Iracema the responsibility as the real seducer. Later, when Martim consciously possesses Iracema, their union is ratified by nature: "A floresta destilava suave fragância e exalava arpejos harmoniosos. Foi a festa do amor e o canto do himeneu" (45). After she leaves her family, Iracema loses her identity and her primordial happiness, but the novel offers Martim's construction of a model patriarchal family as the solution to those problems: "A felicidade do varão é a prole, que nasce dele e faz seu orgulho; cada guerreiro que sai de suas vezes é mais um galho que leva seu nome às nuvens, como a grimpa do cedro. Amado de Tupã, é o guerreiro que tem uma esposa, um amigo e muitos filhos; ele nada mais deseja senão a morte gloriosa" (57).

José Murilo de Carvalho has described political life in the second half of the nineteenth century, marked by a lack of clear direction, a high degree of improvisation and weak institutions, as a "theater of shadows," where form prevails over substance: "A vida política do Segundo Reinado pode ser vista como alternância de sustentação e denúncia do teatro que se desenvolvia. As crises podiam advir seja do excesso de realismo, em geral marca dos conservadores, seja do excesso de ficção, tendência comum entre os liberais" (*Teatro de sombras* 167). Alencar has a profound understanding of this theatricality. There is no question that Alencar's fiction is implicated in the project of national formation devised by the elites. Within the limitations imposed by Romantic literary conventions, Alencar is able, however, to create spaces that allow him to expose both the contradictions in that project and the fragility of the system that the Brazilian elites have established. Reflecting Alencar's ambiguous relationship with the hegemonic ideologies of his time, the flaws in Alencar's "blueprints of national formation" provide a thorough record of and serve as compelling testimony to the ambiguities of Brazil's "golden age."

Notes

[1] For a comprehensive study of the role of the elites in nineteenth-century Brazil see José Murilo de Carvalho's indispensable *A construção da ordem: a elite política imperial* and *Teatro de sombras; a política imperial*. Conceived as companion pieces, the two volumes elaborate the ideas presented in "Elite and State-Building in Imperial Brazil," Carvalho's doctoral dissertation, defended at Stanford University in December, 1974.

[2] See Emília Viotti da Costa's "Introdução ao estudo da emancipação política do Brasil," included in the volume *Da monarquia à república: momentos decisivos*.

[3] As José Murilo de Carvalho explains in *Teatro de sombras*, "se na expressão muitas vezes usada na época, a escravidão era o cancro que corroía a sociedade, ela era também o princípio que minava por dentro as bases do Estado imperial, e que, ao final, acabou por destruí-lo" (50).

[4] According to Richard Graham, the war with Paraguay provided an eloquent proof of that fragility, for it "exacerbated partisan political strife, provoked the return of the Conservatives to power (in 1868) and contributed to the break-up of the middle-of-the-road Progressive League" (155).

[5] In a jointly-written study, Leslie Bethell and José Murilo de Carvalho corroborate this view: "Even leaving aside the regional differences and the deep social and racial divisions, there was still in Brazil too little communication between the provinces, too little economic integration, too little sharing in the government of the country for a positive sense of national identity yet to have developed" (112).

[6] Perhaps too much has been made of the fact that unlike his father, who was a Liberal politician, Alencar was a member of the Conservative party. In reality, in nineteenth-century Brazil party affiliation matters less than individual proclivities. As the debate over the slave traffic proved, the differences separating Conservatives and Liberals in mid-century Brazilian politics were more regional than ideological. The vote was split between northern and southern provinces, rather than along party lines, with the deputies from the southern provinces, dominated by the interests of the coffee barons, voting against suppression of the traffic and the deputies

from the northern provinces, where slavery had become less important, due to the decadence of the sugar plantation system, voting for it.

[7] Alencar's notes for an essay on Brazilian literature are quite direct: "Identidade de raça, mas o solo, o clima, e a natureza é outro. Três elementos: americano, europeu, africano; país novo que mais atrai. Influência, amálgama, ainda a fusão não se fez, está em ebulição. Os que estudam a literatura pátria em vez de se enterrar nas antigüidades da literatura portuguesa, examinam esses elementos." See volume IV of the Aguilar edition of Alencar's *Obra completa*, (10).

[8] "Vós, os propagandistas, os emancipadores a todo transe, não passais de emissários da revolução, de apóstolos da anarquia. Os retrógrados sois vós, que pretendeis recuar o progresso do país, ferindo-o no coração, matando a sua primeira indústria, a lavoura ... Vós quereis a emancipação como uma vã ostentação. Sacrificais os interesses máximos da pátria, a veleidades de glória. Entendeis que libertar é unicamente subtrair ao cativeiro — e não vos lembrais de que a liberdade concedida a essas massas brutas é um dom funesto, é o fogo sagrado entregue ao ímpeto, ao arrojo de um novo e selvagem Prometeu! Nós queremos a redenção de nossos irmãos, como a queria o Cristo. Não basta para vós, dizer à criatura tolhida em sua inteligência, abatida em sua consciência: - Tu és livre; vai, percorre os campos como uma besta fera! Não, senhores, é preciso esclarecer a inteligência embotada, elevar a consciência humilhada, para que um dia, no momento de conceder-lhe a liberdade, possamos dizer — Vós sois homens, sois cidadãos. Nós vos redimimos, não só do cativeiro, como da ignorância, do vício, da miséria, da animalidade em que jazeis." Quoted by Broca (1042).

[9] In his introduction to *Dois escritos políticos de Alencar* Wanderley Guilherme dos Santos proposes that "José de Alencar, até prova em contrário, surge como um dos mais sofisticados teóricos da democracia, escrevendo no século XIX" (50).

[10] In *Imagined Communities: Reflections on the Origins and Spread of Nationalism*, Benedict Anderson defines the nation as "an imagined political community — and imagined as both inherently limited and sovereign" (6).

[11] Sérgio Buarque de Holanda's *Visão do paraíso* is the definitive study of the origins of the Edenic view of Brazil.

[12] "De fato, a 'tendência genealógica' consiste em escolher no passado local os elementos adequados a uma visão que de certo modo é nativista, mas procura se aproximar o mais possível dos ideais e normas européias" ("Literatura de dois gumes" 173). For a much more detailed

study of this tendency, see Cândido's monumental *Formação da literatura brasileira: momentos decisivos.*

[13] Benedict Anderson states that "regardless of the actual inequality and exploitation that may prevail in each, the nation is always conceived as a deep, horizontal comradeship" (7).

[14] For a thorough and cogent study of the links between nature, woman and national identity in Brazilian Romanticism, see Regina Zilberman's article "Natureza e mulher: uma visão do Brasil no romance romântico." The section on *Iracema* is particularly insightful.

[15] As Lucien Goldman convincingly argued in *Towards a Sociology of the Novel*, although literary forms emerge out of a historical, social, and economic reality, literary works are not passive reflections of historical, social, and economic conditions: "The relation between collective ideology and great individual, literary, philosophical, theological, etc. creations resides not in an identity of content, but in a more advanced coherence and a homology of structures which can be expressed in imaginary contents very different from the real content of the collective consciousness" (9).

[16] Doris Sommer has established links between the ideas of José de Alencar concerning race and those of German naturalist Karl Friedrich Philipp von Martius. In his 1843 essay "How the History of Brazil Should Be Written," winner of a contest sponsored by the Instituto Histórico e Geográfico Brasileiro, von Martius proposed that the mixture of races gave the Brazilian people their special stamp (151-153).

[17] In that scene, after opening a glass case where she keeps a vial of curare together with a lock of her mother's hair, Isabel calls her mother's name. What seems to be implied is that Isabel's mother had poisoned herself, most probably out of unrequited love for D. Antônio de Mariz, or perhaps out of shame.

[18] See, for example, "Carta ao Dr. Jaguaribe," appended to the first edition of *Iracema* or the polemical "Cartas sobre *A Confederação dos Tamoios.*"

[19] Regina Zilberman detects a presence in *Iracema* of the ideology that informed the Portuguese discoveries: "O imperialismo português, ao qual Alencar aderira ao se manifestar a favor do mundo cultural [português], explicando os efeitos mágicos presentes no texto, encontra assim uma justificativa: a necessidade imposta num primeiro momento para assegurar a conquista e também a cristianização. Nesse sentido, Martim é antes de tudo um cruzado a serviço do ideal cirstão, absorvendo o autor a ideologia que margeia as grandes descobertas e a colonização, expressa literariamente em *Os Lusíadas*, ou, em outras palavras, *ele adota precisamente a*

cosmovisão da época em que viveu Martim" (*Do mito ao romance* 149-150).

[20] For a more detailed examination of Alencar's problems with the synthesis model and its repercussions in Brazilian literature, see my article "Oswald/Alencar: a Antropofagia revisitada."

[21] In a footnote to this passage, Alencar says the following: "O gavião branco — Baturité chama assim o guerreiro branco, ao passo que trata o neto por narceja; ele profetiza nesse paralelo a destruição de sua raça pela raça branca" (95).

[22] It should be noted that as Peri and Ceci are carried along by the flood, they are going towards the interior and away from the coast. In flowing against the current of the Paquequer river, Peri and Ceci are moving, therefore, in the direction of that primordial cradle of freedom where, as mentioned in the first paragraph, the Paquequer originated. Here Alencar is in the process of creating what is to become a *topos* in Brazilian literature: that authentic Brazil is to be found in the country's hinterland. Less than half a century later, Euclides da Cunha will view the racially-mixed inhabitant of the *sertão* as a quintessential Brazilian figure. More recently one finds an ironic re-reading of that movement in the expedition to the geographic center of Brazil in Antônio Callado's *Quarup*. When the members of the expedition reach the heart of Brazil, they find an anthill.

[23] Quoted by Brennan (45).

[24] José Murilo de Carvalho's comments on this ambiguity are enlightening: "Tanto as idéias e valores que predominavam entre a elite, como as instituições implantadas por esta mesma elite mantinham relação ambígua de ajuste e desajuste com a realidade social do país: uma sociedade escravocrata governada por instituições liberais e representativas; uma sociedade agrária e analfabeta dirigida por uma elite cosmopolita voltada para o modelo europeu de civilização" (*Teatro de sombras* 162).

[25] It is significant that Cecília's room is located directly above the ravine in the back of the house.

Works Cited

Alencar, José de. "Cartas sobre *A Confederação dos Tamoios*." *Obra completa*, vol. IV. Rio de Janeiro: Aguilar, 1960. 863-922.

---. *Dois escritos políticos de Alencar*. Ed. Wanderley Guilherme dos Santos. Rio de Janeiro: Editora da UFRJ, 1991.

---. *O Guarani*. *Obra completa*, vol. II. Rio de Janeiro: Aguilar, 1964. 24-280.

---. *Iracema*. Edição crítica de M. Cavalcanti Proença. São Paulo: EDUSP, 1979.

Anderson, Benedict. *Imagined Communities: Reflections on the Origins and Spread of Nationalism.* Revised edition. London: Verso, 1991.

Bethell, Leslie, and José Murilo de Carvalho. "1822-1850." *Brazil, Empire and Republic: 1822-1930.* Ed. Leslie Bethell. Cambridge: Cambridge U Press, 1989. 45-112.

Brennan, Timothy. "The National Longing for Form." *Nation and Narration.* Ed. Homi K. Bhabha. New York: Routledge, 1990. 44-70.

Broca, Brito. "O drama político de Alencar." *Obra completa de José de Alencar*, vol. IV. Rio de Janeiro: Aguilar: 1960. 1039-1047.

Carvalho, José Murilo. *A construção da ordem: a elite política imperial.* Brasília: Editora Universidade de Brasília, 1981.
---. *Teatro de sombras: a política imperial.* Rio de Janeiro: IUPERJ, 1988.

Cândido, Antônio. *Formação da literatura brasileira: momentos decisivos*, 2 vol. 2nd. edition. São Paulo: Martins, 1964.
---. "Literatura de dois gumes." *A educação pela noite e outros ensaios.* São Paulo: Ática, 1987. 163-181.

Costa, Emília Viotti da. *Da monarquia à república: momentos decisivos.* São Paulo: Grijalbo, 1977.

Franco, Jean. "The Nation as Imagined Community." *New Historicism.* Ed. Aram Veeser. New York: Routledge, 1989. 204-212.

Graham, Richard. "1850-1870." *Brazil, Empire and Republic: 1822-1930.* Ed. Leslie Bethell. Cambridge: Cambridge U. Press, 1989. 113-160.

Holanda, Sérgio Buarque de. *Visão do paraíso: os motivos edênicos no descobrimento e colonização do Brasil.* Rio de Janeiro: José Olympio, 1959.

Malinowski, Bronislaw. "Myth in Primitive Psychology." *Magic, Science and Religion, and Other Essays.* Boston: Beacon Press, 1948. 72-124.

Reis, Roberto. *A permanência do círculo.* Niterói: EDUFF, 1987.

Santiago, Silviano. "Liderança e hierarquia em Alencar." *Vale quanto pesa.* Rio de Janeiro: Paz e Terra, 1982. 89-115.

Sommer, Doris. *Foundational Fictions: The National Romances of Latin America.* Berkeley: U of California Press, 1991.

Valente, Luiz Fernando. "Oswald/Alencar: a Antropofagia revisitada." *Atlântida* 25 (2nd. Semester, 1990). 75-88.

Worsley, Peter. *The Third World.* 2nd. ed. Chicago: U of Chicago Press, 1970.

Zilberman, Regina. *Do mito ao romance: tipologia da ficção brasileira contemporânea.* Caxias do Sul: Universidade de Caxias do Sul, 1977.
---. "Natureza e mulher: uma visão do Brasil no romance romântico." *Modern Language Studies* 19:2 (Spring, 1989). 50-64.

Art and Intention in Mário de Andrade

Randal Johnson

For Alex

Mário de Andrade (1893—1945) was a man of multiple talents and immensely varied activities. Widely acknowledged as the leading figure of the Brazilian modernist movement of the 1920s, he was arguably Brazil's most important and versatile literary personage of the first half of the century. He made intellectual investments of such a magnitude that he eventually touched on almost all of the literary, artistic, and cultural disciplines of the period. He wrote novels, short stories and poetry; he was a literary, art, and music critic and theorist as well as a musicologist, a folklorist and an ethnographer. Through many of the activities he fostered as director of São Paulo's municipal Department of Culture between 1935 and 1938, he also participated in the institutional development of modern social science in Brazil.

The very breadth of Andrade's intellectual undertakings inevitably renders a discussion of only one aspect of his work at best partial and at worst reductive, for none of the different facets of his activities existed in isolation from the others. In this essay I will examine one feature of Andrade's intellectual trajectory that seems to underlie many of his other multiple literary and non-literary endeavors: his view of the social role of artists and intellectuals and, more specifically, his concept of artistic and cultural intention. This concept encompasses such central facets of his work as his theory of artistic nationalism, his notion of the relationship between popular and elite culture, and his view of the relationship between culture and the state.

Historian Carlos Guilherme Mota has suggested that Mário de Andrade may have represented the *consciência-limite* of his generation (105). Perhaps more than any other literary intellectual of his time, Andrade

167

revealed a critical recognition of the contradictions inherent in the artist's objective position in the field of social relations and therefore of the limitations of the social function of art. His most complete expression of this acute critical awareness occurred in what have been termed three major "testaments" written in the early 1940s. In them he attempted to provide an account of his intellectual and artistic achievements and shortcomings. The first was the highly self-critical 1942 lecture "O movimento modernista," which remains, in my opinion, the best single overview of the movement's accomplishments. The second, the long poem "Meditação do Tietê," finished only days before his death in February 1945, summarizes his poetic concerns. The third, which remained unfinished, was *O banquete*, published in book form only in 1977. In it, Andrade synthesized his artistic and aesthetic thought.

The extant fragments of *O banquete* were originally published in a weekly column in a São Paulo newspaper (*Folha da manhã*) starting in May, 1943, under the general title of "Mundo musical." Initially intended as a column on musical culture in general, Mário de Andrade very quickly extended his focus into other areas, discussing such things as folklore, the plastic arts, and the psychology of creativity. Some texts with a unified focus were grouped into irregular series under specific subtitles such as "Vida do cantador" or "Arte inglesa."

O banquete was the longest and most important of such series. The initial installment appeared in May 1944, and subsequent fragments continued to be published until the author's death. *O banquete* differs formally from other series and columns of "Mundo musical" in that it is structured dramatically as an aesthetic-philosophic discussion or "dialogue"—with distant Platonic roots—among five imaginary characters during a luncheon which takes place in Mentira, an imaginary city with all the characteristics of Mário de Andrade's São Paulo. Through the ironic dissimulation inherent in the dialogical situation, Andrade discusses myriad issues related to art, music, literature, aesthetics, and criticism.

The five highly caricatured personages represent in parodic form different positions in the social space of Mentira. They represent, in other words, different positions in the social space in which Mário de Andrade himself was located, which Pierre Bourdieu would characterize as the space of the ruling classes or, in his elaborate conceptual framework, the "field of power" ("Field of Power, Literary Field, and Habitus"). Three characters hold dominant positions in this field: the hostess Sarah Light, satirically described as a "plutocrat" who is "New Yorker by birth, international by profession, and Brazilian by encrustation"; the xenophobic, "naturally fascist" politician of Italian origin, Felix de Cima; and the virtuosic singer of immense vanity and Spanish parents, Siomara Ponga (45).[1] Sarah Light and Felix de Cima occupy dominant positions because of their possession of economic and political capital, Siomara Ponga because of her fame as a musical virtuoso. The other characters, who possess what Bourdieu calls cultural capital, occupy the subordinate pole in this social space.[2] They are the *engagé* composer Janjão, and the rather anarchistic young law student and insurance salesman Pastor Fido.

O banquete comprises three interrelated levels of discussion. The first focuses on the practical problems of artistic culture in Brazil, including the lack of a professional consciousness among musicians, the precarious situation of Brazilian orchestras, and the excessive valuation of individual virtuosity. The second level, which will be the primary focus of this essay, deals with the social function of art, the construction of a national art, the relationship between popular and elite culture, and the social responsibilities of the artist. The third and most abstract level addresses questions of aesthetics per se (Souza).

As a point of departure for a discussion of art and intention in Mário de Andrade, I would like to focus for a moment on the issue that motivates the luncheon to begin with (after, that is, the hostess's sexual attraction for Janjão): the relationship of art and culture to the state. This issue is intricately interwoven with Mário de Andrade's intellectual trajectory, and, in the wake of Fernando Collor de Mello's recent dismantling of the Brazilian government's cultural institutions and, in the United States, the scandal involving the National Endowment for the Arts' indirect support of the Robert Mapplethorpe exhibit, the question has a certain amount of currency.[3]

In *O banquete* Sarah Light decides to hold the luncheon as a means of bringing Janjão and Felix de Cima together, hoping that the politician will agree to some sort of financial support for the composer. She considers supporting Janjão herself as an easy way of buying his love, but she cannot take on the role of patron or Maecenas without ridicule. The upper-class world in which she lives is, as the narrator puts it, an "infectious milieu comprised of snobs who are indifferent to the arts" (46). Thus the idea for the luncheon and the hope for government support for Janjão.

She invites Mentira's sub-prefect Felix de Cima because he is known as the "undisputed protector of the arts in Mentira" (48), despite the fact that he dislikes almost all art except erotic engravings. At one point he says that he is too busy protecting art to learn anything about it. His patronage rests on two basic principles: 1) all requests for support from foreign artists passing through Mentira should be granted so they will not criticize the country abroad; 2) modern art, which he does not understand but which he suspects of communism, should not be supported at all. National artists, as far as Felix de Cima is concerned, can starve to death (49).

Mário de Andrade's portrayal of Felix de Cima as a politician who protects artists for the symbolic and material profits involved, that is, for the direct and indirect benefits to his own career, restates in parodic terms what Alain Viala has called the "logic of recognition" inherent in many forms of artistic patronage. Viala refers to 17th-century France but his comments are, I think, relevant to the question at hand. According to him, a patron's support of an artist is not necessarily disinterested, for the Maecenas often stands to gain prestige through public recognition of his grandeur and good taste, thus legitimizing his power or wealth (54-55). In Andrade's fiction, although totally ignorant in matters of art, Felix de Cima has managed to convert his support of artists into political power and social prestige.

Mário de Andrade dealt with the question of government patronage of the arts on numerous occasions. In his 1935 address to the graduating class of the Musical Conservatory where he taught throughout his adult life, Andrade expressed regret for Brazil's general lack of musical culture. All sectors of society, including the press, artistic organizations, and politicians, preferred the "sensuality of virtuosic tricks" to the "aesthetic and social elevations of art." In Andrade's opinion, the only way to overcome the country's musical poverty was through the "officialization" of musical instruction. Only with government support would the formation of "exemplary elites and the improvement of the people's cultural level" be possible. "Without a basis of official protection the conservatories, orchestras, chorales, chamber groups, and permanent composition would be unable to exist in Brazil" (*Aspectos da música brasileira* 240). He makes much the same point in *O banquete*.

Mário de Andrade's view of the role of the state vis-à-vis culture goes beyond support for elite culture and concerns the perhaps more vital question of accessibility and the need for artistic education for all classes. He provides a concise outline of that view in a 1937 letter to Paulo Duarte:

> In a country like ours, where culture is unfortunately not yet a necessity of daily life, the contrast between a small, truly cultured elite and a people cowered in its uncouth corporeality is intensifying with painful violence. It is necessary to force a greater mutual understanding, a greater leveling of culture which will make it more accessible

to all, and consequently give it a truly functional validity. Of course this leveling cannot consist in cutting off the sun-drenched head of the elites, but rather in stimulating through activity those who are in the shadows, putting them in a position to receive more light. This task belongs to the government. (*Mário de Andrade por ele mesmo*, 153)

According to Andrade, the state's pedagogical function in relation to less fortunate classes should take place on multiple levels, especially through museums and cultural institutes. Museums should be open to all forms of culture, ranging from archaeology, folklore, and history, to indigenous artifacts, the fine arts and industrial design. Visits by workers, students and children would be obligatory and accompanied by trained guides, thus resulting in the visitors' edification.

Andrade wrote this letter while serving as director of the Department of Culture of the municipal government of São Paulo and in a position to attempt to put his ideas into practice. Antonio Candido sees the Department of Culture, along with other cultural, educational and intellectual initiatives which took place at the same time, as a conscious attempt on the part of a "moderate left" within the Partido Democrático—a "cultural vanguard in the shadow of a ruling oligarchy that accepted and supported it," as Candido describes it—to take culture from the privileged and "transform it into a factor for the humanization of the majority through planned institutions" (Prefácio xiv-xvi).

The Department of Culture was an attempt to institutionalize, rationalize, and organize certain aspects of cultural production, leisure activities, and historical preservation in the city of São Paulo. It was charged with stimulating and developing all sorts of educational, artistic, and cultural initiatives, ranging from financial support of music, theater, and cinema, to the organization of libraries and the creation of children's parks and recreational facilities. It established "popular" libraries in working-class neighborhoods, children's libraries, and a bookmobile in which Andrade himself would drive a specially equipped Ford to city parks and lend books to passersby (Dassin 109).

The Department's Division of Cultural Expansion, which Andrade also directed, attempted to make classical music more accessible to a broad, socially and economically diversified audience by sponsoring free concerts in public parks and squares as well as in the Municipal Theater and on radio. It also established a public music library, an archive of recorded folk music, a museum of ethnography and folklore, and a film library. Andrade also planned a series of Casas de Cultura which would include lecture halls with stages for theatrical presentations, game rooms, reading rooms, space for choir rehearsals, and libraries for adults and children.

The lofty designs and good intentions of the Department's programs—which were largely cut short after the decree of the authoritarian Estado Novo in late 1937—cannot efface an element of paternalism in its activities. Based on an analysis of mayor Fábio Prado's description of his own administration's accomplishments, Joan Dassin has written that "a sense of the new and progressive was mixed with an attitude of protectionism toward the *povo*, often expressed in a rather patronizing way" (108, 110).

Even Mário de Andrade's view of the social function and nature of museums, which reflects an openness of spirit and a recognition of the inherent value of different modes of cultural expression, is paternalistic and authoritarian in its desire to impose, through obligatory visits, a specific notion of culture on the working class, students, and children. Despite such contradictions, Andrade was clearly aware of the need for a bi-directional mode of action that would simultaneously attract a broader public to elite culture and make elites more appreciative of popular culture and folklore, and he attempted, at least on the limited scale that the historical conjuncture permitted, to implement his utilitarian notion of cultural change through the pedagogical action of the state.

I dwell on Andrade's participation in the Department of Culture because of its importance for understanding the major underlying impetus of his intellectual trajectory as a whole. Andrade entered the Department of Culture based on a conception of the intellectual's social responsibility, on an awareness of the need to reconcile the artist's inherent individualism with the broader demands of society. The governing concept of much of Andrade's cultural and artistic activity is what has variously been called his "sense of commitment," his "quasi-apostolic consciousness," or, in short, his intention. He possessed a critical awareness of the historical moment in which he lived and of what was needed to transform Brazilian culture. This includes his apparent willingness to sacrifice more personal forms of expression to attempt the necessary modifications. As he put it in "O movimento modernista," very early in his career he had decided "to infuse everything [he] did with a utilitarian value, a practical value of life, something more terrestrial than fiction, aesthetic pleasure, and divine beauty" (*Aspectos da literatura brasileira*, 254).

In a 1935 letter to Sousa da Silveira he explains this utilitarian conception in some detail:

There are . . . artists whose vitality lasts only
during their lifetimes, who are minor creators of
Beauty but strong agents of movement, active
stimulators, of progression more than progress,
malevolent sources of disquiet . . .
Within me is an intimate demagogy that I try to
disguise as much as possible. It was within this order
of ideas, sentiments, and tendencies that I developed
my 'nationalism' . . . [that] I made myself a Brazilian
for Brazil. I decided to work with Brazilian 'material,'
specify it, shape it . . . in its [full] complexity. The
linguistic question is but one corollary of this self-
realization . . . Brazilian musical folklore was
unknown. I initiated the study of Brazilian musical
folklore. There was no art criticism in São Paulo, and
the little Brazilian criticism that existed was worse
than terrible. I therefore wrote art criticism. There
was no modern poetic treatise, adaptable to our times,
so I wrote one. There was no history of music in
Portuguese. Those that existed were simply awful. I
wrote one that was much better than the others.
(*Mário de Andrade escreve cartas*, 149-150).

Mário de Andrade's now voluminous published correspondence is
replete with references to moments in which he consciously attempted to
"force the issue"—of modernist aesthetics, of artistic and linguistic
nationalism, of the need for more systematic study of Brazilian popular
culture, of the creation of more authentically Brazilian modes of expression—
all as a means of instigating change through a utilitarian notion of literary
and cultural practice.

Andrade's insistence on function and participation is evident in
his first book of verse, *Há uma gota de sangue em cada poema*, published
in 1917 under the pseudonym Mário Sobral, which is an impassioned
expression of the poet's pacifism in the wake of the horrors of World War
I. His sense of the contingent nature of artistic production appears in the
"Prefácio interessantíssimo" of *Paulicéia desvairada* (1922), when the writer
creates a new poetic movement—"Desvairismo"—only to declare it defunct
at the end of the same preface and to announce a new movement for his next
book. He recognized that *Paulicéia desvairada* was important more for the
seeds it planted than for its inherent aesthetic value (López 233).

By 1924 Andrade had begun to systematize the connection between the work of art and the necessities of the period and country in which he lived. Especially important in this regard is his extensive research into the specific characteristics of Brazilian speech and popular culture as a means of forging a more authentic cultural identity. This question relates directly to his concept of literary and artistic nationalism.

Andrade conceived of nationalism as the first step in a process of self-discovery that would contribute to universal cultural values to the extent that it was authentic and faithful to itself. His ultimate goal was the integration of Brazilian culture into universal culture, not the closure implied by the more xenophobic currents of nationalism that also found expression within the modernist movement. He recognized the difficulty of creating an authentic national culture in a country permeated by European values and standards. In this regard his 1928 poem, "Improviso do mal da América," is perhaps his most acute expression of the dilemma faced by Brazilian intellectuals. Although he recognizes the diversity of Brazilian society, he is dominated by a "grito imperioso de brancura" ["imperious cry of whiteness"] that impedes his own cultural integration: "Me sinto só branco agora, só branco em minha alma crivada de raças!" ["Now I feel only white, only white in my race-riddled soul!"]. Andrade felt that the dominant whiteness slowly destroyed the potential for cultural differentiation provided by other racial identities.

His artistic answer to this dilemma was to use popular forms of expression structurally, and not merely ornamentally, in elite cultural forms. He began by systematizing errors committed in everyday speech as a means of capturing an authentically national social and psychological character in language itself. By bringing those errors into educated speech and writing, he hoped to help in the formation of a Brazilian literary language. His interest in popular culture as a means of understanding Brazil evolved into the systematic study of Brazilian folklore and the re-creation of popular forms on an erudite level. Knowing and incorporating the foundations of Brazilian popular thought, he felt he could help lead Brazil to self-knowledge and contribute to its passage from nationalism to a universal level in the higher arts. The 1928 novel *Macunaíma*, which is both an etiological myth of national creation and an eschatological myth of national destruction, represents the artistic culmination of Mário de Andrade's research in Brazilian folklore and popular forms of expression (Haberly 159).

Andrade thus saw his role as that of a catalyst, as a "precipitator of fundamental and indispensable changes" (Lafetá 11-13). He conceived of his intellectual practice in functional terms, of his art as an art of "action" or "circumstance," an "interested," as opposed to a "disinterested," form of art. This does not mean, however, that he felt that art should be placed at the service of specific political causes or ideologies.

In *O banquete* Andrade addresses this issue through the voice of Janjão, who had become well-known because of his composition titled "Antifascist Scherzo," in which he had counterpointed the folkloric Brazilian *moda-de-viola* with the Italian fascist hymn, the "Giovinezza." Janjão recognizes his composition as an example of politically "combative art" and a legitimate personal artistic response to "new, collective and socialist forms of life" (63). At the same time he acknowledges that by responding in such a way he risked becoming a puppet (*boneco*) in the service of ideologies which did not necessarily correspond to his intimate convictions and his personal "truth" as an artist. Janjão thus expresses the contradiction of artists who are aware of art's social responsibilities yet who are unable or unwilling to free themselves from their individualism.

Janjão's concept of "combative art" coincides with a position Mário de Andrade increasingly adopted toward the end of his life through an explicit politicization of his concept of artistic function. Andrade's intention had begun to take on a political coloration in the atmosphere of exacerbated ideological tensions surrounding the Revolution of 1930, the unsuccessful 1932 Constitutionalist revolt in São Paulo, and the events leading up to the decree of the authoritarian Estado Novo in 1937. Pressure was intense for intellectuals to define themselves politically, and many opted for radical solutions on the right or the left. Andrade once described his participation in the Department of Culture as a response to a personal political impasse, since he "could no longer tolerate being a writer without a political definition." The Department provided what he called "an objective continuity to his 'art of action'" (*Cartas a Murilo Miranda*, 39).

Yet in the 1942 lecture "O movimento modernista" Andrade confessed that despite having deformed his work through a "focused and obstinate anti-individualism," he had come to realize that in the final analysis it represented no more than an "implacable hyper-individualism" (*Aspectos da literatura brasileira*, 254). Not once, in his words, did he "grab the mask of time and slap it as it deserved" (255). He and his fellow modernists lived in a political age, yet according to his critical self-analysis, they failed when it came to living up to their political responsibilities. They were, rather, abstentionists. At the end of his lecture he calls on the new intellectual generation to reject his generation's example and to march with the masses.

Andrade expressed a similar *engagement* on numerous occasions between the 1942 lecture and his death in early 1945. In an interview granted to the newspaper *Diretrizes* in January, 1944, Andrade harshly denounced intellectuals who had sold out to what he calls the "*donos da vida*" (literally, the "owners of life"), represented in *O banquete* by Sarah Light and Felix de Cima. In his words:

> the artist . . . should never produce a disinterested art. Artists may think they serve nothing other than Art itself, but that is an illusion. In reality, they are serving as tools in the hands of the powerful. The worse thing is that because of the illusion of artistic freedom, honest artists often do not realize that they are serving as a tool, sometimes for terrible things. (*Entrevistas e depoimentos*, 103)

In *O banquete* Andrade extends this critique to the modernist movement itself. He argues, in short, that artists must be responsible to both the public and to society. They must chose which side they are on. We should perhaps recall that at that specific moment, shaped by the struggle against fascism in Europe and authoritarianism in Brazil, the two sides were fairly clearly delineated.

Despite such open calls for participation, Mário de Andrade was very much aware of the place and the limits of artistic practice within the field of social relations. When asked by Pastor Fido if he had composed the "Antifascist Scherzo" for the people, Janjão answers negatively. He suggests that as long as the people are illiterate and conservative, as long as they are folkloric, there will be only one form of art for them, and that is folklore itself (61). He thus implicitly recognizes what the virtuoso Siomara Ponga later explicitly states: aesthetic understanding is not a universally shared quality but rather an unequally distributed acquired disposition. As Bourdieu has suggested, the work of art considered as a symbolic good exists as such only for those who have the means to understand it ("Outline," 594). In this sense art becomes a form of social distinction, and is recognized as such by Sarah Light when she says that "The work of art should always function as pure art. Country people and illiterates do not appreciate the fine arts, and that is what distinguishes us from them" (92).

Continuing with his argument, Janjão contends that artists, and primarily writers, who think they are making art for the people are short-sighted and unable to go beyond their own limited conceptions of artistic practice. He continues by saying that "elite artists who propose a 'proletarian art' [in vogue in Brazil as elsewhere in the 1930s and 1940s] confuse the principle of revolution with sentimentalism . . ." (68). He further suggests that the dominant classes are likely to convert such "'populism' into processes of social distanciation" (67).

Janjão argues that making art for the people is not his role as an artist. He recognizes that in terms of his education and background he is bourgeois and that through the gradual refinement and cultivation of his artistic spirit he had become totally aristocratic. Yet he feels a moral imperative to participate in human struggles. Janjão thus expresses what Bourdieu refers to as the "structural ambiguity" of writers and artists occupying a subordinate position in the field of power. This ambiguity leads them to maintain an ambivalent relationship with the dominant class as well as with the dominated. It leads them, furthermore, to "form an ambiguous image of their own position in social space and of their social function" ("Field of Power"). This ambiguous image is clear in Janjão's confession of his cultural aristocracy followed closely by his description of the artist as "an *out-law*, as extra-economic and without social class or nation" (64).

In the final analysis, Janjão recognizes that his participation, his *engagement*, must take place on the level of high art. That may include incorporating popular elements into his work, but for him to fully adopt a popular perspective would be to falsely accept values that are not his own. He suggests that the best he can do is create an "unhealthy work" (*"obra malsã,"* 65) which will contain toxic and destructive germs that will help demolish society's archaic forms. Such works should be based on what he calls an "aesthetic of the unfinished" which demands a high level spectator participation (61-62). The unfinished is dynamic, suggestive, and inviting and thus appropriate to works of circumstance or combative art. Works based on an "aesthetic of the finished," or what we might call an "aesthetic of closure," do not invite spectator participation and are ultimately dogmatic, dictatorial and imposing.

The "aesthetic of the unfinished" points toward a dialogical conception of artistic practice in which the author ceases to be authoritarian. The artistic utterance anticipates multiple real and imagined interlocutors, permitting intense participation in the construction of meaning. It is based on a critical recognition of the limitations of authorial authority, a shift away from a conception of the artist or even the text as the privileged locus of meaning. This position clearly anticipates what has since come to be called the "postmodern."

Like most of Andrade's creative work, *O banquete* is intertextually dialogical. It also quite literally constitutes an example of the "aesthetic of the unfinished." The fact that Mário de Andrade chose to publish *O banquete* in a newspaper column rather than in the confines of a book or essay, which might seem more appropriate for a discussion of this sort, reveals his long-standing pedagogical intention and a certain level of professorial didacticism. But the ironic dissimulation afforded by the multiple voices of *O banquete*'s dialogical structure, combined with its satirical and parodic nature, creates a space of contradiction, indeterminacy and openness that coincides with and reveals Mário de Andrade's awareness of the contradictions of his own intellectual practice. It also reveals him to be in the vanguard of the Brazilian artistic consciousness of his generation.

Notes

[1] All translations are my own.

[2] Bourdieu defines cultural capital as a form of knowledge, an internalized code or a cognitive acquisition which enables the social agent's empathy toward, appreciation for, or competence in deciphering cultural relations and cultural artifacts (*Distinction*, 12-13).

[3] For documentation on the Mapplethorpe/NEA controversy, see Richard Bolton, ed., *Culture Wars: Documents from the Recent Controversies in the Arts*.

Works Cited

Andrade, Mário de. *Aspectos da literatura brasileira*. 5th ed. São Paulo: Martins, 1974.

---. *Aspectos da música brasileira*. 2nd ed. São Paulo: Martins, Instituto Nacional do Livro, 1975.

---. *O banquete*. São Paulo: Duas Cidades, 1977.

---. *Entrevistas e depoimentos*. Ed. Telê Porto Ancona López. São Paulo: T. A. Queiroz, 1983.

---. *Cartas a Murilo Miranda (1934-1945)*. Rio de Janeiro: Nova Fronteira, 1981.

---. *Mário de Andrade escreve cartas a Alceu, Meyer e outros*. Ed. Lygia Fernandes. Rio de Janeiro: Editora do Autor, 1968.

Bolton, Richard, ed. *Culture Wars: Documents from the Recent Controversies in the Arts*. New York: New Press, 1992.

Bourdieu, Pierre. *Distinction: A Social Critique of the Judgement of Taste*. Tr. Richard Nice. Cambridge: Harvard UP, 1984.

---.   "Field of Power, Literary Field, and Habitus." Christian Gauss
    Lecture in Criticism, Princeton University, 1986. In Bourdieu, *The Field
    of Cultural Production: Essays on Art and Literature.* Ed. Randal
    Johnson. Cambridge, England: Polity Press, 1992.
---.   "Outline of a Sociological Theory of Art Perception." *International
    Social Science Journal* 20 (Winter 1968): 589-612. Also in Bourdieu,
    The Field of Cultural Production: Essays on Art and Literature. Ed.
    Randal Johnson. Cambridge, England: Polity Press, 1992.

Candido, Antonio. "Prefácio." *Mário de Andrade por ele mesmo.* By
    Andrade. Ed. Paulo Duarte. São Paulo: HUCITEC, Secretaria Municipal
    de Cultura, Prefeitura do Município de São Paulo. 1976, xiii-xvii.

Dassin, Joan. *Política e poesia em Mário de Andrade.* São Paulo: Duas
    Cidades, 1978.

Duarte, Paulo, ed. *Mário de Andrade por ele mesmo.* São Paulo: HUCITEC,
    Secretaria Municipal de Cultura, Prefeitura do Município de São
    Paulo, 1976.

Haberly, David. *Three Sad Races: Racial Identity and National
    Consciousness in Brazilian Literature.* Cambridge: Cambridge
    University Press, 1983.

Lafetá, João Luiz. *Figuração da intimidade.* São Paulo: Martins Fontes,
    1986.

López, Telê Porto Ancona. *Mário de Andrade: Ramais e caminho.* São Paulo:
    Duas Cidades, 1972.

Mota, Carlos Guilherme. *Ideologia da cultura brasileira (1933-1974).* 3rd
    ed. São Paulo: Atica, 1977.

Souza, Gilda de Melo e. "Digerindo o banquete de Mário de Andrade."
    Interview granted to Antônio Dimas. *Jornal da Tarde*, 25 February 1978.

Viala, Alain. *Naissance de l'écrivain: Sociologie de la littérature à l'âge
    classique.* Paris: Les Éditions de Minuit, 1985.

Namoros com a Ribalta: Mário de Andrade e o Teatro

Severino J. Albuquerque

No centenário do nascimento
de Mário de Andrade (1893-1945)

Um dos mais caros mitos do Modernismo brasileiro é a propalada falta de participação do teatro no movimento que revolucionou a arte nacional nas décadas de vinte e trinta deste século. Apressados que estavam na tarefa de canonizar tanto o movimento como os seus participantes de maior prestígio, os críticos do Modernismo confundiram um fato real, isto é, a ausência de peças de teatro entre os eventos que formaram o que se convencionou denominar Semana de Arte Moderna, com o mito de que o teatro não integrou o Modernismo. Usando esse foco estrito e estreito, tomaram um período limitado de tempo, aqueles três ou quatro dias de fevereiro de 1922, como se representasse a totalidade dos cerca de vinte anos que constituíram o Modernismo brasileiro. Se tal parâmetro tivesse sido aplicado ao gênero privilegiado pelos canonizadores do Modernismo, ou seja, a poesia, livros fundamentais do movimento, como *Alguma poesia* de Carlos Drummond de Andrade, de 1930, e de fato, o próprio Drummond, estariam excluídos do Modernismo.

A verdade é que os motivos da ausência do teatro tanto da Semana de 22 como do projeto canonizador do Modernismo, ainda ficam por explicar. Talvez a mais sólida entre as raras tentativas de esclarecimento do que realmente ocorreu, seja o capítulo escrito por Décio de Almeida Prado para a coletânea crítica organizada por Affonso Avila, intitulada *O Modernismo*, que embora somente publicada em 1975, fez parte das comemorações do cinqüentenário da Semana.

A explicação de Almeida Prado, aceita sem maiores

questionamentos por críticos e estudiosos do teatro desde sua publicação há quase vinte anos, tem duas premissas básicas. A primeira é que o domínio exercido pelo teatro de costumes— sabidamente medíocre, rasteiro e esgotado—era tal que retardou o aparecimento de um teatro brasileiro moderno; e a segunda, que a complexidade da arte teatral, com sua diversa conjunção signatória (gestos, iluminação, vestuário, sonografia, cenário, etc) não encontrou em nossos acanhados redutos o terreno propício para florescer, ou só o encontraria mais de vinte anos depois da Semana, quando um estrangeiro, um polonês emigrado de nome Zbigniew Ziembinsky (1908-1978), demonstrou todo seu domínio de palco moderno na sua histórica encenação de *Vestido de noiva*, de Nelson Rodrigues (1912-1980), em 28 de dezembro de 1943, data que para muitos marca o verdadeiro começo do teatro brasileiro moderno, senão do próprio teatro brasileiro.

O problema suscitado por essa explicação não é que ela esteja errada, pois não está. É bem mais complicado que isso. O problema é que ela é incompleta e insuficiente. Em primeiro lugar, tal posição ignora o fato de que durante a própria Semana de 22 houve bastante dramaticidade e dramatizações. Dramaticidade nos conflitos entre artistas e público, e dramatizações nos recitais e, talvez ainda mais importante, na postura dos participantes, os quais para todos os efeitos estavam desempenhando papéis, seja para chocar a burguesia, seja para denunciar a fascinação brasileira com tudo que é estrangeiro, seja para ressaltar a caduquice dos modelos parnasianos, e assim em diante. Isso sem esquecer o fato de que os eventos da Semana tomaram lugar em um *teatro*, o Municipal de São Paulo, e não somente em salões, escadarias e outras dependências do prédio, mas no próprio palco do teatro, com os participantes, em cena, atuando mesmo, sendo, por assim dizer, atores.[1]

Almeida Prado, é verdade, se apressa a apontar claras manifestações de teatro moderno ocorridas durante o período áureo do Modernismo brasileiro. Entre os exemplos mais significativos dessas ocorrências, temos a atividade de crítico teatral desempenhada por António de Alcântara Machado (1901-1935) no periódico *Terra Roxa e Outras Terras* e em escritos reunidos na coleção *Cavaquinho e saxofone*; e a criação de dois grupos importantes, embora de curta existência, um no Rio de Janeiro, o Teatro de Brinquedo, fundado em 1927 por dois dos mais destacados modernistas da vertente carioca, Alvaro (1888-1964) e Eugênia Moreyra (1899-1948), e o outro em São Paulo, o Teatro de Experiência, criado em 1933 por Flávio de Carvalho (1899-1973). Foi para o Teatro de Experiência que Oswald de Andrade escreveu *O homem e o cavalo*, peça que foi interditada pela censura na noite de estréia em 1934.

Não é este o lugar nem é meu objetivo aqui analisar o teatro de

Oswald de Andrade (1890-1954), cuja importância tem sido ressaltada por inúmeros críticos. Somente quero enfatizar que as obras de Oswald teriam estreado antes de *Vestido de noiva*, antecipando assim de uma década a renovação do teatro brasileiro, se não fora pela rigidez da censura do regime de Vargas, a qual, a propósito, estava mais interessada em vigiar o palco que os livros, pois *O homem e o cavalo* chegou a ser publicada em 1934, e *O rei da vela* e *A morta*, em um só volume, em 1937. Infelizmente, como sabemos, foi somente em 1967 que o teatro de Oswald chegou aos palcos brasileiros, com a consagração recebida pela montagem tropicalista de *O rei da vela* pelo Teatro Oficina.

Mas é o outro dos três grandes Andrades do Modernismo brasileiro que aqui me interessa na sua relação com o teatro. Refiro-me naturalmente a Mário de Andrade (1893-1945), cujas facetas de poeta, crítico, ficcionista e "correspondente contumaz" têm sido fartamente estudadas, mas com a grande lacuna do teatro à espera da maior atenção que lhe é devida.[2] Este trabalho é uma contribuição ao estudo deste assunto inexplorado-- os flertes de Mário com o teatro, suas tentativas teatrais, suas leituras dramáticas, suas referências ao teatro na poesia e na copiosa correspondência.

Isto sabemos com certeza: que Mário de Andrade rejeitou uma oportunidade sem igual ao recusar o convite que lhe foi feito, em 1936, por Gustavo Capanema, então Ministro da Educação e Saúde, para dirigir o Departamento de Teatros do referido ministério. Os motivos da recusa foram vários—timidez, modéstia, aversão ao mando e ao destaque, ou, como tenta explicar em carta do mesmo ano ao amigo Rodrigo de Mello Franco, uma certa preferência por "um posto que me conserve na obscuridade, subalterno de outros que mandem em mim e a quem obedeça, sem responsabilidade" (Castro 36). Resta-nos somente especular a respeito dos rumos que o teatro brasileiro poderia ter tomado sob a gestão de Mário de Andrade no órgão que depois se transformaria no Serviço Nacional de Teatro.

No entanto, por outro lado, sabemos com certeza que Mário, ao falecer, em 1945, deixou publicadas três peças de teatro, além de ter dado concepção teatral à última secção ("As enfibraturas do Ipiranga"[3]) de sua importante coleção de poemas, *Paulicéia desvairada*, publicada naquele ano chave de 1922. As três peças são: *Moral quotidiana: Tragédia* (publicada em *Estética* [Rio de Janeiro] vol 1, 1925), *Eva* (publicada em *Primeiro andar*, 1926) e *Café: Tragédia secular*, cujo texto somente foi publicado pela primeira vez na terceira edição das *Poesias completas*, fechando o volume saído em 1972 como parte das comemorações do quinquagésimo aniversário da Semana de Arte Moderna (Andrade 1972: ix). Sabemos igualmente que, mais recentemente, algumas de suas narrativas têm sido adaptadas ao palco, como *O banquete*, dirigida por Myriam Muniz em 1979 e por Camila Amado em 1984,[4] e principalmente, *Macunaíma*, dirigida por Antunes Filho em 1978,[5] esta última indiscutivelmente o evento teatral mais importante do teatro brasileiro da década de setenta.

Ao organizar suas *Obras completas*, quase duas décadas após a publicação de suas primeiras obras modernistas, Mário de Andrade voltou à coleção de textos que ele tinha chamado de *Primeiro andar* (1926). Embora seja geralmente descrito como um "livro de contos," *Primeiro andar* continha os textos de duas peças de teatro, "Eva" e "Moral quotidiana." Ao efetuar a revisão, Mário, de olho na posteridade, descartou alguns textos e conservou outros, os quais foram acrescentados a alguns poemas e um longo ensaio de estética, para assim formar uma nova coleção, por ele próprio intitulada de *Obra imatura*,[6] que mais tarde veio a ser o Primeiro Volume das *Obras completas*, publicadas pela Editora Martins de São Paulo (Andrade 1960).

Entre os textos de *Primeiro andar* que Mário achou por bem conservar, apesar de rotulá-los de "imaturos," estavam "Eva" e "Moral quotidiana." No entanto, os dois textos continuam sendo identificados no sumário como "contos" e não se nota nenhuma ênfase na sua dessemelhança das outras narrativas que compõem esta secção de *Obra imatura*. As duas peças nem sequer aparecem juntas na seqüência textual, estando separadas por dois contos, "Brasília" e "História sem data." Embora inicialmente surpreendente, esta classificação de "Eva" e "Moral quotidiana" como "contos" faz mais sentido quando lembramos que, ao escrever esses textos (em 1919 e 1922, respectivamente), o autor estava em busca de inovações formais ou alternativas inovadoras no campo do conto.

Com ironia e humor característicos da primeira onda modernista, "Eva" e "Moral quotidiana" subvertem as convenções não somente do conto mas também do drama. Rejeitando por completo o formato de um conto tradicional, ambas adotam a voz homodiegética do diálogo aliada à voz heterodiegética da rubrica (Genette 1980: 228-31, 245). "Eva," a menos elaborada das duas peças de *Obra imatura*, transpõe a cena da tentação em Gênesis 3.1-6 para um "pomar ridiculamente europeu de cidade sulamericana civilizada" (Andrade 1960: 106), onde Eva, uma garota de oito anos de idade, agindo em nome do "Desejo, personagem principal" (104), leva seu primo Julinho, de doze anos, a comer uma maçã do pomar, desobedecendo assim as ordens explícitas da dona da chácara.

Em "Moral quotidiana," antes mesmo de iniciar-se o texto dramático propriamente dito, o subtítulo de "Tragédia," aposto ao título da obra, vem acompanhado de uma nota de rodapé que diz, "Juro que é tragédia" (Andrade 1925: 133), solapando assim a seriedade tradicionalmente associada ao gênero.[7] A peça tem apenas um ato, chamado "Terceiro e Unico Ato," cujas duas cenas são separadas por um intervalo de dois minutos, um intervalo que não é exatamente um intervalo, pois a ação continua ininterrupta durante os dois minutos de sua suposta duração. A *dramatis personae* é apresentada deste modo: "A Amante - primadona; A Mulher - coisa que acontece; O Marido - joguete nas Mãos do Destino."[8] O Marido só aparece na Segunda Cena e, mesmo assim, de maneira limitada, de modo que a ação propriamente dita se restringe às duas mulheres. Além das protagonistas, o texto secundário (side text) nos informa que também são vistos no palco: "*um criado pendurado impassível na porta,*" o qual permanece calado durante todo o desenrolar dos acontecimentos; e quatro Coros, que somente intervêm na Segunda Cena (o Coro das Senhoras Casadas, o Coro dos Senhores Casados, o Coro das Senhoras Idosas, e o Coro dos Senhores Idosos).

A ação acontece no tempo "presente," numa tarde ensolarada de verão no terraço de um hotel, com "*Mesas. Cadeiras de vime. Tudo chique,*" no balneário de Guarujá, no litoral de São Paulo. A esposa, uma jovem brasileira, "*brasileirinha ... viva,*" morena de 24 anos, e a amante do marido desta, uma francesa de 35 anos, alta, ruiva, "*belíssima,*" disputam a primazia do amor do Marido. O que se inicia como um jogo de evasivas logo se torna uma verdadeira batalha verbal na qual a esposa vai aos poucos prevalecendo sobre a amante, a qual estará totalmente vencida ao término da Primeira Cena.

O Intermédio, como já mencionei, não chega a sê-lo, pois a amante humilhada agride fisicamente a vencedora da batalha verbal, começando assim uma altercação que é descrita pelo texto secundário em termos de luta de boxe. Ao fim da briga, a brasileira está outra vez vitoriosa. Ao se arranjar, ofegante, deixando para trás a francesa caída no chão e soluçando alto, a esposa é confrontada pelos quatro Coros, que tinham entrado em cena atraídos pelos gritos da francesa a pedir socorro. Inicia-se assim a Segunda Cena, a qual é essencialmente a expressão das noções burguesas de moralidade, fidelidade e manutenção das aparências a todo custo, o objetivo da cena sendo, evidentemente, a denúncia da hipocrisia então vigente. Em intervenções que se alternam, o Coro das Senhoras Casadas critica o comportamento público da esposa; o Coro dos Senhores Casados defende o direito do Marido de ter amantes e condena os ciúmes da esposa; o Coro das Senhoras Idosas insiste que a existência de amantes é parte normal da vida de casado; e finalmente, o Coro dos Senhores Idosos, fascinado pela beleza da francesa, expressa pena e dó pelo sofrimento da coitada (138-39). O Marido, agora em cena, ilustra a ficção burguesa do protetor da mulher e esposo galante ao oferecer-lhe "vinte dúzias de cravos paulistanos" e defendê-la das acusações da francesa e dos Coros. Unido, o casal retira-se de cena, aos gritos de "Fora! Fora!" dados em *fortissimo* pelos quatro Coros, e de acordo com as indicações do texto secundário, sob "*Aplausos frenéticos da assistência*" (139-40), ocorrência precoce da técnica de distanciamento no teatro brasileiro moderno, assim como a luta de boxe entre as duas mulheres e o criado "pendurado na porta" evidenciam familiaridade com técnicas do expressionismo teatral.

Sem perder a oportunidade de fazer gozação de dois de seus alvos favoritos, ou seja, o nativismo cego dos românticos tardios e as teorias de Graça Aranha, Mário de Andrade faz que o Marido e a Mulher digam em uníssono ao sair de cena:

> Adeus! Adeus! Adeus! Oh Civilização! Vamos livrar
> o nosso amor maravilhoso do teu contágio pernicioso!
> ... Lá longe, dentro dos matos americanos, onde as
> iraras pulam, os chocalhos das cascavéis charram,
> onde zumbem milhões de insetos venenígeros,
> seguiremos o conselho de Rousseau, de João Jaques
> Rousseau, e segundo as bonitas teorias do sr. Graça
> Aranha, nos integraremos no Todo Universal! (140).

Fica em cena, sozinha, a francesa, que, "*desesperada,*" entoa seu lamento de morte, a "Cavatina da Abandonada," tendo como fundo musical um arranjo do "Matuto," de Marcelo Tupinambá, "*pra flauta, 3 violões e gramofone*" (140). A Cavatina não passa de uma longa paródia onde se acumulam numerosos clichês românticos, eivados de sentimentalismo e pena de si mesma. O texto se encerra com a última rubrica do autor, que descreve o que ocorre após a morte da francesa:

> *O coro das senhoras idosas, com gestos chaplineanos*
> *de deploração, estende sobre a morta um grande*
> *manto branco. Os senhores idosos e senhores casados*
> *dançam em torno do cadáver num hiporquema grave*
> *e gracioso, desfolhando sobre a amante as 20 dúzias*
> *de cravos, que o smoking [o criado] fora buscar nas*
> *mãos da Mulher e repartira entre eles. As senhoras*
> *casadas desnastrando as respectivas comas sobre o*
> *rosto, levantam nos ombros alvíssimos, aquela que*
> *sempre viva se conservará na memória dos mortais.*
> *E então, tendo na frente um abundantíssimo Jazz*

[band] que executa a Marcha Fúnebre de Chopin,
Op. 35, o cortejo desfila, desfilará pela Terra inteira
e pelas civilizações futuras até a vinda, por todos os
humanos desejada, do Anticristo. (142)

Ao fim da página, logo antes do nome do autor, aparecem em maiúsculas os nomes de cinco produtos comerciais, provavelmente representando o consumismo desvairado e o comercialismo barato que já naquela época preocupavam o nacionalista Mário de Andrade:

LACTA   SALUS
GUARANA   ESPUMANTE
BELLA COR   DUNLOP[9]

Como "Eva" e "Moral quotidiana," "Café" também se encontra em *Primeiro andar* e em *Obra imatura*. Porém, ao contrário das duas outras peças, cujos textos iniciais já eram praticamente suas formas definitivas, o texto de "Café" que aparece em *Primeiro andar* e *Obra imatura* é um conto curto intitulado "Os sírios" e identificado ao final como um "fragmento do romance *Café*" (Andrade 1960: 194).[10] A metamorfose de conto ou fragmento de romance para poema dramático ou ópera coral[11] foi comentada pelo próprio autor em entrevista concedida a Mário da Silva Brito.[12] Na entrevista, Mário de Andrade explica que depois de trabalhar vários anos no texto de um romance que seria intitulado *Café*,[13] resolvera interromper a escrita sem pretender retomá-la, e ajunta que inclusive já tinha publicado trechos da narrativa sob outras formas, tais como "crônicas musicais," por exemplo (Andrade 1983: 97).[14] Para surpresa do entrevistador, Mário declara que a maior parte do texto havia sido transformada em libreto para uma ópera coral cuja partitura seria composta por Francisco Mignone (1897-1986),[15] e que tal "concepção melodramática" fazia parte de um projeto seu de "dignificação da ópera."[16] Mário confessa ademais ter trabalhado no libreto umas quatorze a quinze horas por dia entre outubro e dezembro de 1942,[17] "cigarro na boca e uísque ao lado," o resultado sendo, segundo os amigos que tinham lido o manuscrito, "a melhor coisa que já fiz" (Andrade 1983: 97).[18]

A peça propriamente dita, denominada "Café: Tragédia secular" (Andrade 1987: 423-49) vem precedida de um longo texto, intitulado "Café: Concepção melodramática," datado de 15 de dezembro de 1942, no qual o autor fornece comentários detalhados sobre cada cena da peça (399-422), e de um curto "Apêndice" contendo fragmentos de uma "Primeira versão para ser musicada" e de uma "Segunda versão para ser musicada" (451-55).

Café é, nas palavras do próprio autor, uma "ópera coral . . . em três atos, inteiramente de massa, sendo os seus personagens grupos sociais em movimento" (Andrade 1983: 97). Graças ao teor francamente contestatório da peça, a primeira tentativa de encenação de *Café*, em julho de 1968, foi proibida pela ditadura militar, através do Serviço de Censura de Diversões Públicas, com a peça sendo acusada de "provocar incitamento contra o regime, a ordem pública, e as autoridades constituídas" ("Censura proíbe Andrade" 72; ver também Michalski 1979: 69). Foi somente em 1986 que *Café* chegou aos palcos brasileiros,[19] numa montagem realizada no Teatro Experimental Cacilda Becker, com o elenco da Escola de Teatro Martins Pena, sob a direção geral de Luís Fernando Lobo e direção musical de Charles Kahn ("Mário de Andrade ... em Cena" 27). Vale salientar, no entanto, que houve pelo menos duas leituras de *Café* na década de quarenta, mais de vinte anos antes da tentativa malograda de encenar a peça em 1968. A primeira leitura realizou-se, no início de janeiro de 1943, na casa do próprio Mário, à rua Lopes Chaves, com a presença de Antônio Cândido e Gilda de Mello e Souza, Oneida e Sílvio Alvarenga, Luis Saia, e Norberto Frontini ("Carta de Mário sobre *Café*" 4); a segunda teve lugar no auditório da Biblioteca Municipal de São Paulo-- atualmente denominada Biblioteca Municipal Mário de Andrade—na tarde de 25 de fevereiro de 1946, como parte das comemorações do primeiro aniversário do falecimento do escritor ("Noticiário da Semana de Mário de Andrade" 187).

O elo de ligação entre as duas leituras—além, naturalmente, do texto da obra—é a figura do crítico Antônio Cândido, que se encontrava presente na primeira ocasião, e que na segunda funcionou como leitor e comentarista do texto deixado por seu grande amigo. Muito antes da segunda leitura, Antônio Cândido já havia despertado para a importância de *Café*. De fato, passados apenas alguns dias da primeira leitura (feita aparentemente pelo próprio Mário com seu inimitável vozeirão), Antônio Cândido enviou a Mário um comentário que ele havia escrito sobre a obra. Mário respondeu em pouco tempo, com uma longa carta (datada de 19 de janeiro de 1943), descrita pelos editores do *Suplemento Literário do Estado de São Paulo*, onde foi primeiramente publicada, como "um documento de intensa lucidez, dos mais importantes que um artista já escreveu no Brasil sobre os próprios métodos de trabalho e sobre o processo da criação" ("Carta de Mário sobre *Café*" 4).

Na carta a Antônio Cândido, Mário tece considerações gerais sobre as fontes onde buscou a "inspiração" para a obra (tragédias gregas, Shakespeare, folclore nacional, e poetas celtas, estes últimos sendo apontados, surpreendentemente, como a origem da revelação criadora da peça), admite sua insatisfação a respeito da cena da discussão entre donos e colonos (concordando, assim, com a opinião do casal Mello e Souza), e confessa-se particularmente preocupado com o impacto das cenas de maior conteúdo político sobre os diversos componentes da platéia. Além disso, escreve sobre mudanças introduzidas por ele próprio na seqüência das cenas.[20] Para evitar que a comicidade da "Câmara- Ballet" tivesse um efeito "desmoralizador [sobre] um público geral," facilitando, ao mesmo tempo, "a gradativa intensificação dramática do assunto," Mário explica haver transferido a citada cena para o início do Segundo Ato, permitindo assim que o comovente "Exodo" encerrasse o mesmo ato. Com a transposição das duas cenas, o autor revela haver detectado uma "modulação rítmica urbano > rural," a qual ele decide obedecer também nos dois outros atos, sendo necessário para tal introduzir novas mudanças seqüenciais. Em esquema proposto pelo próprio dramaturgo, esta seria a segmentação rítmica definitiva de *Café*:

Primeiro Ato	Segundo Ato	Terceiro Ato
urbano > rural	> urbano > rural >	urbano
Porto Parado > Comp.	Cafeeira > Camara > Exodo >	Dia Novo

Enquanto o tom de protesto já é bastante evidente nos dois primeiros atos, o Terceiro Ato, intitulado "Dia Novo," louva abertamente a Revolução que "convulsiona a cidade" (Andrade 1987: 444). Era a Revolução prenunciada nos dois atos anteriores como sendo inevitável e absolutamente necessária para a redenção das massas oprimidas. Estas são representadas pelo Homem Zangado, louvado pelo "Coral da Vida" como "o herói do coração múltiplo,/ O justiçador moreno, o esmurrador com mil punhos/ Amassando os gigantes da mina e peidando para os anões" (442). Os nove curtos quadros que formam o último ato da peça se sucedem num crescendo irresistível, tão irresistível como a vitória das massas sobre "os gigantes [encurralados] nos seus palácios confortáveis, defendidos pelos anões subterrâneos" (444). A rápida sucessão dos eventos que levam à vitória final é veiculada por meio de transmissões radiofônicas e coros de revolucionários, até chegar à "Apoteose final, em grande quadro imóvel," cantada pela Mãe Revolucionária, que se identifica dessa maneira no "Hino da Fonte da Vida":

Eu sou a fonte da vida
Do meu corpo nasce a terra

Na minha boca floresce
A palavra que será.
....
Eu sou a fonte da vida:
Força, amor, trabalho, paz. (448-49)

A crítica social, a empatia com o sofrimento das massas, o protesto contra a exploração do operariado, e um tom geral de insatisfação com o status quo fazem de *Café* uma peça politicamente engajada, colocando-a, deste modo, muito além da costumeira neutralidade ideológica encontrada nas obras de Mário de Andrade. Além da consciência política do autor, *Café* também demonstra que Mário estava perfeitamente ciente do fato de que estava fazendo teatro e, ainda mais, de que ele se preocupava com a necessidade de alcançar as massas com o seu teatro:

> Teatro é fundamentalmente e essencialmente povo, e si [sic] um de nós, ressequidos de cultura e erudição, é mais ou menos refratário a essa funcionalidade educativa do teatro, eu não queria e não quero esquecer que fiz uma obra voluntariosamente popular. Pra povo. ("Carta de Mário sobre *Café*" 4)

Esta consciência política encontrada em *Café*, aliada a outros aspectos das primeiras peças, como o humor modernista de *Eva* e o uso de certas técnicas expressionistas e de distanciamento em *Moral quotidiana*, plenamente justificam a necessidade de maior atenção crítica para o teatro de Mário de Andrade. Igualmente digno de mais amplo escrutínio é o assunto da relação ou relacionamento entre a pessoa ou a figura de Mário e o teatro do Brasil como instituição tradicionalmente dependente do apoio dos órgãos de cultura do governo. Para este fim, a volumosa correspondência de Mário de Andrade aguarda o pesquisador desejoso de dar validez e realce a esta até agora pouco explorada faceta daquele que foi a mais importante figura da cultura brasileira deste século.

Notas

[1] Não é de se estranhar, portanto, que o autor de *A Semana* tenha escolhido o veículo teatral para ficcionalizar o ocorrido em fevereiro de 1922, nem que Mário de Andrade ocupe papel de destaque na peça (Telles 1972), destaque que se repetirá em outra obra do mesmo dramaturgo (Telles 1975).

[2] Entre muitos outros casos, veja-se por exemplo a conspícua ausência do teatro entre os capítulos de um dos mais consultados estudos introdutórios à obra do autor de *Macunaíma*. O sumário do livro de Henrique L. Alves, *Mário de Andrade*, apresenta uma lista de oito capítulos, dedicados cada um a uma faceta da obra de Mário: "Mário de Andrade e . . ." [a poesia; o conto; o romance; a crítica; o folclore; a música; as artes plásticas; as cartas.]

[3] "As enfibraturas do Ipiranga", subtitulada "Oratório profano", tem por epígrafe a fala de Ofélia, "O, woe is me / To have seen what I have seen, see what I see" (*Hamlet* III i: 160-62). Quatro grupos de vozes (Os Orientalismos Convencionais, As Senectudes Tremulinas, Os Sandapilários Indiferentes, e As Juvenilidades Auriverdes) e a solista (um soprano ligeiro chamado "Minha Loucura") são acompanhados de orquestra e banda, "perto de cinco mil instrumentistas dirigidos por maestros . . . vindos do estrangeiro," que tocam na esplanada do Teatro Municipal. Os coros (compostos de um total de 550.000 cantores) estão espalhados pela área adjacente ao Teatro Municipal, no centro da cidade de São Paulo, mas somente as Juvenilidades Auriverdes, representantes que são dos modernistas renovadores, têm "os pés enterrados no solo" (Andrade 1987: 103-104).

[4] *O banquete*, uma compilação de crônicas musicais em forma de diálogo publicadas na *Folha da Manhã* de São Paulo entre 1943 e 1945, foi uma das obras que Mário deixou incompletas ao falecer. Nas crônicas, cujo texto somente foi publicado em forma de livro pela primeira vez na década de setenta (Andrade 1977), cinco estranhos personagens se encontram num almoço onde discutem problemas ligados à criação artística num contexto de dependência econômica e cultural. Na montagem de 1979 a adaptação teatral foi feita por José Rubens Siqueira para o Grupo Teatro do Ator; várias resenhas dessa produção aparecem em Moreira 1981: 62-71. Na montagem de 1984, a adaptação do texto para o palco foi de autoria da diretora, Camila Amado.

[5] Sobre a montagem teatral deste texto seminal do Modernismo brasileiro, ver George (1983; 1985; 1990) e Moreira (1981: 72- 202). No dizer de Mariângela Alves de Lima, "a encenação de *Macunaíma* ... não é apenas a transposição cênica de uma obra, mas também da contribuição crítica de Mário de Andrade para a compreensão da cultura brasileira. Para pôr em cena o imaginário e o dinamismo das forças subterrâneas da cultura, o espetáculo recorria a procedimentos de Mário de Andrade, notadamente à dissolução das antinomias arcaico/moderno, rural/urbano e selvagem/ europeu" ("Dois livros de teatro" 195).

[6] O volume tem três secções: a primeira, tirada do livro de estréia de Mário de Andrade, reúne uma seleção de poemas da coleção *Há uma gota*

de sangue em cada poema, publicada em 1917, de caráter ainda evidentemente parnasiano-simbolista; a segunda é composta dos textos selecionados de *Primeiro andar*; e a terceira reproduz a poética modernista de Mário de Andrade, *A escrava que não é Isaura*, publicada pela primeira vez em 1925.

[7] Seriedade que o próprio Mário louvaria mais tarde em "Do trágico," artigo datado de 10 de setembro de 1939, no qual resenha as *Três tragédias à sombra da cruz*, de Otávio de Faria. As tragédias de Faria, Mário escreve, "não me parecem bem sucedidas," devido a "um certo confusionismo conceptivo e uma forma bastante bamba, desprovida daquela arquitetura nobre que a tragédia exige" (Andrade 1955: 109).

[8] Aqui e através do artigo, a ortografia dos textos citados foi mudada para conformar-se ao uso atual.

[9] Em *Obra imatura*, a posição das duas palavras da primeira linha se encontra invertida, e somente o "s" inicial de Salus aparece em maiúsculas (163).

[10] Na sua "Nota para a Segunda Edição" de *Primeiro andar* (melhor descrita como fazendo parte da primeira edição de *Obra imatura*), Mário reitera a classificação de "conto" para o trecho de *Café* (Andrade 1960: 48). O cotejamento da data da Nota (novembro de 1943) com a da carta enviada a Antônio Cândido (janeiro de 1943), citada mais abaixo, e principalmente, com as datas no frontispício da "Concepção Melodramática" de "Café" (1933-1939- 1942) sugere que ao escrever a Nota, Mário já havia terminado de efetuar as mudanças diegéticas que resultaram no texto definitivo de "Café: Tragédia secular."

[11] As dificuldades genéricas e terminológicas confundiram o próprio autor de *Café*. Ver, por exemplo, a carta de Mário a Francisco Mignone, datada de 9 de novembro de 1942, onde se confessava incerto quanto à classificação da obra (Andrade s.d.: 110). A mesma missiva é citada por Marta Moraes da Costa como parte de suas perspicazes observações sobre o gênero a que pertence *Café* (Costa 1988: 126-31).

[12] A entrevista foi publicada inicialmente no *Diário de São Paulo* de 2 de dezembro de 1943 e reproduzida em Andrade 1983 (93- 98), sob o longo título de "1943: Uma excursão pelo fichário de *Macunaíma*; Reedições, novas obras e planos de futuros trabalhos de Mário de Andrade, o mais organizado intelectual do Brasil." Ver também a cronologia das referências, feitas por Mário na sua correspondência, sobre a composição e as transformações de *Café*, em Costa (1988: 116-21).

[13] Ver, por exemplo, a carta a Manuel Bandeira, datada de 28 de março de 1931, na qual Mário informa o amigo de como anda a composição

do romance: "Tenho escrito um bocado dele, mas vai lerdo, aos arrancos, porque não só as preocupações e trabalhos me estão peiando, como os horríveis sofrimentos diante da vida, da feição que está tomando o Brasil e o mundo me deixam abandonado, sem coragem pra nenhuma empreitada contínua e eficaz às direitas. Mas enfim sempre o romance continua e talvez nestes dois ou três anos esteja pronto" (*Cartas a Manuel Bandeira* 339).

[14] Segundo Telê Lopez, o projeto original de *Café* se tornou eventualmente *Vida do cantador* (Costa 1988: 119).

[15] Mignone e sua esposa, Liddy Chiafarelli, a quem o texto de "Café: Concepção Melodramática" está dedicado, integravam o círculo de amizades de Mário; o autor presenteou o casal os originais de "Café," os quais foram por estes cedidos ao editor Martins e à família Mário de Andrade para serem publicados na terceira edição das *Poesias completas* (Andrade 1972: ix). A partitura que Mignone deveria elaborar para "Café" nunca foi concluída (Andrade 1987: 522).

[16] Este não foi o primeiro libreto escrito por Mário: em 1928 ele havia colaborado com o maestro e compositor Camargo Guarnieri (1907) na ópera *Malazarte*. Ver referência, por exemplo, em carta a Manuel Bandeira de 10 de setembro de 1928 (Andrade 1966: 262-64). O projeto de "dignificação da ópera" fica melhor explicitado à luz do seguinte trecho de uma carta de Mário a Paulo Duarte, datada de 18 de outubro de 1942: "o teatro cantado sempre existiu e com dignidade humana. Se chamou tragédia grega, se chamou Chegança e Bumba-meu-Boi, teatro Nô, etc. e tal. Até que um dia perdendo validade social, também careceu mudar de nome e se chamou "ópera", Tosca e Manon. Como tornar à dignidade e eficiência humana do teatro cantado em referência ao nosso tempo? Então parti da força coletivizadora do coro e imaginei um melodrama exclusivamente coral, onde em vez de personagens solistas, os personagens são massas corais" (Duarte 1977: 254).

[17] Apesar de já estar bastante enfermo nessas alturas, Mário continuava a trabalhar arduamente nos seus manuscritos. Foi-lhe possível dedicar tantas horas ao projeto de *Café* por estar de licença médica e por ter desistido de terminar o romance *Quatro pessoas*, pois com a queda de Paris, "não era mais possível preocupar-me com o destino de quatro indivíduos—envolvidos em dois casos de amor—quando o mundo sofria tanto e a cultura recebia um golpe profundo" (Andrade 1983: 96). O manuscrito inconcluso de *Quatro pessoas* só foi publicado na década de oitenta, graças aos esforços editoriais de Maria Zélia Galvão de Almeida (Andrade 1985).

[18] Em seu excelente artigo sobre *Café*, Marta Morais da Costa considera a obra como sendo "a síntese do pensamento social e da inserção

histórica de Mário de Andrade na realidade e na arte de seu tempo" (1988: 115).

[19] Isto significa que a primeira vez que Mário de Andrade chegou efetivamente aos palcos brasileiros foi através da consagrada montagem de *Macunaíma*, estreada em 1978, sob a direção de Antunes Filho.

[20] No formato definitivo da peça, as duas partes do Primeiro Ato estão subdivididas em cenas curtas: "Porto Parado" é composto de "Coral do Queixume," "Madrigal do Truco," "Coral das Famintas," e "Imploração da Fome;" "Companhia Cafeeira," por sua vez, está formada de: "Coral do Provérbio," "A Discussão," e "Coral do Abandono." Cada uma das duas partes do Segundo Ato tem três cenas: "Camara-Ballet" está subdividida em "Quinteto dos Serventes," "A Embolada da Ferrugem," e "A Endeixa da Mãe," enquanto que "O Exodo" está constituído de "Coral Puríssimo," "Coral da Vida," e "Coral do Exodo." O Terceiro Ato, chamado "Dia Novo," tem nove cenas curtas: "O Parlato do Rádio," "Cânone das Assustadas," "Estância de Combate," "Estância da Revolta," "Fugato Coral," "Segundo Parlato do Rádio," "Grande Coral de Luta," "O Rádio da Vitória," e o "Hino da Fonte da Vida."

Obras Citadas

Alves, Henrique L. 1983. *Mário de Andrade*. 2a. ed. São Paulo: Ibrasa.

Andrade, Mário de. 1925. "Moral quotidiana." *Estética* 2 (Janeiro - Março) 133-42. [Reproduzida em *Obra imatura* 154-63]

---. 1955. *O empalhador de passarinho*. São Paulo: Livraria Martins Editora.

---. 1960. "Eva." (1926). *Obra imatura*. São Paulo: Livraria Martins Editora. 104-12.

---. 1966. *Cartas a Manuel Bandeira*. Org. Manuel Bandeira. Rio de Janeiro: Edições de Ouro.

---. 1972. "Café." *Poesias completas*. 3a. ed. São Paulo: Livraria Martins Editora. 317-75. [Reproduzida na edição definitiva, Andrade 1987: 399-455.]

---. 1977. *O banquete*. Org. Jorge Coli e Luís Carlos da Silva Dantas. São Paulo: Duas Cidades.

---. 1982. *Correspondente contumaz: Cartas a Pedro Nava, 1925-1944*. Org. Fernando da Rocha Pires. Rio de Janeiro: Editora Nova Fronteira.

---. 1983. *Entrevistas e depoimentos*. Org. Telê Porto Ancona Lopez. São Paulo: T. A. Queiroz.

---. 1985. *Quatro pessoas*. Org. Maria Zélia Galvão de Almeida. Belo Horizonte: Editora Itatiaia.

---. 1987. *Poesias completas*. Org. Dilea Zanotto Manfio. Belo Horizonte e São Paulo: Editora Itatiaia e Editora da Universidade de São Paulo.
---. 1988. *Macunaíma, o herói sem nenhum caráter* (1928). Org. Telê Porto Ancona Lopez. Paris e Brasília: Association Archives de la Littérature Latino-Américaine, des Caraïbes, et Africaines du XXème Siècle / Conselho Nacional de Pesquisas.
---. s.d. *71 cartas de Mário de Andrade*. Org. Lygia Fernandes. Rio de Janeiro: Livraria São José.

Andrade, Oswald de. 1934. *O homem e o cavalo*.
---. 1976. *A morta. O rei da vela. O homem e o cavalo* (1937). Rio de Janeiro: Editora Civilização Brasileira.
"Carta de Mário sobre *Café*." 1960. *Suplemento Literário do Estado de São Paulo* 171 (27 de fevereiro) 4.

Castro, Moacir Werneck de. 1989. *Mário de Andrade: Exílio no Rio*. Rio de Janeiro: Rocco.
"Censura proíbe Andrade." 1968. *Folha de São Paulo* (19 de julho). [Reproduzida em Moreira (1981: 72)].

Coli, Jorge, e Luis Carlos da Silva Dantas. 1977. "Sobre *O banquete*." Em Andrade 1977: 9-41.

Costa, Marta Morais da. 1988. "Um poeta verdadeiro conta seu sonho: Teatro e revoulção em *Café*, de Mário de Andrade." *Revista Letras* 37: 115-41.

Duarte, Paulo. 1977. *Mário de Andrade por ele mesmo*. 2a. ed. rev. São Paulo: HUCITEC / Secretaria da Cultura, Ciência e Tecnologia.

Genette, Gérard. 1980. *Narrative Discourse*. Trans. Jane E. Lewin. Ithaca: Cornell University Press.

George, David. 1983. "The Staging of *Macunaíma* and the Search for National Theatre." *Latin American Theatre Review* 17.1: 47- 58.
---. 1985. "A montagem de *Macunaíma*." *Teatro e antropofagia*. São Paulo: Global Editora. 61-84.
---. 1990. "*Macunaíma*." *Grupo Macunaíma: Carnavalização e mito*. São Paulo: Editora Perspectiva. 41-77.

Lima, Mariângela Alves de. 1990-91. "Dois livros de teatro." *Revista USP*

8 (Dezembro-Janeiro-Fevereiro) 193-96.

"Mário de Andrade e Nélson Rodrigues estiveram em cena no Teatro Cacilda Becker." 1986. *Revista de Teatro* 459 (Julho - Setembro) 27.

Michalski, Yan. 1979. *O palco amordaçado*. Rio de Janeiro: Avenir Editora.

Moreira, Amélia Maria, et al. 1981. *Nossos autores através da crítica*. Vol. 2. São Paulo: Associação Museu Lasar Segall.

"Noticiário da Semana de Mário de Andrade." 1946. *Revista do Arquivo Municipal de São Paulo* 106 (Jan - Fev) 179-91.

"Fictions" of Gender in Contemporary Brazilian Literature

Lucia Helena

Since patterns of gender are constructed in Brazilian society through a patriarchal perspective, this essay will investigate the way in which two contemporary female writers focus on this issue. The essay will take as representative examples of these writers' works the collections of stories *O Ultimo Verão de Copacabana* by Sonia Coutinho (1986) and *Diana Caçadora* by Márcia Denser (1986).

1. The social formation of gender

Though political independence in Brazil was formally declared early in the XIX century, there remained an ambivalent character which determined the profile of Brazilian society during both the colonial and imperial periods.[1] This profile is clarified by the fact that the ruling elite always presented a Janus-faced attitude, which Roberto Schwarz has called "ideas out of place."[2] That is, since the XVIII century, the ruling elite has behaved in accordance with what Paulo Mercadante has referred to, in *A Consciência Conservadora no Brasil*,[3] as the profile of the "senhor dos domínios" — liberal in his commercial transactions with foreigners but patriarchal in the administration of his property. Among the property of these landowners there were two human commodities —slaves and women — controlled by the force of a perverse power and an ingenious technology of gender, a concept which will later be discussed in detail.

In a cultural universe such as the one briefly outlined above, Brazilian literature can offer rich material for the investigation of gender relations. However, to deepen this analysis it is necessary to acknowledge that Brazilian society's "Janus face" determines, as a social construct, the strategies of gender.

196

This "social construct" has produced discourses of all types (within the family, the school, and juridical, economic, political and religious institutions), establishing not only conceptions of power, but also a genderization of culture. Within the discourse of science, for example, Evelyn Fox Keller argues in *Reflections on Gender and Science*, that there is a "deeply rooted mythology that casts objectivity, reason, and mind as male, and subjectivity, feeling, and nature as female" (6-7). In Keller's terms,[4] there is a division of emotional and intellectual labor which attributes to women the domain of the personal, the emotional, and the particular, whereas science is the preserve of men, the province par excellence of the impersonal, the rational, and the general. The consequence of such a division is not simply the exclusion of women from the practice of science, but is also the symptom of a wider and deeper form of genderization, which affects and permeates the whole set of social practices and discourses, contributing to the formation of the genderization of culture.

The hegemonic cultural values of Brazilian national identity present woman as the symbol of the land, interconnecting these images with values of emotionalism and uncontrolled nature. In so doing, Brazilian society offers an understanding of gender as the synonym of sex and establishes a rigid binary opposition, connecting masculinity and femininity to man/woman. In such an understanding of gender the question of cultural and individual (emotional, sexual) identity is not being addressed. What is needed is a theoretical perspective which has the power to dismantle the metaphysical bases of the canon of literary history, questioning the humanism which underlies the binary opposition between masculine and feminine as "natural" essences within a universal culture.

Such a perspective is to be found in de Lauretis's attempt[5] to subvert the grounds of western metaphysics. One of de Lauretis's main objectives is to theorize about gender beyond the limits of sexual difference and of the reductive dimensions of biological determinism. Focusing on the web of power relations, de Lauretis sees gender as a product of a variety of social technologies which operate simultaneously, as a set of techniques of sex which have been developed by the bourgeoisie since the end of the eighteenth century. Those techniques are mechanisms for the elaboration of discourses — pedagogy, medicine, demography and economics — and were supported by the institutions of the state (especially the family).[6] These techniques disseminate modes of knowledge into each individual through the family and other institutions. In short, we could state that the construction of gender is achieved today

> through the various technologies of gender (e.g.
> cinema) and institutional discourses (e.g. theory) with
> power to control the field of social meaning and thus
> produce, promote and "implant" representations of
> gender. (de Lauretis, *The Technology*... 18)

As the above passage suggests, in de Lauretis's analysis the connection between gender and ideology is crucial. The concepts of man and woman are constructed in culture according to the aims of society's dominant class. Far from being biologically determined, the categories of masculinity and femininity are historically constructed, and ideology is a primary element in this construction. In this way, persuasive metaphors of gender are to be found throughout the web of discourses of life in society, relating nature, woman, and emotionalism and science, man, and rationality, thus opposing the feminine and the masculine domains and offering images of truth from these representations, making them appear as the natural essences of daily life. This also occurs in the area of literature, myth and social mythologies (in Barthes's meaning of the term). In the mythical text there are two central characters, the hero (the mythical subject) and the obstacle (which delimits a barrier to the hero's trajectory). The hero who overcomes the obstacle is a representation of the active principle of the culture,[7] which creates and establishes social differences. As a counterpart there is a feminine principle insusceptible of transformation, an element identified with creation, the mother, and space.

Since the novels which celebrated national independence — the historic novels of the romantic period, and most especially *Iracema* (José de Alencar, 1865) — the native woman has been depicted as a South American virgin Indian, living in the hidden forest, and identified with the sap of nationality. In Alencar's novel, the female protagonist (Iracema) gives herself freely to the white colonizer and hero, Martim, after forsaking her own tribe and traditions. In the novel, Iracema represents the passive principle of culture, even though Alencar's conscious intention was to praise American Indian traditions. He transforms Iracema into the image of "mother land," passive and emotional. All the power of conquering is in the hands of Martim. The white man is the active principle of culture and the masculine character ends up being the heroic winner, responsible for establishing the cultural basis of the new land.[8]

Due to the ethnocentric perspective of Alencar's romanticism in approaching Indian culture, to one conscious project of representation and definition of nationality the writer opposes another unconscious project, deeply rooted in the colonizer's ideology. In this way, Alencar elaborates

Iracema[9] within the patterns of a mythical narrative which (transforming the white Martim into the mythical subject) becomes the symbol of the genderization of Brazilian culture depicted in white and western terms.

At the same time in which this occurs, the definition of Brazilian nationality has given ever-increasing support to patriarchal, white, western and European values, which were used to dominate the newly discovered land. The forces which have intertwined, since the XVI century, in the formation of Brazilian society have established not only conceptions of power, but also a technology of social representations from which the way of being of the state and of individuals is defined in their internal and external articulations.

By focusing on the Other and otherness, systematically undermined by this dominant ideology (of which *Iracema* is an impressive example), the contribution of feminist theory has been enormous because it brings about a subtle criticism of the western epistemological tradition. But even before feminist criticism was consistently discussed in Brazil, two (among other) female writers articulated an opposition to the patriarchal tradition depicted in Alencar's *Iracema*.

2. Gender and literature

The works of Sonia Coutinho and Márcia Denser focus on the above mentioned issues and undermine the traditional concepts of a patriarchal society. In their narratives, contrary to Alencar, they elaborate a female character who no longer represents the passive principle of culture but a contradictory and split subject, questioning the inherited concepts of culture, subjectivity, tradition and the place of woman in Brazilian society. *O Ultimo Verão de Copacabana* and *Diana Caçadora* enter the discussion of the gender question because of the way in which these collections of stories are structured. Otherness is their main issue; they highlight the rigidity of the patriarchal binary opposition and deconstruct the ideological genderization of Brazilian society.

2.1 Female solitude in *O Ultimo Verão de Copacabana*, by Sonia Coutinho

In the fourteen stories which comprise *O Ultimo Verão de Copacabana*, the tragic feeling of existence and the impossibility of determining, *a priori*, the justness of one's choices achieves lucid expression. Coutinho presents literature as a way of understanding the erotic experience in a world of loneliness, lack of communication, obsessions and inner disintegration. Many of her works present a female character who moves from a small town in the state of Bahia to a "splendid" metropolis — Rio de Janeiro — the symbol of glamour, social climbing and magnificence.

The short story "Toda Lana Turner tem seu Jonny Stompanato" can be taken as a synthesis of Coutinho's work. The story is about Lana Turner, the American movie star, but also refers to any other woman who tries to become glamorous and awakens from this dream as if it were a nightmare. Alluding to Lana Turner but at the same time addressing another woman who is presented without a name and without biography, the narrative indicates the split identity of the "women" depicted. Between both, the myth and the Other, several names of women are evoked by the narrator:

> Pois Lana Turner, como Madame Bovary para Flaubert, Lana Turner *c'est moi*. Foi o que também pensou a segunda mulher, a outra, o espeiho. (Chama-se Melissa? Ou será Teresa? Quem sabe Joaquina? Dorotéia?). Folheava uma revista, na varandinha de seu apartamento, quando encontrou, com um repentino susto de reconhecimento, com uma estranha e cúmplice compreensão (ela, independente, mitificada, distorcida), o retrato não muito antigo de Lana, numa reportagem nostálgica sobre grandes estrelas do passado. ("Toda Lana..." 4-5)

In contrast to the profiles of the housewives and the nuclear family presented, for example, in Clarice Lispector's *Laços de Família* (1960), Coutinho's protagonists belong to a new cast of women: independent, working outside of the home, appearing sexually free and conscious of their rights. Paradoxically, these women are split into two contrary forces: one is related to consciousness and freedom, the other to unconscious forces that make them feel lonely and guilty because of the freedom they have conquered. To speak about these split women, their dreams and conflicts, is the goal of Coutinho's short narratives.

In "Toda Lana Turner tem seu Jonny Stompanato" Coutinho creates one of the best symbols for this confused human being, lost in the impersonal and aloof atmosphere of the big city. By using the myth of Lana Turner the narrative combines, in this image, two peculiar traits common to the world of the women portrayed by Coutinho: first, the crude reality opposed to the character's dreams and, second, the consumer society which transforms human beings into commodities. In so doing, *O Ultimo Verão de Copacabana* promotes the deconstruction of two female images: the romantic profile of the naive girl who comes from the provincial town and the glamorous woman who inhabits the urban setting.

The result of this process is to induce the reader to uncover and question one of the most striking characteristics of contemporary consumer society: the loss of identity. Such a society transforms things and human beings into an image, a *simulacrum*. Consumer society sells not only commodities but images which people embody, without knowing exactly why.

In Coutinho's narratives, the female character is frequently "buying" myths (the protagonist is imprisoned by the chain of a repetitive and neurotic idealization) and pseudo-truths, even though the women represented are intelligent and well informed, be they writers, artists, or journalists. In a way, these female characters are trapped in a game of ventriloquism. In such a game, the narrative alternates first and third person and the pronoun "I" does not indicate wholeness or complete identity. On the contrary, this "I" who is the subject of the enunciation is a split self. The protagonist is divided between different behaviors and feelings.

In *O Ultimo Verão de Copacabana* Coutinho uses an interesting narrative strategy to indicate this lack of identity: the protagonist's name is rhetorically underlined by the "narrator's text" (in Mieke Bal's terminology). As in the aforementioned example, the female character can be named Melissa, Joaquina, Dorotéia, Teresa, or even Lana.

Through this technique, the narrator alludes to a myth (Lana, the American movie star), to Flaubert's character, Emma Bovary, and to several other "fictions" of a modern and urban profile of woman. The *moi* ("Pois Lana Turner, como madame Bovary para Flaubert, Lana Turner *c'est moi*"), this inner portion of the self, is not — in Coutinho's short story — the synonym of a metaphysical essence. The *moi* is a multiple singularity, formed by contradictory forces, impulses, historical and fictional references. Sometimes the character is depicted as idealistic and romantic like Emma Bovary, sometimes as a modern and independent woman like Lana Turner — and ends up being both at once.

The critical narrative attitude is to demonstrate that the character's quest for identity is undermined by an individual void as well as by the emptiness of a world which denies the metaphysical grounds of humanism, but has not yet succeeded in finding new values to establish and indicate as a possible path to be followed. Coutinho tries to reproduce, in her own process of textualization, the social structure of contemporary society. In this way, her location is, most of the time, a glamorous city: Rio de Janeiro, Hollywood, New York. This setting attracts the female character and develops a compensatory fantasy. At the same time, this attractive city is contrasted with another city without any glamour, which represents the anonymous daily life of an anonymous woman, full of dreams of fame and romantic happiness. The character's split self is located in a split space (glamourous city *vs.* countryside) and confronted with a sex-gender system which confines to opposite sides the "feminine" and the "masculine" domains. Stressing this opposition, Coutinho's narrative points to its despotic and restraining social role.

Trying to avoid an obvious and explicit style, Coutinho adopts — as a sharpened weapon — a subtle and bitter irony with which she "cuts" through the heavy load of myths which envelop the feelings of her female characters. In general, this happens at the moments the female character is about to fall for the tricks of her own imagination. Coutinho also destroys the hypothesis of wholeness and happy endings. Her characters do not "find" their own identities, or "life's truth." They are struggling to dismantle their middle-class mythologies. Sonia Coutinho's characters are internally debating the split between the consciousness of their own loneliness and their romantic dreams. In her narrative the woman is confronted with the deep desolation of solitude, and with the price she sometimes has to pay in order to avoid it. Coutinho's female characters live the loneliness of the modern woman, conscious of solitude's "crespa mordida num sábado à tarde."[10] In Coutinho's narrative the protagonists do not exemplify anymore, as they did in Alencar's novels, the passive principle of culture. They include both male and female conventional roles in their inner configuration and question the pseudo-stability of these functions.

2.2 - The "Janus-faced" woman in *Diana Caçadora*, by Márcia Denser

"Tigresa" is the eighth[11] short story of the collection *Diana Caçadora*, by Márcia Denser. This story narrates Diana Marini's quest for identity, and it is worth saying that Marini is the explicit protagonist of three other short stories of Denser's collection,[12] although the anonymous female protagonists (simply called "I") of the other stories can be taken as a version of the same prototype Diana represents: the upper middle-class woman of the Southeast of Brazil, socially independent but emotionally immature.

Resolute Diana Marini is a woman of many facets. She is a successful journalist who works at an advertising agency as well as a short story writer (a frequent metafictional device in Denser's narrative which enables the narrator to double as the character, while simulating a biographical narrative). Diana Marini is about to leave her work place when she receives a phone call from a fan:

      - Alô!
      - Eu quero falar com Diana Marini.

> - É ela. Atendi o telefone no escuro da agência
> deserta, estava de saída para um coquetel. [....]
> - Meu nome é Lila. Você não me conhece. Estou
> ligando porque ficaria maluca se não te conhecesse.
> Li teu conto na revista. Achei sensacional. Você deve
> ser uma mulher incrível. Preciso te conhecer.
> - Claro, respondi, irrefletidamente impostando o tom
> condescendente de ídolo para o fã. Meu ego
> estremecera até as raízes. ("Tigresa," 121-122)

Diana Marini — as expressed in the above passage — has a weakness: her ego is "touched" by the fan's affection. Since the first lines of the story the reader is told that Diana is a split self: on the one hand, she is strong and independent — she is the hunter, in a metaphorical image of her ability to hunt, that is, to occupy a place conventionally assigned to a man. On the other, she is emotionally dependent, capable of being the prey of another hunter, in this case her fan's prey.

Diana is at once the woman who "vai à luta," socially, sexually and professionally speaking, but she represents a paradoxical woman. On the one hand, she competes with men in the work place, outside the limits of the four walls of the home, an attitude which suggests that she is free; on the other hand, she lives in her parents' household, even though she is more than thirty years old.

As in Coutinho's works, Diana is not only the hunter, but also the prey of another hunter in the sense that she dramatizes the threatening territory between compensatory fantasy and the sense of reality.

But differently from Coutinho's short stories, which insinuate more than demonstrate, Denser's narrative has the tendency to highlight the female protagonist's sensuality, almost in a neo-naturalistic approach:

> [...] o sexo se esticava num lamento em nossas cordas
> vocais como pianinhos de Natal, tinha o sabor amargo
> e perfumado de nozes e avelãs, nossos ventres
> exaustos cultivavam uma excitação estranha, oca,
> vinda não sabíamos de onde [...] eu ficava tão
> molhada, tão doida e tão derretida ao simples roçar
> da tua boca na minha [...]. ("Frutas Secas," 104)

There is something grotesque in Diana Marini, this hedonistic and independent woman, as indicated in the above passage. The narrator has the tendency to highlight the sexual freedom of Diana, who has liberated herself from the constraints of the rigid sex-gender system. But since to be a liberated woman is so hard in a repressive society, this freedom is presented through a grotesque perspective. For example, in another short story in the same collection, "Welcome to Diana," the character drinks heavily and is treated like a prostitute by Fernando, who gives her money after they have gone to bed in a São Paulo motel.[13]

Alcoholism, sexual brutality, homosexual and heterosexual intercourse, all these practices have been experienced by Diana Marini. In "Ladies First," the homosexual allusion is used as a narrative device to stress the quest for identity and illustrates the deconstructionist approach of Denser's style in relation to the sex-gender system's binary opposition:

> Ladies Drinks é um lugar escuríssimo, mas após meia hora, quando você tiver acomodado suas pupilas e começar de fato a distinguir o ambiente, ainda levará um bom tempo até que consiga perceber que o esbelto rapaz sentado na mesa ao lado é mulher, e que aquele gordinho de camisa xadrez, duas mesas à direita, outra mulher [....]. E assim por diante, e daí você talvez ficará um tanto confuso sobre quem *realmente* será mulher lá dentro, embora as haja. *Eu*, por exemplo, era uma mulher, não restava a menor dúvida. Ou restava? Em meio a essa crise de identidades (ou identificações), Das Graças convidou-me para dançar. ("Ladies First," 90-91)

In the above passage, the first person narrator emphasizes the usual sex-gender system's opposition between man/woman: the supposed "esbelto rapaz" is, in fact, a "mulher" as well as "aquele gordinho de camisa xadrez". The expected binary opposition between man/woman or "mulher/rapaz" is misplaced in order to dismantle the reader's expectations, and in so doing the text demonstrates that these "ideas" of gender are "out of place." In order to make the reader criticize the sex-gender code, the first person narrator clarifies even more the narrative device: "*Eu*, por exemplo, era mulher, não restava a menor dúvida. Ou restava?"

As stated before, Denser's characters are a representation of a paradoxical woman. Despite the character's irony and social consciousness of her own marginality, there is a kind of late romanticism in this postmodern woman, who wishes to be loved and to be free at the same time, as in "O animal dos motéis" in the same collection:

> Como se fosse possível o amor, como se fosse fácil,
> muito simples. Possível. Fácil. Simples. Do diâmetro
> de uma moeda de prata. Uma fresta úmida. O ponto
> exato. Amor. (49)

Another important device in Denser's character's quest for identity is the attempt to double, mirror, duplicate one image into another. In *Diana Caçadora*, as in Coutinho's narrative, the reader is confronted by a female character who multiplies herself in several Others. But, whereas in Coutinho's stories the character's split self is more psychologically than sexually suggested, Denser's characters adopt a grotesque narrative mannerism close to the naturalist novel. In this sense, Denser employs a postmodern characteristic: the literature of exhaustion, in which the grotesque functions as the way of demonstrating the erosion of traditional values in the violent and self-destructive urban setting of a well developed consumer society like the city of São Paulo.

What is at stake in Denser's narrative, besides the quest for identity and the discussion of the place of woman in contemporary Brazilian society, is the category of *representation* itself. Denser's work poses a challenge to the ideology of the repressive sex-gender system. Her narrative is the refusal of the masculine desire to fix the woman in a stable and stabilizing identity, as well as the successful attempt to unmask the male-centered frame of mind of Brazilian patriarchalism.

In pointing to Diana Marini's world of repressive binary opposition (the hunter *vs.* the prey; active *vs.* passive; maleness *vs.* femaleness, etc) Marcia Denser's works emphasize that the terrain between the character's social prescriptions and individual subjectivity is one that leaves the female subject hopelessly caught in patriarchal chains. However, the fiction this female character inspires, contains, and dismantles the representations of gender which render it possible.

This postmodernist trait of Denser's narrative questions the entire series of interconnected concepts that have come to be associated with liberal humanism: uniqueness, certainty, unity, transcendence, wholeness. When Denser's short narrative puts these concepts into question it is not to deny them, but to examine their relation to human experience and to literature. Her texts confirm and withdraw these contested notions in an insightful deconstructionist strategy. This also happens, for example, when Denser's text becomes metafictional, as in the following passage:

> E tudo isso quer dizer literatura: a requintada
> crueldade de poder observar as próprias vísceras
> expostas refletidas no espelho e imaginando não ser
> as nossas, como se este refletisse toda a humanidade
> agora — a desumanidade estará dentro de nós, como
> o olho cego da câmara fotográfica, as lâminas frias
> da cortina que fecha e abre a objetiva, o vidro da
> lente, inopinadamente a sangrar, a sangrar, amigos, a
> sangrar, o fluxo maldito chamado literatura, a
> sangrar... ("Relatório Final," 140).

As Craig Owen argues, "when the postmodern work speaks of itself, it is no longer to proclaim its autonomy, its self-sufficiency, its transcendence; rather, it is to narrate its own contingency."[14]

In the above passage, the "maldito fluxo chamado literatura, a sangrar..." is to be related to another flowing. If women were once thought to be the sap of national identity — as a passive principle of the culture as in Alencar's novel — in Denser's narrative they are focused upon through a different perspective, and this process of focusing offers an awareness of the diversity of history and the culture of women and their place in modern society.

3. Untying the knots of the patriarchal tradition

With their critical enterprise, both Coutinho and Denser question the genderization of culture promoted by the patriarchal tradition (represented, for example, in Alencar's novel *Iracema*) with which they, nevertheless, enter into dialogue. In the texts examined in this essay, these two writers criticize the technology of gender which has generated the images of women as the land, passive principle of culture and uncontrolled nature.

Taking the images of the naive provincial girl who dreams of Copacabana (Coutinho) and of the independent journalist Diana Marini (Denser), both writers question the limits of the narrow social background these women come from. They intertwine their critical perspective with the bourgeois mythology the characters both represent and question: the quest for glamour, wholeness, happy endings through marriage, or the guilty rupture from the social roles designed to be followed by them.

Coutinho and Denser break the stability of the patterns of gender (and of the sex-gender system) they are simultaneously depicting and criticizing. In Coutinho's narrative this happens through an acute and bitter demonstration of how devastating the romantic idealization can be for woman's inner and outer world. Apparently free, Coutinho's female characters are bound by the knots of their personal fantasy and social mythology. In Denser's short stories, this happens through versions of a "single developmental tale that provides patterns of female possibilities, vulnerabilities, and power" (Peixoto, 1983, 296). Diana Marini, Denser's main character, is also Denser's leading narrative symbol: the free woman, living in her unbearable loneliness, but "limpa do pseudo-romantismo retórico que caracteriza boa parte do romance brasileiro moderno."[15]

The importance of Coutinho's and Denser's contribution is enormous for the present state of Brazilian society: they highlight the need to dismantle myths and idealization in favor of a conscious sense of the perverse social pressures of a culture which has a split image of itself.

Both *O Ultimo Verão de Copacabana* and *Diana Caçadora* highlight the bitter violence of consumer society relations, with their powerful and corrosive links. These intensely urban upper middle-class short narratives reflect the inward processes familiar to feminist discourse. Thus, the cultural repression of women, produced by patriarchy, is placed within a critical perspective. By means of this perspective, their narrative technique of repetition points to the existence of a paradoxical relationship between the female protagonists and others, as well as within themselves.

The richness of the world of Coutinho's and Denser's characters is a paradoxical one. On the one hand, the elements of imprisonment (daydreams, idealizations, compensatory fantasies, sex-gender prescriptive roles) develop dialectically into their contrary (the consciousness of their split selves and loneliness as a price to be paid for their freedom and independence). On the other hand, the movement directed towards freedom always turns back on itself, thus indicating that *freedom is not a product* but a process, a continuous movement against unconscious constraining forces, both individual and social. There is no "happyending" or easy solution for the conflicts the characters confront. There is no absolute freedom or absolute imprisonment to triumph over. The social technologies of the patriarchal sex-gender system cannot be naively redeemed. At the same time the narrator does not promise to free women from their crushing family and social background.

In these two collections of stories, both Coutinho's and Denser's characters' conclusions correspond to the tenets of some feminist critics today (working outside Brazil) and this could raise some interesting questions that could be addressed: Does it posit a "sameness" to female experience across cultures or at least within all western cultures (or within the Americas)? I think it does not posit a "sameness", nor indicates the presence of an universal "essence" connecting feminist experience across the Americas. But I do think it suggests the existence of an intercultural dialogue between these two Brazilian female writers and European and North American feminist critics and writers, since both Coutinho's and Denser's works present the relations of gender and power as an entangled web of complex interrelationships whose patterns point to a *"labirinto especular no qual continuo vagando, os pés feridos nos meus próprios cacos, armadilhas obstinadas a me reter, infinitamente, destruir-me, reconstruir-me, incessantemente, em dor e em pó"* (Denser, "Welcome...," 29).

Rejecting muteness and passivity both for themselves and for the other women to whom they allude, Coutinho's and Denser's female protagonists are woven into the fabric of a new conception of gender relations. They are part of a new signifying system of culture, and therein lies their meaning and their value.

Notes

[1] See Roberto Schwarz (1977) and Paulo Mercadante (1972).

[2] On this question, see my article "A personagem feminina na ficção brasileira dos anos 80: problemas históricos e teóricos," in *Luso-Brazilian Review* 26.2 (Winter 1989): 43-57.

[3] See Mercadante (1972), 59.

[4] Another important contribution to be considered in these remarks about gender is Elaine Showalter's observations in her essay "Feminism and Literature." Showalter states that "the latest and most rapidly growing mode of American feminist criticism is gender theory" (Showalter (1990), 196). Referring to the work of Joan W. Scott, Showalter identifies three theoretical objectives within gender theory: first, the need to replace biological determinism with the analysis of social constructions in the discussion of sexual difference; second, to develop a specific discipline for the comparative study of man and woman; and third, to transform the current paradigm of these disciplines through the introduction of gender as an analytical category. Although Showalter's analysis opens up many interesting questions in relation to gender, it is necessary to go beyond her view of gynocriticism. Above all, her feminist perspective has its interpretive potential increased if we consider the contribution made by deconstructionism. In this way, the insights of gynocriticism can be enriched, for example, by Teresa de Lauretis's theoretical perspective in *Technologies of Gender*.

[5] See de Lauretis's *Technologies of Gender*.

[6] de Lauretis is using an Althusserian approach in which the family is included in the ideological state apparatuses.

[7] See de Lauretis (1987), 43.

[8] Instead of being biologically determined, the categories of masculinity and femininity are historically constructed, and ideology is a primary set of this construction, as I have said elsewhere. The position assigned to men/women by Alencar in his novel is a position within social life, and the fact that Martim is the conqueror exemplifies the masculine as a sign of power in the sex-gender system of Brazilian society in the nineteenth century.

[9] It is worth remembering that the novel has the suggestive subtitle of "lenda do Ceará" even though Alencar intended to write a historical novel.

[10] See Coutinho (1986), 11.

[11] The book comprises nine short stories.

[12] See, in the same book, "Welcome to Diana," "Hell's Angels," and "Ladies First" (titles in English in the original).

[13] See Denser (1986), 43-44.

[14] Taken from Hutcheon (1988), 59-60.

[15] See Paulo Francis's commentary in Denser (1986), book cover.

Works Cited

Bal, Mieke. *Narratology.* Toronto, Buffalo, London: University of Toronto P., 1985.

Coutinho, Sonia. *O Ultimo Verão de Copacabana.* Rio de Janeiro: José Olympio, 1986.

Denser, Márcia. *Diana Caçadora.* São Paulo: Global, 1986.

Helena, Lucia. "Genre and Gender in Lispector's 'The Imitation of the Rose'." *Style* 24.2 (1990): 215-27.

Hutcheon, Linda. *A Poetics of Postmodernism.* New York and London: Rutledge, 1988.

Keller, Evelyn Fox. *Reflections on Gender and Science.* New Haven: Yale, 1985.

Lauretis, Teresa de. "The Technology of Gender." *Technologies of Gender:*

Essays on Theory, Film, and Fiction. Bloomington: Indiana UP, 1987.
---. "The Violence of Rhetoric: Considerations on Representation and Gender." Lauretis.

Mercadante, Paulo. *A Consciência Conservadora no Brasil*. 2.ed. Rio de Janeiro: Civilização Brasileira, 1972.

Peixoto, Marta. "Family Ties: Female Development in Clarice Lispector." *The Voyage In: Fictions of Female Development*. Ed. Elizabeth Abel, Marianne Hirsch, and Elizabeth Langland. Connecticut: UP of New England, 1983.

Showalter, Elaine. "Feminism and Literature." *Literary Theory Today*. Ed. Petter Collier and Helga Geyer-Ryan. Ithaca: Cornell UP, 1990.
--- . "Women's Time, Women's Space: Writing the History of Female Criticism." *Feminist Issues in Literary Scholarship*. Ed. Shari Benstock. Bloomington: Indiana UP, 1987.

Schwarz, Roberto. *Ao Vencedor as Batatas*. São Paulo: Duas Cidades, 1977.

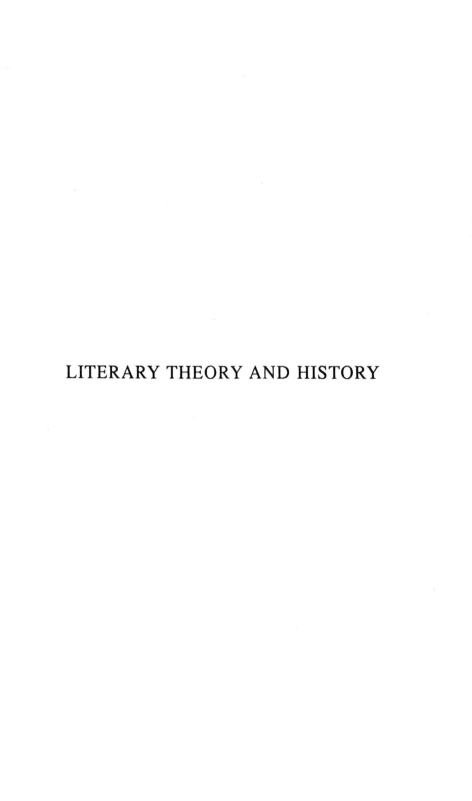

LITERARY THEORY AND HISTORY

Beyond Cannibalism:
Recent Theories of Brazilian
Literature and Culture

Bobby J. Chamberlain

I

When in May, 1928, Oswald de Andrade launched his *Manifesto antropófago* in the first issue of the *Revista da antropofagia* in São Paulo he was attempting to come to grips with a problem that had long bedeviled colonial and post-colonial intellectuals: the matter of cultural dependence and of how to treat metropolitan cultural imports.[1] In short, Oswald's solution was that Brazilians should assimilate European literary and cultural models irreverently, "against the grain," as it were, with an eye to laying bare their capriciousness and partiality. Rather than imitating such models submissively in the manner of the "good" or "noble savage," Brazilians were called upon to emulate the "bad savage," the cannibal, and perform a critical deglutition and digestion of the Western cultural legacy, a renovation by way of absorption and desacralization.

Given the impracticality, indeed, the impossibility, of a wholesale renunciation of imposed European cultural values—political and socio-economic systems, religion, ideological and aesthetic traditions, and, yes, even the Portuguese language—this was, then, the only alternative open to Brazilians other than buying into a cultural matrix inappropriate to their specificity and by which they would forever be judged deficient. Through parodying rather than parroting the discourse of the Portuguese colonizer and his European and American successors, Brazilians could best seek their own cultural and literary voice. Sameness should yield to difference. Subversion and mockery became the order of the day; the self-proclaimed logic of the European *ratio* was traded in for what Lévy-Bruhl had

213

ethnocentrically branded the "prelogical mentality" of the savage. Oswald was thus attempting to effect an axiological inversion of sorts. Allegiance to cherished Portuguese and European cultural traditions was to be replaced by a spiritual identification with the defiance and anthropophagy of some of the very indigenous peoples whom the former had demonized and brutally exterminated as being unworthy of "civilized" treatment. As with other Oswaldian creations, the manifesto was, of course, not without its shock dimension, its desire to épater le bourgeois.

In the sixty-three years since this formulation, particularly in the last twenty, a number of Brazilian literary and cultural critics have grappled with some of the same issues. I do not propose here to discuss all of them; one cannot be exhaustive within the confines of a short presentation. Nor do I seek in the following remarks to valorize them according to some notion of greater or lesser appropriateness. Indeed, let me say from the outset that it seems to me that all of them may validly be used to explicate certain facets of Brazilian literature and culture. But perhaps not simultaneously. I would thus invoke the principle of complementarity here and tend to downplay the importance of any apparent contradictions between one theory and another. What I would like to do, then, is to concentrate on some of the theories put forth by Brazilian literary and cultural critics in the last twenty years. In so doing, I shall try to give special attention to such questions as the appropriation of European and American cultural models and the erection of counter-models grounded on a seemingly irrationalist aesthetic.

II

Antonio Candido, in his 1972 article "Literatura y subdesarrollo," published the following year as "Literatura e subdesenvolvimento" in the journal Argumento, asserts that it is fatuous to try to eliminate all contacts and influences from outside the Brazilian literary tradition. "As nossas literaturas latino-americanas, como também as da América do Norte, são basicamente galhos das metropolitanas" (151), he states in the Portuguese version, echoing a similar affirmation made in his earlier Formação da literatura brasileira (1959).[2] "Sabemos, pois, que somos parte de uma cultura mais ampla, da qual participamos como variedade cultural" (154), he continues. By virtue of its status as a product of European colonization, then, Brazil cannot escape its cultural dependence.

Brazilian literature began as a poor simulacrum of Portuguese or Spanish literature, he contends, and later replaced its imitation of Lusitanian models with allegiance to those of France and, most recently, the United States. Throughout much of the early period, Brazilian writers, deprived of an adequate cultural climate and a sufficient domestic readership, acted as if their ideal reading public were in Europe, he states. Thus, despite periods, such as neoclassicism and romanticism, in which a certain glorification of the exotic wonders of the *país novo* of Brazil was widespread, often to the point of *ufanismo*,[3] there has long existed in Brazil, as in the rest of Latin America, a gulf between a largely illiterate majority and a literate and literary minority often perceived as having little to do with it. It was during the modern period of regionalism and social realism in the 1930s and 40s, in which aesthetics was frequently sacrificed for the sake of documentation, that awareness of "underdevelopment" first came to the fore. Indeed, the persistence of regionalism, he asserts, was itself largely a manifestation of the country's continued perception of itself as a socially and culturally backward nation.

Although he considers outside influences as inevitable and as not necessarily undesirable, Candido regards Brazil and Latin America in general as a "continente sob intervenção" (146) by the mass culture of the developed world, particularly the United States. This, he believes, is undesirable and must be resisted to the extent that it inculcates in Brazilians and other Latin Americans the values and interests of the metropolitan countries from which such films, television programs and other forms of popular culture emanate. For, instead of helping to initiate Latin America's masses into the world of literacy, to introduce them to literature and art, metropolitan popular culture as conveyed by the electronic media (i.e., what has been termed the "culture industry" by the Frankfurt School) has in many cases propelled them from a traditional folk culture straight into what Candido calls "essa espécie de folclore urbano que é a cultura massificada" (145). And in the process, he adds, it has imposed on them "valores duvidosos e bem diferentes dos que o homem culto busca na arte e na literatura" (145).

Alien ideas and exogenous values are again the subject of a collection of essays published by Roberto Schwarz in 1977 under the title *Ao vencedor as batatas*. In what has become one of the most influential critical theories in recent years, Schwarz emphasizes the inappropriateness of imported European concepts and models to the reality of Brazil throughout the latter's history. Among these *idéias fora do lugar*, he cites the European ideology of liberalism, which was totally inappropriate to nineteenth-century Brazilian slavocracy. Brazilians came to use the vocabulary of liberalism largely as ornamentation, as window dressing to conceal their backwardness, for in most cases it had no corresponding referent in Brazilian society and could thus be employed only improperly in the manner of a *catachresis*. In their passage from their origin in the European cultural center to the cultural periphery that was Brazil, European ideas no longer made sense. He feels that such misfits give rise to a series of contradictions, incongruities, and anachronisms in literature, especially in the works of novelists like Alencar, where they emerge, often involuntarily, through the cracks of the work as seeming defects. Many of these inconsistencies, marginal in Alencar, would be consciously recognized and foregrounded in the works of Machado de Assis, he adds:

> One may be tempted to equate Schwarz's theory of *as idéias fora do lugar* with those of earlier Latin American thinkers. The Mexican Samuel Ramos readily comes to mind. In his 1934 study entitled *El perfil del hombre y la cultura en México*, Ramos decries his country's traditional importation of European values and standards inappropriate to it. If Mexicans continue to judge themselves by the standards of others, he claims, they are forever doomed to failure. But whereas he goes on to posit the consequent existence of a national inferiority complex, making use of Adlerian psychology, the Brazilian Schwarz, by contrast, concentrates on the deformations wrought by such inappropriate cultural importations on the society and literature of his country, producing a two-tiered reality that came to be identified with Brazil by those who knew it well and valorizing the role of the favor and the *agregado* as necessary mediations.[4]

In an article published in 1978 in the volume *Uma literatura nos trópicos: Ensaios sobre dependência cultural*, Silviano Santiago asserts that the literary discourse of Brazilians and other Latin Americans takes place in an *entre-lugar*, or "space in between." Brazilians, indeed Latin Americans in general, have replaced racial "purity" with miscegenation. Culturally, they have subverted or hybridized everything from the Portuguese colonizer's language to his religion and aesthetics. Dialogism has come to supplant monologism. It is up to them, then, to continue to transgress European models by "playing with" the sign-systems on which they are grounded. "Entre o sacrifício e o jogo, entre a prisão e a transgressão, entre a submissão ao código e a agressão, entre a obediência e a rebelião, entre a assimilação e a expressão,—ali, nesse lugar aparentemente vazio, seu templo e seu lugar de clandestinidade, ali, se realiza o ritual antropófago da literatura latino-americana" ("O entre-lugar..." 28). Latin Americans are inextricably bound to the European tradition, but let them subvert the imported European models rather than slavishly imitating them. Citing Borges' story of Pierre Menard and his rewriting of the *Quijote*, he notes that "a liberdade, em Menard, é controlada pelo modelo original, assim como a liberdade dos cidadãos dos países colonizados é vigiada de perto pelas forças da metrópole. A presença de Menard — diferença, escritura, originalidade — se instala na transgressão ao modelo, no movimento imperceptível e sutil de conversão, de perversão, de reviravolta" (26-27). The "copy" is, thus, no longer inferior to the "original," but, if anything, is richer and better for the anthropophagic play of difference.[5]

Interestingly, Schwarz has recently written on this same subject. In an article entitled "Nacional por subtração," appearing in the book *Que horas são?* (1987), he seems to agree to some extent with Candido in claiming that it is illusory to imagine that by eliminating all foreign influences one can somehow arrive at an authentically Brazilian culture. At first, he appears also to concur with Silviano regarding the matter of copy and original. "Por que dizer que o anterior prima sobre o posterior, o modelo sobre a imitação, o central sobre o periférico, a infra-estrutura econômica sobre a vida cultural e assim por diante? . . . Seria mais exato e neutro imaginar uma seqüência infinita de transformações, sem começo nem fim, sem primeiro ou segundo, pior ou melhor" (35).

He hastens to add:

> Salta à vista o alívio proporcionado ao amor-próprio
> e também à inquietação do mundo subdesenvolvido,
> tributário, como diz o nome, dos países centrais. De
> atrasados passaríamos a adiantados, de desvio a
> paradigma, de inferiores a superiores . . . isto porque
> os países que vivem na humilhação da cópia explícita
> e inevitável estão mais preparados que a metrópole
> para abrir mão das ilusões da origem primeira. . . .
> Sobretudo o problema da cultura reflexa deixa de ser
> particularmente nosso, e, de certo ângulo, em lugar
> da almejada europeização ou americanização da
> América Latina, assistiríamos à latino-americanização
> das culturas centrais" (35)

Schwarz makes it clear that he rejects this view as well, but cites as recent examples of it the aforementioned article of Silviano's ("O entre-lugar do discurso latino-americano") and another published in 1982 by the *paulista* critic and Concrete poet, Haroldo de Campos.

The article in question was published by Campos as "De la razón antropofágica: Diálogo y diferencia en la cultura brasileña" and appeared in the journal *Vuelta*. It came out the following year in Portuguese in the *Boletim bibliográfico da Biblioteca Mário de Andrade*. Like Silviano's essay, it explicitly identifies itself with Oswald's *antropofagia* and seems, as Schwarz claims, to propound the notion that the "copy" is indeed superior to the "original." Campos posits the existence of a *nacionalismo ontológico* and a contrasting *nacionalismo modal o diferencial*. The first, he associates with an organicist and teleological view of the world, with the search for origins and for the appearance or *parousia* of a national logos. Citing Derrida in this regard, he considers this brand of nationalism to be based on what the latter has called a Western "metaphysics of presence." Trying to detect such *logofanías*, he asserts, leads to the suppression of difference—"las disrupciones, las infracciones, los márgenes, lo 'monstruoso'" (13). By contrast, a modal or differential brand of nationalism, he proclaims, foregrounds such difference, eschewing the quest for essences and *teloi*. It represents a dialogic movement and stresses the discontinuous, heterogeneous and fragmentary side of history, while repudiating what he terms the "metáfora sustancialista de la evolución natural, gradualista, harmónica" (13).

Campos sees only minor differences between the sociological criticism of Antonio Candido, mentioned above, and the more aesthetically oriented approach of the other prominent literary historiographer, Afrânio Coutinho, usually identified with Anglo-American New Criticism. Whatever their differences, both are engaged in the same essentialist search, he states. However, he praises Candido's well-known article on Manuel Antônio de Almeida's *Memórias de um sargento de milícias* (1852-53) ("Dialética da malandragem," 1970) for its detection of a "*malandro* tradition" in Brazilian literature. For it is this marginal tradition, which may be equated, he notes, with Bakhtinian carnivalization, that best characterizes *antropófago* authors running from Gregório de Matos to Sousândrade, to Mário de Andrade, Oswald de Andrade, the Concretist poets and *tropicalista* musicians, among others. Campos casts all of these authors as belonging to an anti-normative tradition in Brazilian literature, as deconstructors of the official logocentric discourse.

Lúcia Helena, in her 1983 book, *Uma literatura antropofágica*, confirms many of Campos' assertions. Moreover, she notes that Brazilian culture has been characterized by a dialectic structuring in which two "linhas de força" have interacted with one another:

uma matriz judaico-cristã, de influência da colonização européia, a que chamaremos de *linha do bom senso e do bom gosto*, acentuadamente marcada por um progressivo modelo racionalizante, e que é literariamente expressa por uma retórica clássica de cunho realista e referencial; e uma matriz carnavalizante, a que chamaremos de *linha do muito riso e do pouco siso*, que se explicita num estilo 'dionisíaco', contestador, cuja principal marca é a crítica da cultura dominante realizada por um acervo de gestos marginais, dentre eles o veio popularizante do riso aberto e desabrido que destroniza o poder. (91)

III

I should like, if I had the time, to discuss the theories and findings of other contemporary Brazilian critics: the *relacionalismo* proposed by Roberto Da Matta as a kind of Brazilian aesthetic par excellence; Flora Süssekind's analysis in her "Tal país, qual romance?" of the three periods of Brazilian "naturalism" from the point of view of filiation and similarity; and the study of hierarchy in the Brazilian novel by Roberto Reis in his *A permanência do círculo* using the *centro/periferia*, or *núcleo/nebulosa*, models borrowed from the social sciences. The inclusion of such works, however, is regrettably beyond the purview of the present paper and will thus have to wait for future critical undertakings.

Still, it should be possible to draw several conclusions from the foregoing discussion. But for minor discrepancies, it would appear that all of the critics surveyed agree that Brazilian literature and culture are irrevocably linked to the Western cultural legacy and in great part derive their sustenance from it. Some of the formulations are, of course, primarily descriptive while others are of a more prescriptive tenor. Moreover, all but Candido and Schwarz seem to advocate the *antropofágico* point of view, that there is, or should be, a strong tendency in Brazilian literature to "cannibalize" imported European or American cultural and literary models in a critical or parodic fashion. My title, "Beyond Cannibalism," might better be formulated, then, not as a statement of reality, but as an interrogation. Indeed, can we speak about having gone beyond *antropofagia* if a large number of the contemporary theories of Brazilian literature and culture simply engage in working out the details of what in Kuhnian fashion might be dubbed the "anthropophagic critical paradigm"?[6]

To regard such theoretizations as Silviano's "entre-lugar do discurso latino-americano" and Campos' and Lúcia Helena's efforts to delineate anthropophagic currents in Brazilian literature as a mere rehashing of Oswaldian notions or even a working out of the details of the relationship of *antropofagia* to the works of specific Brazilian authors does not, to my mind, do justice to the critics and projects in question, however. To be sure, such projects might better be characterized as attempts to relate *antropofagia* to other, non-Brazilian critical theories, such as Bakhtinian dialogism and carnivalization, Derridean deconstruction or the various formulations of the baroque and neobaroque, in a word, to bring Brazilian critical theory into a dialogue with its metropolitan counterparts. And, in the case of critics such as Candido and Schwarz, it would, of course, be erroneous to speak of anthropophagic affiliations, at least on the basis of the works discussed.

Just as all of the critics mentioned subscribe to the notion of Brazilian culture's inevitable ties to the larger Western cultural matrix, they likewise feel free to draw on the cultural and literary theories of the First World and to mold them to the specificities of Brazilian literature and culture. I am reminded here of the remarks made on this topic by Gayatri Chakravorty Spivak, herself an Indian postcolonial critic schooled in Marxism, feminism, and deconstruction. "I am . . . far from averse to learning from the work of Western theorists," she observes, "though I have learned to insist on marking their positionality as investigating subjects" (296).[7] By the same token, it seems to me that Brazilian critics for the most part do not hesitate to make use of European and American critical theory provided that they can appropriate it *critically* or employ it "under erasure," as Derrida would say, thus indirectly circumscribing the positionality of its authors. What is more, they frequently seek to dialogue with it, knowing very well that neither First-World nor Brazilian or other Third-World theory developed in a vacuum, indeed, that all theoretical discourse is eminently intertextual. Theories such as *antropofagia*, Silviano's "entre-lugar do discurso latino-americano" and Da Matta's *relacionalismo* are themselves deliberately grounded on intertexuality.[8] And, to the extent, that Brazilians invoke metropolitan theories "against the grain," or at least with some skepticism, they too may be said to fulfill Oswald's anthropophagic exhortation.[9]

That there exists a radical power disparity, or *anisocracy*, between metropolitan and Brazilian or other Third-World critical discourse is, of course, acknowledged. Indeed, for the most part, critical discursive exchange between the First and Third Worlds has traditionally been less a Rortian dialogue than a one-way street.[10] Talal Asad, in an essay published as part of the 1986 volume on the poetics and politics of ethnography, *Writing Culture*, has affirmed the existence of what he calls "weak" and "strong" languages, noting that the former "are more likely to submit to forcible transformation in the translation process than the other way around" (157-58). Here, I would hasten to add that much the same dichotomy exists, and has long existed, with respect to discursive impact. Even a metropolitan language such as Portuguese has frequently been characterized with regret by some of its most illustrious authors as a *beco-sem-saída* providing no international outlet. In the case of Brazilian and other Third-World critical theory, then, translation into English or French, in light of Asad's observations, yields only a partially satisfactory solution.

In writing and researching the present remarks, I was frequently reminded of Roberto Fernández Retamar's 1971 essay, "Calibán," itself an eminently anthropophagic piece, to my way of thinking. In it, he resumes the defiant, irreverent posture of Oswald de Andrade in recommending the adoption of Calibán, the cannibal or "bad savage," as a symbol for Latin Americans, turning what was once meant as a scornful insult into a badge of pride.[11] I would submit that this is also essentially what Oswald attempted to do, albeit in a satirical, farcical context, that is, to erect a figure threatening to self-perceived European and American rationalism and civility, to espouse the abhorrent, the illogical.

It has long been a stereotype for Europeans and North Americans to regard Latin Americans as an emotionally driven people, as someone less rational than themselves. Jack Pizzey, in one episode of his documentary film series "South American Journey," seen in the United States on public television, remarks: "They're not a profound people, these Cariocas." He then goes on to assert that they are not likely to produce a Tolstoy or some other great intellectual, oblivious to the existence of Machado de Assis, Clarice Lispector and other eminent Brazilian writers. But, such stereotypes are frequently forthcoming from Latin Americans themselves, even from contemporary Latin American intellectuals. César Fernández Moreno, in the introduction to *América Latina en su literatura*, the very volume in which Candido published his "Literatura y subdesarrollo," reinforces this negative image when he warns the reader about the following essays: "No se espere, pues, un rigor científico, una precisión sociológica o estética, una ordenación histórica, sino el nervioso saltar del pensamiento sobre una realidad que también se desplaza imprevisiblemente, como un potro sin domar" (16). Some of the more perceptive critics of Latin American culture and literature, both Latin American and non-Latin American, have wondered in recent years about the negative fallout deriving from the characterization of Latin Americans, particularly in the narrative of the *boom*, as a people given more to "magical realism" than to rational or logical thought.[12]

I do not wish to quibble about the positive or negative subtext of the *Manifesto antropófago* or, for that matter, of Fernández Retamar's "Calibán." Nor do I wish to tar latter-day theories of Brazilian literature and culture with an irrationalist brush. Indeed, all of the aforementioned pieces, enthusiastic though they may be for the *antropofágico* creed, are located solidly within the realm of contemporary Western academic scholarship. If anything, they are cast in a rationalist mold. And, for better or for worse, none of them seems to possess quite the same enthusiasm for espousing the irrational that some would impute to Oswald, notwithstanding his tongue-in-cheek manner. Suffice it to say, then, that reveling in the negative stereotypes, particularly as a means of ridiculing them or their creators is quite a different matter from taking them seriously or apologizing for their accuracy. The *tropicalismo* of the 1960s attests to this point. There is undoubtedly a danger of perpetuating the irrationalist stereotype of Latin Americans, and we should all be aware of it. But, in my opinion, what Oswald and many of his more recent adherents have sought to do is not to perpetuate them but to disarm them.

Beyond cannibalism, then, a number of the recent theories acknowledge their debt to Oswald de Andrade and a few of them seek to extend his arguments. Others have chosen different directions, but, in fact, sometimes appear still to be reacting to the *antropofágico* stimulus, albeit negatively. All of them, whatever their leaning, seem to have in common a desire to relate the Brazilian critical experience to that of a larger Western tradition. Not only by imitating that tradition, but also by affirming the radical difference between it and themselves.

Notes

[1] A facsimile edition of the various issues of the *Revista da antropofagia* (1928-29), introduced by Augusto de Campos, was published in 1975. In addition, the text of the manifesto may be found in Oswald de Andrade, *Obras completas* (Vol. 6, *Do Pau-Brasil à Antropofagia e às utopias*, pp. 11-19) and in many anthologies, including Teles (293-300) and Candido and Castello (III, 66-74). For a discussion of the manifesto and of *antropofagia*, see, for example, Campos, Helena, Nunes, and Larsen (78-86); see also Bary, "Civilization, Barbarism, 'Cannibalism,'" and its later, expanded version, "The Tropical Modernist as Literary Cannibal."

[2] In *Formação*... (I, 9, 10), he states: "A nossa literatura é galho secundário da portuguesa, por sua vez arbusto de segunda ordem no jardim das Musas... (. . .) Comparada às grandes, a nossa literatura é pobre e fraca. Mas é ela, não outra, que nos exprime."

[3] The term *ufanismo* denotes excessive patriotic bragging, especially in literature, where it often takes the form of extolling Brazil's ostensibly boundless natural resources.

[4] *Agregado* designates a boarder who lives with a family almost as one of its members.

[5] Silviano also treats the subject of copy and original in the article "Apesar de dependente, universal." Cf. Costa Lima ("Posfácio"): "Deixar de ser colônia também significa perguntar-se pelo espectro de racionalidade que nos tem sido proposto e reconhecer as áreas que esse espectro tem domesticado. Aceitar esse desafio significa deixar de nos vermos como repetidores da cultura metropolitana. Qualquer pois que seja a eficácia da hipótese do controle parece pelo menos inquestionável que ela manifesta a possibilidade doutro modo de relacionamento de nós, latino-americanos, com a cultura ocidental. Em vez de seus repetidores, podemos ser seus interlocutores."

[6] Kuhn, in his *The Structure of Scientific Revolutions*, regards the history of science as a succession of interpretive "paradigms," which change only rarely. In his opinion, science develops through paralogism, or quantum leaps, rather than by evolution or sheer accumulation. Indeed, most "normal science," consists, as he sees it, of a working out of the details of the dominant paradigm.

[7] Lucas (73, 76-77) espouses an opposing view with respect to the importation of First-World theory by Third-World countries. "Quando se importa o método, repita-se, importa-se o pensamento" (76). For an examination of First-World studies of Third-World literature—specifically that of Latin America—see Franco and Chamberlain.

[8] Indeed, it would not be amiss, I think, to regard *antropofagia* and similar notions as theories of *intertextuality*, in the same manner that Bloom's account of the coming into being of a poem through an oedipal confrontation between a poetic newcomer and a predecessor text has been so regarded. See Bloom, *The Anxiety of Influence*, and Culler, *The Pursuit of Signs*, 107-11.

[9] Rama (32-56) invokes not the notion of intertextuality but that of *transculturation* to describe the process of appropriation of the culture of the European or North American metropolis by Latin Americans. He quotes the Cuban Fernando Ortiz (*Contrapunteo cubano del tabaco y el*

azúcar. [Caracas: Biblioteca Ayacucho, 1978], p. 86): "Entendemos que el vocablo *transculturación* expresa mejor las diferentes fases del proceso transitivo de una cultura a otra, porque éste no consiste solamente en adquirir una cultura, que es lo que en rigor indica la voz anglo-americana *aculturación*, sino que el proceso implica necesariamente la pérdida o desarraigo de una cultura precedente, lo que pudiera decirse una parcial desculturación, y, además, significa la consiguiente creación de nuevos fenómenos culturales que pudieran denominarse *neoculturación*" (Rama 32-33). Interestingly, he notes that Latin Americans' exercise of independence and selectivity in importing such exogenous cultural elements has often led them to appropriate the marginal, the heterodox, "selecciona[ndo] los elementos recusadores del sistema europeo o norteamericano que se producían en las metrópolis, desgajándolos de su contexto y haciéndolos suyos en un riesgoso modo abstracto" (39).

[10] Said ("Representing..." 210) makes this observation, noting that Rorty, Bakhtin, and Habermas seem to ignore this power-ladenness in their respective theoretical formulations; cf. Said (*The World...* 48): ". . . far from being a type of conversation between equals, the discursive situation is more usually like the unequal relation between colonizer and colonized, oppressor and oppressed."

[11] States Fernández Retamar (14): "Our symbol then is not Ariel, as Rodó thought, but rather Caliban. This is something that we, the *mestizo* inhabitants of these same isles where Caliban lived, see with particular clarity: Prospero invaded the islands, killed our ancestors, enslaved Caliban, and taught him his language to make himself understood. What else can Caliban do but use that same language—today he has no other—to curse him, to wish that the 'red plague' [invoked by Shakespeare's Caliban in reproaching his master, Prospero] would fall on him? I know no other metaphor more expressive of our cultural situation, of our reality." The essayist goes on to observe (16): "In proposing Caliban as our symbol, I am aware that it is not entirely ours, that it is also an alien elaboration, although in this case based on our concrete realities. But how can this alien quality be entirely avoided? The most venerated word in Cuba—*mambí*—was disparagingly imposed on us by our enemies at the time of the war for independence, and we still have not totally deciphered its meaning. It seems to have an African root, and in the mouth of the Spanish colonists implied the idea that all *independentistas* were so many black slaves—emancipated by that very war for independence—who of course constituted the bulk of the liberation army. The *independentistas*, white and black, adopted with honor something that colonialism meant as an insult. This is

the dialectic of Caliban." Cf. Gates (63): "The ironic reversal of a received racist image of the [North American] black as simianlike, the Signifying Monkey—he who dwells at the margins of discourse, ever punning, ever troping, ever embodying the ambiguities of language—is our trope for repetition and revision, indeed, is our trope of chiasmus itself, repeating and simultaneously reversing in one deft, discursive act. If Vico and Burke, or Nietzsche, Paul de Man, and Harold Bloom, are correct in identifying 'master tropes,' then we might think of these as the 'master's tropes,' and of *signifying* as the slave's trope, the trope of tropes . . ." Gates goes on to relate the Signifying Monkey to Èsù-Elegbára (Exu, Legba, Echu-Legua, Papa Legba, Papa La Bas), the messenger god and trickster figure of Yoruba, Afro-Caribbean, African-American and Afro-Brazilian religious tradition.

[12] Franco (504-05), in particular, makes this point in her discussion of metropolitan discourse on the Third World.

Works Cited

Andrade, Oswald de. "Manifesto antropofágico." *Revista da antropofagia* 1, 1 (maio de 1928): 3, 7.

---. *Obras completas.* Vol. 6, *Do Pau-Brasil à Antropofagia e às utopias: Manifestos, teses de concursos e ensaios.* Rio de Janeiro: Civilização Brasileira, 1972.

Asad, Talal. "The Concept of Cultural Translation in British Social Anthropology." In *Writing Culture: The Poetics and Politics of Ethnography.* Ed. James Clifford and George E. Marcus. Berkeley: Univ. of California Press, 1986. 141-64.

Bary, Leslie. "Civilization, Barbarism, 'Cannibalism': The Question of National Culture in Oswald de Andrade." *Toward Socio-Criticism: Selected Proceedings of the Conference 'Luso-Brazilian Literatures, A Socio-Critical Approach'.* Ed. Roberto Reis. Tempe, AZ: Arizona State University, Center for Latin American Studies, 1991. 95-100.

---. "The Tropical Modernist as Literary Cannibal: Cultural Identity in Oswald de Andrade." *Chasqui* 20. 2 (noviembre 1991): 10-19.

Bloom, Harold. *The Anxiety of Influence.* New York: Oxford Univ. Press, 1973.

226　　　　　Bobby J. Chamberlain

Campos, Haroldo de. "De la razón antropofágica: Diálogo y diferencia en la cultura brasileña." *Vuelta* 68. 6 (1982): 12-19. [A Portuguese version, entitled "Da razão antropofágica: Diálogo e diferença na cultura brasileira," was published in the *Boletim bibliográfico Biblioteca Mário de Andrade* 44 (1983): 107-25.]

Candido, Antonio. "Dialética da malandragem: Caracterização das *Memórias de um sargento de milícias*." *Revista do Instituto de Estudos Brasileiros* 8 (1970): 67-89.

---. *Formação da literatura brasileira: Momentos decisivos*. 3ª ed. 2 vols. São Paulo: Martins, 1969. [1st ed., 1959]

---. "Literatura e subdesenvolvimento." *A educação pela noite e outros ensaios*. São Paulo: Ática, 1987. 140-62. [Published originally in Spanish as "Literatura y subdesarrollo" in César Fernández Moreno, ed. *América Latina en su literatura*. México: Siglo Veintiuno, 1972, and later in Portuguese in *Argumento* 1 (outubro de 1973): 7-24.]

Candido, Antonio, and José Aderaldo Castello. *Presença da literatura brasileira*. 2ª ed. 3 vols. São Paulo: Difusão Européia do Livro, 1966.

Chamberlain, Bobby J. "Through Eagle Eyes: U.S. Brazilianists and Their Relationship to Brazilian Literature." *Hispania* 74. 3 (September 1991): 604-09.

Culler, Jonathan. *The Pursuit of Signs: Semiotics, Literature, Deconstruction*. Ithaca, NY: Cornell Univ. Press, 1981.

Da Matta, Roberto. "*Dona Flor e seus dois maridos*: Um romance relacional." *Tempo Brasileiro 74: Jorge Amado, Km 70* (julho-setembro de 1983): 3-33.

Fernández Moreno, César. "Introducción." *América Latina en su literatura*. Ed. César Fernández Moreno. México: Siglo Veintiuno, 1972. 5-18.

Fernández Retamar, Roberto. "Caliban." *Caliban and Other Essays*. Trans. Edward Baker. Minneapolis: Univ. of Minnesota Press. 3-45.

Franco, Jean. "Beyond Ethnocentrism: Gender, Power, and the Third-World Intelligentsia." In *Marxism and the Interpretation of Culture*. Ed. Cary Nelson and Lawrence Grossberg. Urbana, IL: Univ. of Illinois Press, 1988. 503-15.

Gates, Henry Louis, Jr. "The 'Blackness of Blackness': A Critique of the Sign and Signifying Monkey." In *Contemporary Literary Criticism: Literary and Cultural Studies.* Ed. Robert Con Davis and Ronald Schleifer. 2nd ed. New York: Longman, 1989. 629-58.

Helena, Lucia. *Uma literatura antropofágica.* Fortaleza: Univ. Federal do Ceará, 1983.

Kuhn, Thomas S. *The Structure of Scientific Revolutions.* 2nd ed., enlarged. Chicago: Univ. of Chicago Press, 1970. [1st ed., 1962]

Larsen, Neil. *Modernism and Hegemony: A Materialist Critique of Aesthetic Agencies.* Minneapolis: Univ. of Minnesota Press, 1990.

Lévy-Bruhl, Lucien. *How Natives Think.* Trans. Lilian A. Clare. New York: Knopf, 1966.

Lima, Luiz Costa. "Posfácio." *O controle do imaginário: Razão e imaginação no Ocidente.* 2ª ed. São Paulo: Brasiliense, 1989.

Lucas, Fábio. *Vanguarda, história e ideologia da literatura.* São Paulo: Ícone, 1985.

Nunes, Benedito. "Antropofagia ao alcance de todos." In Oswald de Andrade. *Obras completas.* Vol. 6, *Do Pau-Brasil à Antropofagia e às utopias: Manifestos, teses de concursos e ensaios.* Rio de Janeiro: Civilização Brasileira, 1972. xi-liii.

Rama, Ángel. *Transculturación narrativa en América Latina.* México: Siglo Veintiuno, 1982.

Ramos, Samuel. *El perfil del hombre y la cultura en México.* México, 1934.

Reis, Roberto. *A permanência do círculo: Hierarquia no romance brasileiro.* Niterói: EDUFF; Brasília: INL, 1987.

Revista da antropofagia. Edição fac-similar. Introdução de Augusto de Campos. São Paulo: Abril-Metal Leve, 1975.

Said, Edward W. "Representing the Colonized: Anthropology's Interlocutors." *Critical Inquiry* 15 (Winter 1989): 205-25.

---. *The World, the Text, and the Critic.* Cambridge, MA: Harvard Univ. Press, 1983.

Santiago, Silviano. "Apesar de dependente, universal." *Vale quanto pesa: Ensaios sobre questões político-culturais.* Rio de Janeiro: Paz e Terra, 1982. 13-24.
---. "O entre-lugar do discurso latino-americano." *Uma literatura nos trópicos: Ensaios sobre dependência cultural.* São Paulo: Perspectiva, 1978. 11-28.

Schwarz, Roberto. *Ao vencedor as batatas.* São Paulo: Duas Cidades, 1977. [See especially "As idéias fora do lugar," pp. 13-28, and "A importação do romance e suas contradições em Alencar," pp. 29-60]
---. "Nacional por Subtração." *Que horas são?* São Paulo: Companhia das Letras, 1987. 29-48.

Spivak, Gayatri Chakravorty. "Can the Subaltern Speak?" In *Marxism and the Interpretation of Culture.* Ed. Cary Nelson and Lawrence Grossberg. Urbana, IL: Univ. of Illinois Press, 1988. 271-313.

Süssekind, M. Flora. "Tal Brasil, qual romance?" M.A. thesis PUC Rio de Janeiro 1982.

Teles, Gilberto Mendonça. *Vanguarda européia e modernismo brasileiro.* 3ª ed., rev. e aum. Petrópolis: Vozes; Brasília, INL, 1976.

A Respeito da Questão da Pós-Modernidade no Brasil

Francisco Caetano Lopes Junior

"La gare pleure les voyageurs..."
René Char

"Everybody comes from the other side of the world."
Janet Frame

Na década passada (e, sem dúvida alguma, até os dias de hoje), a discussão a respeito da pós-modernidade tomou conta de alguns setores acadêmicos numa dimensão inimaginável. A princípio, tomada como mais um "modismo", depois com mais "seriedade", encorpando lentamente, crescendo e marcando uma presença forte, decidida. A bibliografia cresceu avassaladora e rapidamente, deixando, no entanto, margem para que as controvérsias se estabelecessem e, de alguma maneira, criassem raízes. Este panorama que podia ser visto de uma ponte européia ou norte-americana frutificou em terras de Brasil. Mais uma novidade importada, diriam alguns, tendo como limite a polêmica estabelecida entre Lyotard e Habermas ou os artigos mapeadores de Jameson; sem dúvida alguma, uma questão candente, expressariam convictamente outros, tentando entender mais concretamente o que aconteceria com tais indagações em terras tupiniquins.

Antes de continuarmos, devemos dizer que a velha pergunta a respeito da nossa identidade foi, de novo e mais uma vez, levantada, pois não se tinha nenhuma certeza a respeito de que tipo de contribuição o

229

debate traria para a nossa afirmação cultural e artística (e não só). A velha querela entre a nossa atitude de seres autóctones ou meros reprodutores de idéias (fora ou não do lugar) voltava com alguma força e fazia com que as respostas mais díspares fossem dadas, sem se fechar, como não poderia deixar de ser, o debate. Este continua até hoje e, assumindo outras faces, continua a tirar o sono de muita gente boa...

Mais ainda, a questão a respeito da pós-modernidade recolocava no Brasil (bem como em toda a América Latina e outros centros chamados de "periféricos", com todas as aspas possíveis e imagináveis) problemas de ordem política, moral e ética. A discussão, longe de encontrar um denominador comum (como não poderia deixar de ser em se tratando da matéria sobre a qual refletia), fazia mortos à direita e à esquerda (dicotomia ainda existente em terras de Seu Cabral) ou como nos diz muito acertadamente Luiz Costa Lima:

> Mas convertê-la (a questão da pós-modernidade) em pura manifestação de estilo, que se rebelaria contra as normas institucionalizadas do alto modernismo, significa perder a oportunidade de repensar seriamente nossas próprias condições de vida. (Costa Lima, 1991, 136)

Antes de continuarmos nesta trilha, façamos um pouco de história a respeito dessa "idéia fixa" cuja presença nos causa tantos dissabores. Fincando a bandeira em terra nem sempre fértil, alguns especialistas brasileiros (via de regra com excelentes conexões com o panorama intelectual do além-mar) começam a discutir a questão, abrindo o debate não só para o que se poderia encontrar no estrangeiro mas também para que os pressupostos teóricos em formação fossem empregados estrategicamente para o entendimento da nossa própria realidade. Em cursos oferecidos no meio da década dos anos oitenta, para sermos mais específicos no segundo semestre de 1985, o professor Silviano Santiago, neste tempo trabalhando nos programas de pós-graduação da Pontifícia Universidade Católica do Rio de Janeiro, acendia a chama de tal debate e convocava seus estudantes e pares a uma reflexão a respeito do assunto. Ainda neste mesmo ano, mas em outra ponta do eixo cultural brasileiro, aparecia na revista *Novos estudos CEBRAP* uma tradução de uma conferência do professor Fredric Jameson intitulada "Pós-modernismo e sociedade de consumo". Os ventos da dúvida e da perplexidade varriam nossos campos e, mais uma vez, causava uma série de danos, por vezes irreparáveis. Mas a estória não pára por aí.

Mais tarde, em 1988, o debate se perpetuava com o aparecimento de um livro fino na quantidade de folhas, mas extremamente polêmico no que que diz respeito às questões trazidas para o debate, trata-se da obra *Pós-modernidade*, publicada pela editora da Universidade de Campinas. Muito recentemente, um novo trabalho reacende a fogueira de tais paixões, estamos falando do volume de ensaios organizado pela professora Heloísa Buarque de Holanda, intitulado *Pós-modernidade e política*. As dúvidas e os rancores continuam, como se pode ver, no centro de tais discussões a respeito de um assunto tão polêmico e controvertido, como sói ser este a respeito da pós-modernidade. Os artigos dos professores Luiz Costa Lima e Silviano Santiago também contribuem para trazer lenha à fogueira, no caso do primeiro, tentando a divulgação da polêmica entre Habermas e Lyotard e ajudando-nos a pensar a nossa condição específica de "sociedade à margem" ("Pós-modernidade: contraponto tropical"); já no do segundo, oferecendo-nos uma possibilidade de teorizar sobre as características e configurações possíveis do narrador pós-moderno a partir da obra do contista brasileiro Edilberto Coutinho ("O narrador pós-moderno").

Antes ainda de ir em frente, devemos dizer que esta nossa escolha acima mencionada é parcial nos seus dois sentidos da palavra: primeiro, faz um recorte bastante resumido da questão, como não poderia deixar de ser, já que todos somos humanos e a totalidade não parece ser a matéria com a qual estamos mais familiarizados; segundo, opta por um determinado lado do problema, esquecendo, de propósito (e nem sempre), outras vertentes que também poderiam ser escolhidas como válidas para a leitura do problema. Feitas estas ressalvas necessárias e oportunas, podemos continuar este nosso trajeto nesta nau dos insensatos...

Comecemos, então, por estabelecer um elo que, a nosso ver, reveste-se de profunda importância: a relação entre literatura pós-colonial e pós-modernidade[1]. Como já sabemos de longa data, a escritura literária pós-colonial e os questionamentos efetuados pela teoria da literatura pós-estruturalista (e aqui estamos também incluindo as vertentes do pós-marxismo e do feminismo) se tangenciam em vários e múltiplos pontos. Tais formulações teóricas dialogam extensivamente com estas literaturas "periféricas" (conservando-se todas as aspas possíveis e imagináveis mais uma vez), trazendo para o centro do debate questões candentes e importantes para que se possa desconstruir, com mais eficácia, o edifício da empresa colonial e pós-colonial. É evidente que não estamos querendo dizer que foram estas teorias que "descobriram" tais questões no que diz respeito à literatura brasileira, muito pelo contrário, do diálogo estabelecido surge um atrito (por vezes bastante forte) que faz com que o debate cresça e frutifique (para continuarmos na mesma cadeia semântica do universo de Vieira).

Não devemos cair na arapuca de que tal discussão obscurece ou coloca em segundo plano a nossa fundamental questão do local e do particular, também não devemos cair no outro campo (minado) da nossa total e completa independência: somos autóctones e tudo que se refere a nós nasce em nosso próprio solo.

Estamos mais do que conscientes de que a utilizacão totalmente acrítica daquele casamento (sempre por interesse) pode conduzir-nos à incorporação de seus pressupostos teóricos num sentido internacional e universalista, repetição sem graça e aguada do velho paradigma da dominação. Tal modelo de operacionalização faz com que o pós-modernismo chegue até nós em duas vertentes distintas (uma de resistência e outra de reação, para utilizarmos a nomenclatura proposta pela professora Heloísa Buarque de Holanda), levando-nos, por vezes, a comprar gato por lebre. Como nos explica muito claramente a referida professora acima citada:

> Este último (o pós-modernismo de reação) é o que geralmente informa o senso comum sobre a noção de pós-moderno. É aquele que, liderados pelos neoconservadores, rejeita o modernismo em nome dos males da modernização e impõe uma cultura "afirmativa". O pós-modernismo de resistência, por sua vez, surge como uma contraprática não só da cultura oficial do modernismo mas também da "falsa normatividade" de um pósmodernismo reacionário. (Hollanda, 1991, 8-9)

Há também o perigo (sempre muito presente em termos da ideologia da cultura brasileira) de essa apropriação de teorias européias e norte-americanas incoporar-nos a um discurso internacional pós-moderno, reproduzindo mais uma vez e deslocadamente antigas técnicas da empresa colonial. Como sabemos de longa data, a história (oficial) da literatura e os movimentos críticos que fizeram a sua leitura no século XX sempre andaram de mãos dadas com o próprio imperialismo (basta que pensemos na rigidez de espartilhos dos efeitos do "new criticism" em termos da formação do cânone da Literatura Brasileira), isto sem levarmos em conta as leituras "antropológicas" feitas sobre o Brasil elaboradas por intelectuais nativos que estudaram nos Estados Unidos.

Temos muito claramente em nossas mentes que a relação entre o modernismo (recuamos um pouco mais no tempo a fim de trazermos mais luzes para o centro do debate) e as suas diversas formas de experimentação é um produto (evidentemente não terminado, estabelecendo aqui um diálogo

com Habermas) do contacto entre as culturas ditas "centrais" e as "outras".
Assim, como todos sabemos, enquanto a Europa descobria as máscaras
africanas e de outros lugares também "exóticos", o modernismo brasileiro
recuperava suas próprias raízes, vinculando sua literatura de cariz "branco"
às "fontes" indígenas e africanas. Sinteticamente, tal encontro pode ser
achado na "blague" de um dos mais controvertidos modernistas brasileiros,
Oswald de Andrade: "Descobri o Brasil olhando a Plâce Clichy". A partir
de tal movimento artístico, descobre-se que há outras possibilidades de
representação da realidade brasileira que pode passar por diferentes
caminhos, múltiplos desvãos. As viagens feitas pelos modernistas assumem
um caráter interno, de busca incessante da realidade nacional (Macunaíma
seria o exemplo mais evidente de tal procura). Com faca incisiva a cortar os
tecidos mais rígidos da nossa ideologia cultural, Silviano Santiago nos
aponta singularmente as contradições do movimento:

SEU SENNA — III

Mas o Osvardo
(depois do manifesto pau-brasil assim chamado)
jura que jamais tivera
a intenção de abandonar Paris
para vir encontrar o
Senna
em São João d'el Rei. (Santiago, 1989, 73)

Como se pode ver pelos exemplos acima citados, as contradições
trazidas pelo Modernismo explodem, arremessando estilhaços para todos
os lados. Neste movimento dos barcos, constata-se que a arte que se vinha
imitando até o momento comportava outras formas de representação e
brechas eram estabelecidas no continuum da cultura literária canônica de
até então. Neste sentido, é interessante notar como o espelho brasileiro
reflete de forma alucinada as imagens de uma Europa que se encontrava
também em crise de identidade por ocasião dos anos um pouco anteriores e
posteriores à Primeira Guerra Mundial.(A nossa esquizofrenia saía
despudoramente pelas ruas, gritando, na tentativa de encontrar o seu
próprio nome.)
        É nesse momento que se estão a elaborar os grandes textos
modernistas e é através desse contacto tão crucial com o "Outro" que se
formula a sua "nova" estética e futura dispersão. A arte européia (neste
momento, considerada como pedra de toque para o imaginário brasileiro)
se "redescobre" nos elementos advindos das culturas pós-coloniais e, a

partir desse encontro, somente poderá reproduzir-se em função da presença de tais elementos. O processo de "contaminação" (já que estamos numa época pós-AIDS, esta também uma doença pós-moderna) afeta incondicionalmente os critérios de representação de ambas as manifestações artísticas. Tanto lá como cá há sabiás que se embebedam com kir e não perdem um filme de Godard (para continuarmos com o discurso da blague proposto por Oswald de Andrade.) Todos estes elementos se apresentam como solo profícuo para a desmontagem estabelecida pelo pós-modernismo no seu questionamento incondicional da estabilidade, da autoridade e dos discursos explicativos totalizadores (Lyotard está aí mesmo e não nos deixa mentir). Os elementos dionisíacos se infiltravam sorrateiramente na textura bem orquestrada apolineamente pela sociedade burguesa de entao (Oswald é inclusive chamado de "palhaço da burguesia) mas não conseguiram romper com estas malhas tão bem urdidas. Como nos diz muito bem o crítico Silviano Santiago a respeito deste movimento literário:

> Terminaria esta nossa conversa de hoje sobre a permanência do discurso da tradição no modernismo quase sem palavras, ou com pequenas palavras, dizendo que talvez seja irremediável o fato que, dentro da estética da ruptura característica da modernidade e do modernismo, nas vezes em que fomos buscar o traço forte da tradição, ou até mesmo o traço pouco vincado, nos aproximamos mais e mais de uma poesia, de uma produção poética que se desliga do social enquanto dimensão do histórico vivenciado pelo poeta. Isso às vezes pode beirar — e muitas vezes beira — o neoconservadorismo. (Santiago, 1989, 112)

Com o fim da Segunda Guerra Mundial e a conseqüente redistribuição dos espaços de influência por parte das grandes potências vitoriosas, podemos verificar também a presença de uma "nova" maneira de ler os textos, uma "nova" concepção no estabelecimento e ratificação do cânone (não seria nada leviano recordar o esforço feito pelos teóricos norte-americanos do "new criticism" no sentido de postular um "novo" cânone para a literatura de língua inglesa, desafiando os antigos mestres da Inglaterra). A questão fundamental para esta escola que se apresentava como nova no horizonte da crítica literária estava estribada na unicidade irreversível de cada texto, na sua idiossincrasia mais radical. Este movimento, por sua vez, teve um efeito ambíguo no que se refere à literatura pós-colonial, pois, se, por um lado, continua a vê-la como um ramo secundário na árvore do jardim das musas (para retomarmos a metáfora estabelecida por Antônio Cânido), por outro, dava-lhe voz (num sentido paternalista, escusado seria dizer). No horizonte dos estudos críticos literários brasileiros, estas (e outras) contradições se tornam evidentes quando observamos mais de perto os trabalhos do professor Afrânio Coutinho.

Depois de sua estada prolongada nos Estados Unidos, tendo entrado em contacto muito diretamente com o "new criticism", a volta deste crítico para o Brasil faz com que ele seja o responsável por um novo mapeamento da nossa literatura através do estabelecimento oficial de um "novo" cânone. Mais uma vez, tal importação tem um efeito negativo em terras "cabralinas" uma vez que impede (obscurece) mesmo o aparecimento de uma teoria autóctone, forjada a partir das necessidades culturais aparecidas em solo pátrio. Ao invés de se buscar uma linhagem crítico-cultural em nosso próprio percurso, de novo, tinha-se em mente um horizonte que não era nosso nem seria capaz de dar conta das nossas próprias especificidades. Como nos diria ainda mestre Cândido, a idéia de "sistema" não tinha encontrado o solo fértil para que a fruta nascesse. Adiava-se tal "descoberta" para um outro tempo. De forma bastante ampla, o advento da escola crítica do "new criticism" no Brasil impediu que a nossa literatura fosse vista como um produto cultural radicalmente novo, distinto, específico, inclusive podendo funcionar como uma desconstrução radical dos valores chegados das grandes metrópoles. Sua presença entre nós fez com que a possibilidade do surgimento de uma teoria crítica radical "autóctone" fose ofuscada, relegada a um segundo plano. Nem mesmo o híbrido era levado em consideração, já que a cegueira etnocêntrica deste movimento era assustadora.

Este caminho pelo qual estamos seguindo nos conduz ao questionamento mais do que evidente de formações discursivas que nos ajudam a entender, de forma muito mais precisa, a nossa própria especificidade, fazendo com que percamos a idéia do "universal" e do totalizador/zante. Esta seria a fórmula encontrada por teóricos que, indo de Heidegger/Sartre a Foucault, nos ensinam que a história objetiva é uma ficção e a sua reconstrução, uma arqueologia violenta imposta aos fatos por uma determinada interpretação. Ou como nos diz muito bem o crítico anglo-saxão Hayden White:

> . . .it is possible to view historical consciousness as a specifically western prejudice, by which the presumed superiority of modern, industrial society can be retroactively substantiated. (White, 1973, 1-2)

Neste sentido, fica evidente que o sentido de reconstrução (ou até mesmo de elaboração) do cânone está indissoluvelmente preso a uma categoria totalmente etnocêntrica, teoricamente falando. E aqui, através desse viés de matiz monológico, podemos estabelecer a ligação com um determinado tipo de escritura pós-modernista e com as teorias literárias pós-estruturalistas, uma vez que ambos têm como bandeira uma crise de autoridade, no seu sentido mais europeocêntrico:

> Decentered, allegorical, schizophrenic. . . however we choose to diagnose its symptoms, postmodernism is usually treated, by its protagonists and antagonists alike, as a crisis of cultural authority, specifically of the authority vested in Western European culture and its institutions. That the hegemony of European civilization is drawing to a close is hardly a new perception; since the mid-fifties, at least, we have recognized the necessity of encountering different cultures by means other than the shock of domination and conquest. (Owens, 1983, 57)

É evidente que houve um tremendo investimento no que diz respeito à questão da alteridade por parte dos estruturalistas e pós-estruturalistas tanto europeus como norte-americanos, mas este investimento, como se pode imaginar, articulou-se homologamente às estratégias também empreendidas pela História no sentido, de mais uma vez, domesticar e vigiar (e futuramente punir os trangressores, para fazer ecoar a voz de Foucault neste trabalho) o "outro". Obviamente que todas estas questões ficam totalmente obscurecidas uma vez que o discurso (algum discurso, seria melhor dizê-lo) pós-moderno se apresenta como salvador da pátria, um guerrilheiro revolucionário que tem como meta a destruição dos códigos epistemológicos do ocidente. Ou como resume muito bem a questão a professora Heloísa Buarque de Holanda:

> Já me referi anteriormente às freqüentes recusas em se refletir sobre o pós-moderno no Brasil ou em qualquer dos países que se pensam a partir do modelo metrópole/periferia. No caso da América Latina, temos mais um complicador: o caráter altamente problemático da participação democrática e da multiplicação dos espaços públicos em sociedades até muito recentemente marcadas pelos estados

militares. *Assim, além da associação usual com as*
posições conservadoras e "politicamente incorretas",
que identificam o pós-moderno deforma direta com
as ideologias do consumo e com as políticas
neoliberais, em se tratando de países periféricos
esse debate adquire intensidade e gravidade
particulares. (Hollanda, 1991, 11. Grifos nossos).

Neste sentido, "pós-colonial", "pós-estruturalista" e "pós-moderno" (principalmente) podem ser considerados como termos que recobrem uma extensa camada de práticas literárias, culturais e sociais.[2] A presença deste debate em solo brasileiro faz com que vejamos a nossa capacidade disruptora como uma força concreta que merece ser explorada, (re-)estudada, estabelecida. Embora, sem dúvida alguma, os modelos teóricos importados da Europa e dos Estados Unidos estejam vincadamente presentes em nossa arena social, começa-se a ver esta influência não com os óculos da inferioridade mas com as lentes binoculares da desconstrução. Muito antes de o pós-modernismo ser visto única e exclusivamente como um espaço de forças em-se-descentrando, uma categoria de desautomatização da autoridade, sua presença pode ser encontrada no encaminhamento de forças subversivas que tentam questionar violentamente a idéia de centro, suas formas de aprisionamento e suas esperanças em relação a uma cultura "secundária". Nessa medida, parece-nos, a grande importância das estratégias pós-modernistas reside no fato de a Literatura Brasileira recapturar e reapropriar-se da sua própria maneira de escrever, resgatando-se de uma história de "mentiras e infâmias". A fim de complexificar ainda mais o debate, abramos um parênteses.

Seria importante que a Literatura Portuguesa, até então afastada destas questões, porque vista como colonial, também questionasse a sua posição atual e se juntasse a outras literaturas de expressão portuguesa de cunho pós-colonial.[3] A afirmação de tal diferença por parte da Literatura Portuguesa faria com que a sua história literária fosse reavaliada e reconcebida, tomando o pós-modernismo como agente possibilitador de uma sua inserção numa atmosfera "pós-colonial" e apontando-lhe a diferença. Tal diferença não seria mais vista como "inferioridade" ou "cópia", mas muito pelo contrário uma forma de vigor criativo, de potência fundadora. Fechemos, pois, os parênteses e continuemos o debate.

Muitas são as preocupações que unem os escritores pós-modernistas brasileiros e os teóricos pós-estruturalistas no sentido de questionar as certezas que regem os conceitos de linguagem, escritura e crítica, mais ainda, de acentuar a enorme presença de relações ideológicas que presidem a fatura dos textos pós-coloniais. Antes de prosseguir nesta malha interpretativa, abramos um outro parêntesis para falar de uma questão que nos parece fundamental para o debate da questão do pós-modernismo no Brasil.

No verão de 1991,[4] fizemos várias entrevistas com críticos brasileiros do eixo cultural Rio de Janeiro/São Paulo. Uma das perguntas feitas era a seguinte: "Que autores você citaria como pós-modernos no Brasil?". (Em nossa mente, a questão da rearticulação de um novo (ou outro cânone) encontrava-se presente.) Uma das respostas mais interessantes nos foi dada pelo crítico Silviano Santiago, mais uma vez apontando-nos para a complexidade incomensurável da questão em solo tupiniquim:

> . . .acho extremamente precário tentar levantar o elenco dos autores que seriam enquadrados pela etiqueta de pós-modernistas, como outros o foram no passado pela de modernistas. É uma tarefa que compete mais ao futuro historiador da literatura, do que a alguém que tenta refletir sobre o problema sedutor que é a forma como a atualidade se apresenta ao intelectual que a tenta pensar e sobre ela agir. (...) Diante da atualidade somos sempre cartógrafos do precário. Desenhamos um mapa para logo em seguida descobrir que habitantes, grupos, fronteiras, tudo mudou. No caso do Brasil, e até segunda ordem, diria que pós-modernos são TODOS os autores que publicaram livros a partir da época que se convencionou chamar de "abertura". Quem é Guilherme de Alemida, Plínio Salgado, Cassiano Ricardo, Mário de Andrade, Guimarães Rosa ou Clarice Lispector? só o tempo dirá. (Silviano Santiago, em entrevista concedida ao autor em 1.9.91)

Fechemos o parênteses da questão cronológica e voltemos às nossas velhas problemáticas teóricas. A preocupação com o questionar do edifício da epistemologia ocidental (e estamos pensando evidentemente nos postulados feitos por Jean-François Lyotard) encontra eco nos críticos literários pós-coloniais mais perspicazes, uma vez que este diálogo pode servir para uma compreensão mais radical da nossa própria realidade. O artigo do professor Luiza Costa Lima, intitulado "Pós-modernidade: contraponto tropical" é fundamental neste sentido, mostrando-nos metonimicamente no seu título as sendas que serão ali percorridas. Em forma de técnica recolectiva barroca, assevera-nos o autor:

> Marx escrevia que "a apropriação da vontade alheia é
> o pressuposto da relação de domínio. Pode-se servir,
> como os animais, pela perda da vontade, mas isso
> não converte o propietário em senhor" (Marx, K.:
> 1857-8, 400). Nossa experiência mostra a busca dessa
> apropriação por um método antes adequado aos
> animais: pelo terror causado pela perda ou iminência
> de perda da base para a sobrevivência material. O
> convencimento pode vir depois: afinal, para isso, os
> aparelhos de TV continuam ligados. Será esse o
> primeiro ato da chegada do pós-moderno entre nós?
> Ou ao contrário é um instante de exceção? O único
> que desde logo podemos saber é que a possibilidade
> positiva acima exposta ou inexiste ou se adia. (Costa
> Lima, 1991, 137)

Essa "apropriação da vontade alheia" estabelece o privilégio da competência, relegando-se a segundo plano o conhecimento (forjado no/a partir do) cotidiano. Tudo isso faz com que a percepção social das formas cognitivas sejam apreendidas de acordo com as relações sociais ideologicamente determinadas e enquadradas no universo da "objetividade", categoria, sem dúvida alguma, neste modelo conceptual, acima de qualquer suspeita.

> Narratives. . . determine criteria of competence and/
> or illustrate how they are to be applied. They thus
> define what has the right to be said and done in the
> culture in question, and since they are themselves a
> part of that culture, they are legitimised by the simple
> fact that they do what they do. (Lyotard, 1979, 23)

A ciência, perseguindo ainda a trilha aberta por Lyotard, contrapõe-se às afirmações narrativas e, neste sentido, funciona como uma assertiva primária no sentido de legitimar o "ocidente", fazendo com que este decida, ao fim e ao cabo, o que é ou não verdade(eiro). A ciência classifica, pois, estas outras narrativas como pertencentes a um mundo que pode ser configurado enquanto "selvagem", "primitivo", "subdesenvolvido", "terceiro-mundista" (mantendo-se todas as aspas possíveis e imagináveis), colocando-nos, mais uma vez, "à margem da vida". Deste cadinho sairá, como bem sabemos, todos os projetos de dominação imperial ocidental, aprisionando-nos num quarto escuro a fim de que não prossigamos no/com o debate. Na mesma medida em que Lyotard critica o projeto do edifício do conhecimento ocidental, ele também vê como extremamente problemática a recuperação do sentido de "tradicional":

> There is no question here of proposing a "pure" alternative to the system: we all now know that an attempt at an alternative of that kind would end up resembling the system it was meant to replace.
> (Lyotard, 1979, 66)

Para o crítico francês, como bem podemos imaginar, a configuração de conceitos como pós-moderno não significa, de maneira nenhuma, o nascimento de novas "metanarrativas", não quer dizer, em momento algum, o ressurgimento de um discurso monolítico, central(do) de legitimização, sua perspectiva deve ser antes vista como a possibilidade de engendramento de práticas nascidas do particular e do local. Lyotard, num certo sentido utilizando-se de uma técnica também cara a Jacques Derrida, formula o conceito de verdade a partir de sua característica local, o conhecimento, enquanto "criado do sujeito", não mais o sujeito em si mesmo. As "verdades" forjadas nas práticas sociais merecem tanto respeito quanto aquelas que se desenvolvem (desenvolveram) de forma abstrata. A única diferença, como nos assegura Derrida, baseia-se em que a primeira se formula num ambiente pós-colonial. Metaforicamente diz-nos o crítico Silviano Santiago, misturando discursos antes irreconciliáveis; hoje, possibilidade concreta de existência:

> O olhar pós-moderno (em nada camuflado, apenas enigmático) olha nos olhos do sol. Volta-se para a luz, o prazer, a alegria, o riso, e assim por diante, com todas as variantes do hedonismo dionisíaco. O espetáculo da vida hoje se contrapõe ao espetáculo da morte ontem. Olha-se um corpo em vida, energia e potencial de uma experiência impossível de ser fechada na sua totalidade mortal, porque ela se abre no agora em mil possibilidades. Todos os caminhos o caminho. O corpo que olha prazeroso (já dissemos), olha prazeroso um outro corpo prazeroso (acrescentemos) em ação. (Santiago, 1989, 50)

Se, neste excerto, a metáfora funciona como elemento que engendra o discurso, na abertura deste seu livro (*Nas malhas da letra*), o crítico chama a atenção do seu leitor para as quatro questões básicas que norteiam as suas preocupações de intelectual no contexto cultural brasileiro. Duas, para efeito deste trabalho, são fundamentais e as transcrevemos abaixo:

> Uma primeira preocupação é com os contemporâneos, isto é, aqueles autores de obras com quem convive a minha própria escrita ficcional e poética. É a maneira como, analisando e avaliando a produção literária pós-64, mapeio escritas, traços temáticos e problemas para melhor me situar. (...) Retomo a questão das relações entre Europa e as Américas, agora pelo viés de um ensaio de Umberto Eco e pela crítica de uma inesperada forma de censura artística em país tão democratizado quanto a Alemanha pós-hitleriana. (Santiago, 1989, 7)

Como se pode constatar, o multifacetado intelectual se apropria da matéria crítica elaborada alhures para emprestar-lhe um valor tipicamente nosso, enquanto elemento em diferença. Não algo puro, sem manchas, mas o espaço configurador do híbrido, do "entre", como nos dizia ele em outro seu artigo ("O entre-lugar do discurso latino-americano").

O conceito de "discurso" proposto por Michel Foucault (mais tarde desenvolvido ou questionado por Said, Althusser, Pêcheux e outros) apresenta-se como fundamental no sentido da determinação das regras que funcionam como elementos de controle, seleção, organização e (re)distribuição de um certo número de procedimentos, cujas principais zonas de interdição estão ligadas à sexualidade e à política. Um discurso, no sentido foucaultiano do termo, deve ser entendido como a formulação de uma possibilidade de conhecimento. O que nos faz reconhecer um texto como literário? Que bússola temos de usar para encontrar o caminho da classificação ou do sistema? Neste sentido, Edward Said nos dá algumas pistas no sentido de que vejamos como foi efetuada a construção do discurso a respeito do "oriente" em mentes ocidentais:

> The Orient is not merely there. Just as the Occident itself is not just there either. We must take seriously Vico's great observation that men make their own history, that what they can know is what they have made, and extend it to geography: as both

> geographical and cultural entities — to say nothing
> of historical entities — such locals, regions,
> geographical sectors as "Orient" and "Occident" are
> man-made. (Said, 1978, 5)

Da mesma maneira como as duas entidades acima citadas (Oriente-Ocidente) se refletem, assim também a Literatura Brasileira numa época pós-moderna configura sua identidade enquanto diferença, negando a possibilidade de constituição de uma "essência". Sua configuração enquanto um "outro" diferente da metrópole (ou das metrópoles, para globlalizar ainda mais a nossa perspectiva) somada a um distanciamento do centro (ou centros) possibilitam-lhe a elaboração da sua identidade, a fim de repensar os conceitos de linguagem, verdade, poder e suas possíveis e inumeráveis relações (para seguir a trilha aberta tanto por Foucault como por Said). A verdade nada mais é do que a verificação de determinadas regras no universo de um discurso particular e específico; o poder se configura enquanto aquele elemento que determina e verifica a verdade (previamente estabelecida). A relação entre poder e verdade se estabelece enquanto uma relação intrínseca e indissociável: o poder não pode ser exercido sem que haja, ao mesmo tempo e no mesmo espaço, a produção da verdade (continuando a ouvir os ecos da teoria de Foucault). Neste sentido, algumas instâncias da Literatura Brasileira enquanto situadas no espaço pós-colonial se arvoram numa luta pelo poder que, em última instância, encontra-se intimamente ligado à linguagem de fatura metropolitana. Mas seria, de fato, este o seu espaço de legitimação? Reproduzir não seria evidentemente criar, mas refletir de forma integral a imagem que vinha da metrópole. De novo, Silviano corre em nosso auxílio para mostrar-nos como seria possível entender este problema:

> O pós-modernismo tem duas pernas, ora manca de
> uma, ora manca da outra, e sempre manca
> surrealisticamente das duas. Uma perna se apóia na
> pós-modernidade européia e norte-americana; outra
> perna se apóia no modernismo brasileiro propriamente
> dito. Ambas as pernas tentam sustentar e erguer o
> corpo físico do atual no que ele tem de problemático
> e sedutor para o intelectual e o artista brasileiros.
> Problema sedutor, a atualidade repugna e atrai. Mais
> repugna por estar o Brasil (e a América Latina)
> atravessando as suas piores décadas do século; mais
> solícita porque impossível ficar indiferente ante ao

desmoronamento de uma esperança (uma "colonização do futuro", diz Octavio Paz) que foi constituída pela ação e pensamento dos modernistas brasileiros. (Santiago, S., entrevista concedida ao autor em 1.9.91).

O poder está concentrado na língua(gem) (não sendo à toa que Cortez precisou decididamente de La Malinche) porque, através da utilização desta, a verdade daquele pode ser constituída e, posteriormente, preservada. A luta pelo poder, então, no espaço pós-colonial, num certo sentido, imita (como nos diz Homi Bhabha, aliás um de seus artigos aparece traduzido no livro Pós-modernidade e política da professora Heloísa Buarque de Hollanda) os impulsos de dominação usados na "metrópole". A fim de evitar tal tipo de "imitação" é preciso que os espaços fora da "metrópole" utilizem outras fórmulas para os mesmos elementos em jogo, colocando em circulação estratégias que se liguem à diferença, à liberdade e à criatividade. Será, por assim dizer, um discurso "entre", para utilizar uma das categorias acima citadas, proposta pelo crítico Silviano Santiago em relação à nossa especificidade de latino-americanos (Santiago, 1978).

Neste sentido, podemos aprender com a teoria crítica bebida aos pensadores europeus e norte-americanos mecanismos que nos ajudem a desenvolver um contra-discurso para a desconstrução do edifício do (neo)colonialismo. Indo mais longe, diríamos que temos condições de apropriar-nos das teorias européias e norte-americanas no sentido de desenvolvermos (perdoem-nos o termo por demais ligado ao século XIX) mecanismos discursivos que nos permitam conhecer melhor "la cara del villano". Na intersecção destes discursos, afinal de contas, encontramos a presença de "outras" vozes que juntando-se às nossas fazem com que possamos encontrar uma saída (talvez muitas, várias, já que estamos em pleno período da morte de metarranativas e certezas absolutas). Num período de questionamentos múltiplos, de descentramento total, as teorias pós-estruturalistas funcionam como aquele marco que ajuda a colocar as literaturas pós-coloniais no mapa "mundi". A questão da pós-modernidade, assim, não significa apenas reelaborar o espaço do universo pós-colonial, muito pelo contrário, este movimento faz com que os questionamentos a respeito do "centro" incorporem lugares "outros", pertencentes a uma cartografia até então deixada de lado pelas instâncias de dominação e hegemonia da sociedade ocidental branca, privilegiada, masculina, etc. e tal. A auto-reflexividade do pós-modernismo traz para o centro de discussão todas as vozes que fazem (e devem necessariamente fazer) parte do debate, não deixando (ou pelo menos não querendo deixar) que apenas os ecos dessas mesmas vozes sejam ouvidos. Não mais a mímica (ou até ela mesma) pura e simples, mas o simulacro como possibilidade de potência e afirmação, tudo, no mundo pós-moderno, tornou-se reflexo do reflexo, do reflexo e assim infinitamente. A cena primitiva não existe mais enquanto instância fundadora, muito pelo contrário, ela aponta apenas para um "abandono universal":

> . . .to ask whose interests are served by "universal abandon" is not to hark back to a more straightforward kind of oppositional politics — our interests or their interests? — in which the left clearly "owned" or appropriated what the right had lost. On the contrary, it is to problematize the very question of interests in an age when interests can no longer be universalized, and for a politics in which identities are not already there, to be reflected as unitary in already constituted forms of struggle. (Ross, 1988, XVII)

Como bem sabemos, existe uma forte corrente em toda a América Latina que quer convencer-nos a não aceitar os valores alienígenos das teorias importadas (este tipo de reação é menos evidente e menos violenta em terras de Brasil), postulando-nos que, mais uma vez, estamos dando vez a vozes que não são as nossas. O que esta corrente perde de ver é que esta apropriação possível (e, por vezes, necessária) compõe dramaticamente o nosso existir: somos híbridos por natureza ("heróis sem caráter", como dizia mestre Mário de Andrade) e esta especificidade é a nossa dupla marca de seres textuais pós-coloniais. Não podemos (nem devemos) cair na teia armada pela nossa "diferença" única e específica, pois, de novo, estaríamos repetindo o conto do centro, da essência e da busca da unicidade absoluta. Uma apropriação radical dessa realidade integra todos os elementos de nossa aldeia global. De Nova Iorque a Paris, a La Paz ou Sucre, a Sidney (e estamos esquecendo, sem dúvida alguma, muitas outras possibilidades), existe a presença de todos em tudo (para parodiarmos as palavras de George Yúdice num congresso sobre teoria literária latino-americana, realizado em Dartmouth College, em 1987). O caos não é mais uma característica marcante apenas (e tão somente) das margens, mas está devidamente incorporado ao movimento global do mundo, que tem de incluir simultaneamente as devastações feitas na Amazônia e a incapacidade de salvar corujas nas florestas do noroeste norte-americano, para citarmos uns poucos exemplos de anti-ecologia. A pós-modernidade mais uma vez recoloca-nos a questão (hoje mais do que nunca) fundamental da natureza enquanto reserva ecológica. Unindo elementos, antes irreconciliáveis, o cacique de uma tribo indígena brasileira nos dá uma resposta extremamente aguda:

> As pessoas costumam ver na atitude do povo indígena uma espécie de sentimento místico, porque nós somos um povo muito simples, então a gente teria muita imaginação. . . a natureza é poderosa, pode matar a gente. . . Em função desse medo, respeitamos a natureza. Isso é bobagem. Respeitamos a natureza por ela ter durante milhares de anos embalado nossos sonhos, nos dado casa, alimentos, sem nunca ter falhado, porque a central de energia dela nunca desliga. Então, esse jeito de respeitar a natureza é anterior ao conceito ecológico de preservar a natureza. Uma coisa muito perigosa nesse conceito de proteger, preservar, que eu vejo no pensamento das chamadas sociedades civilizadas, é que elas podem transformar a natureza em refém da humanidade. (. . .) aquilo que você pode proteger você pode também submeter (. .) a floresta é refém da humanidade. (Moriconi, 1991, 92)

Se, por um lado, o debate a respeito da pós-modernidade põe em cheque os valores há muito perpetrados pela nossa situação de país pós-colonial, por outro, vem reforçar a diferença existente entre uma pequena parcela da população que tem acesso a este

> (. . .) debate, mínimo é verdade, tem se restringido aos suplementos literários da grande imprensa escrita. (Santiago, 1991, entrevista concedida ao autor)

e a imensa massa de analfabetos que continua a existir no país. Neste sentido, seria oportuno terminar o trabalho com as palavras premonitórias de um crítico já bastante citado ao longo deste artigo, cuja clarividência nos ajuda a entender mais detalhada e nuançadamente a questão do pós-moderno no Brasil: ·

> É neste sentido que vale enfatizar: o problema da pós-modernidade é fundamentalmente de ordem política. (Costa Lima, 1991, 136)

tecendo-as em malhas outras que, do "centro", olham a "periferia" de uma maneira "diferente":

> The Christian Base Communities use the biblical scriptures as the vehicles for hearing the voices of the oppressed; we must also avail ourselves of such vehicles that are possible within our secular culture and that do not run counter to our own struggles among racial, ethnic, sexual, and class minorities. There are no guarantees, of course, that articulations across our own social movements, on the one hand, and with oppressed groups abroad, will be possible and/or successful. Our ethical practice, then, is the political art of seeking articulations among all the "marginalized" and oppressed, in the interests of our own survival. (Ross, 1989, 230-1)

Como se pode constatar, o debate está apenas começando e já incendeia coracões e mentes, resta-nos esperar que o futuro comece a contar a sua própria estória. Este trabalho, parcial como só ele, iniciou o debate, o resto virá com o tempo. . .

Notas

[1] Estamos usando os termos pós-modernismo e pós-modernidade como intercambiáveis. Nesta altura da nossa discussão, parece-nos desnecessária a dicotomização teórica radical. Assim, a diferença parece-nos assustadoramente "superficial".

[2] Seria interessante notar como até mesmo a cultura norte-americana está descobrindo a sua "força" numa possibilidade de se autodenominar como "pós-colonial". A influência do pós-estruturalismo francês, na esfera dos estudos crítico-literários, revela esta face outra e disruptora do espaço discursivo norte-americano. O seu ar de inferioridade em relação à Literatura Inglesa vai desaparecendo na medida em que esta nova literatura se assume como variedade e não mais como "um ramo" no jardim daquela velha senhora inglesa.

[3] Neste sentido, o discurso do presidente português Mário Soares por ocasião da transferência da capital da Comunidade Européia para Lisboa em 1.1.92 é crucial. Contrastando com a mensagem do Primeiro Ministro português (Cavaco e Silva), o presidente lembrava aos "europeus novo-ricos" que as relações portuguesas não poderiam (nem deveriam)

esquecer-se do Brasil nem da África. Havia um matrimônio entre Portugal e o resto da Europa, mas este era um "casamento de interesses", sem dúvida alguma, pois o amor estava deslocadamente em outro lugar. [4] Esta viagem de pesquisa somente foi possível graças à bolsa de estudos oferecida pelo Latin American Center da Stanford University, instituições que recebem aqui, de público, o nosso agradecimento.

Bibliographia

Ayres, Miriam de Mello. *Interpretações culturais da sociedade pós-industrial*. Rio de Janeiro: Pontifícia Universidade Católica, 1989. (Dissertação de mestrado, inédita).

Buarque de Hollanda, Heloísa (org.). *Pós-modernismo e política*. Rio de Janeiro: Rocco, 1991.

Coelho, Teixeira. *Moderno Pós-moderno*. São Paulo, LPM, 1986.

Foucault, Michel. *The Order of Things: an Archaeology of the Human Sciences*. London: Tavistock, 1966.
---. *The Archaeology of Knowledge*. London: Tavistock, 1972.
---. *Language. Counter-Memory. Practice*. Oxford, Basil Blackwell, 1977.

Lima, Luiz Costa. *Pensando nos trópicos*. Rio de Janeiro: Rocco, 1991.

Lopes, Jr., Francisco Caetano. *Crescendo durante a guerra numa província ultramarina, de Silviano Santiago: construção da memória esquecida*. Niterói: Universidade Federal Fluminense, 1982. (Dissertação de mestrado, inédita).

Lyotard, Jean-François. *The Postmodern Condition — a Report on Knowledge*. Manchester: Manchester University Press, 1979.

Morioni, Italo. *Pós-modernidade e razão histórica (exercícios de configuração metateórica)*. Rio de Janeiro: Pontifícia Universidade Católica, 1991. (Tese de doutorado, inédita).

Oliveira, Roberto Cardoso (et allii). *Pós-modernidade*. Campinas, Editora da UNICAMP, 1988.

Owens, Craig. "The Discourse of Others: Feminists and Postmodernism". *The Anti-Aesthetic: Essays on Postomdern Culture*. Ed. Hal Foster. Port Toursont: Bay Press, 1983.

Revista *Novos Estudos*, CEBRAP, São Paulo, n. 12, junho 1985.

Ross, Andrew, ed. *Universal Abandon? The Politics of Postmodernism*. Minnesota: University of Minnesota Press, 1988.

Santiago, Silviano. *Nas malhas da letra*. São Paulo: Companhia das Letras, 1989.
---. *Uma literatura nos trópicos*. São Paulo: Perspectiva, 1978.

Said, Edward. *Orientalism*. New York: Pantheon, 1978.

White, Hayden. *Metahistory*. Baltimore: Johns Hopkins, 1973.

Fogos de Artifício —
Anotações para o Estudo do Sistema Intelectual Brasileiro

Roberto Reis

Essa parte da intelectualidade torna-se [...] incapaz de refletir criticamente sobre seu próprio drama e sobre as transformações que vive, como seria seu papel, confundida pela barreira de fogos de artifício que ela própria fabrica.
— Luciano Martins.

O quadro descrito por Edward Said, numa passagem na qual ele se referia à crítica de esquerda nos Estados Unidos (que se debruça sobre problemas de vária ordem, menoscabando porém a noção de autoridade) é ainda válido para dar conta do estágio em que se encontram os estudos literários sobre o Brasil. Em livro publicado em 1983, ele escrevia que naquela crítica não se achava

> a serious study of what authority is, either with reference to the way authority is carried historically and circumstancially from the State down into a society saturated with authority or with reference to the actual workings of culture, the role of intellectuals, institutions, and establishments. (Said 172)

Não vem ao caso examinar os motivos por que a crítica que tem por objeto o *corpus* literário brasileiro, em suas linhas mais gerais, tampouco se politizou, no sentido de argüir temas como o caráter autoritário que assume o discurso cultural no Brasil. Muito menos quero taxá-la de desatualizada. No entanto, se tivermos em mente uma visão panorâmica, a verdade é que os estudiosos que se interessam pela literatura brasileira — e isso me parece pertinente também para os que se dedicam a tal atividade no estrangeiro, sejam eles brasileiros natos ou não — via de regra passam ao largo de candentes questões, emprestando ao trabalho crítico um perfil insípido e neutro, que em muito pouco contribui para colocar em xeque o contexto histórico e social. E isso num momento em que o debate travado no interior das Ciências Humanas em torno da linguagem, da textualidade, da interpretação, das instituições, do ficcional em sua relação com o histórico tendem a valorizar os contornos ideológicos de todo o discurso, cuja semantização parece estar diretamente conectada às marcas de poder. As exceções ao que ficou dito acima, no caso, só fazem confirmar a regra, e a crítica, o mais das vezes, se transforma numa empresa escorpiônica, a morder a própria cauda.

Não é, pois, simples coincidência — principalmente se reivindicamos um gesto de leitura que esteja enraizado na História e no social — que algumas das contribuições mais interessantes para o escrutínio da literatura brasileira publicadas nos últimos anos tenham sido assinadas por investigadores de outras disciplinas — historiadores, sociólogos, antropólogos, filósofos, cientistas políticos.[1] Parte deste menosprezo se deveria à ainda forte influência que as *close readings* e os -ismos de toda sorte exercem nos assédios ao fenômeno literário brasileiro, em larga medida estigmatizados pelo enfoque imanentista e estetizante. Mais uma vez, os que fogem ao paradigma predominante apenas nos certificam de que não há injustiça no diagnóstico aqui delineado.

Se transpomos nossa curiosidade para as áreas afins há pouco enumeradas, contudo, nos deparamos com sucessivas análises ressaltando a feição autoritária da política, das instituições ou da cultura brasileiras.[2] Marilena Chauí, por exemplo, é bem contundente ao sustentar que nossa sociedade é autoritária "na medida em que não consegue, até o limiar do século XXI, concretizar sequer os princípios (velhos de três séculos) do liberalismo e do republicanismo" (Chauí, *Conformismo e resistência* 47). Ao abordarmos o discurso cultural brasileiro, salta aos olhos a recorrência de um padrão autoritário vigente desde a Colônia (resultante da presença da metrópole), que passa pelo Império e pela República Velha (quando o senhoriato agrário-exportador domina hegemonicamente e garante que a visada que atende a seus interesses prevaleça) e encontra sua formulação mais cabal no instante em que se sedimenta o Estado, forte e centralizador, ao longo dos anos 30 e, recentemente, por ocasião das seqüelas legadas pelo "fascismo" militar de 64. Enquanto prática discursiva, este discurso é autoritário por não consentir que circulem em seu interior vozes e significados dissonantes, estando presidido, em seus limites, pela angulação dos grupos dirigentes, impedindo assim a eclosão da diferença. Mas meu propósito não é empreender uma radiografia do autoritarismo brasileiro. Pretendo, ao invés, examinar, e de maneira não exaustiva, o comprometimento da elite letrada com este projeto, com o fito de sugerir que seria imperioso levar em consideração o sistema intelectual ao se interrogar o artefato literário produzido no Brasil, sob pena de se incorrer em deformações interpretativas de toda sorte.[3] Para isso, tomarei como apoio alguns textos, ora glosando-os, ora pontuando-os, ora insinuando bifurcações. O enfrentamento destes tópicos implicará, por outra parte, em retomar o trecho transcrito de Said, no qual ele aludia ao papel da *intelligentsia* e de algumas instituições e à *performance* da cultura, na expectativa de que o que se segue evidencie, não importando tanto que corte se faça, o caráter autoritário do discurso cultural brasileiro produzido pelos segmentos letrados.

*   *   *

São escassos os estudos dedicados ao levantamento das contradições ideológicas de críticos e historiadores literários e esta é uma tarefa que está por se fazer. Existem, entretanto, vários trabalhos sobre os intelectuais brasileiros em geral[4] e, não por casualidade, se os tomamos em conjunto, nota-se uma constante subjacente a todos eles: a elite pensante da sociedade brasileira pactuou com a construção de um Estado nacional forte, centralizado e autoritário, tendo sido cooptada ou parasitado à sombra do poder, buscando usufruir das benesses de comendas e cargos, o que, sem dúvida, em muito esvazia a atividade intelectual de sua contundência. A *intelligentsia* sempre se atribuiu o papel de porta-voz da nação. Longe de assumir um perfil realmente crítico e problematizador, o grosso do pensamento brasileiro está atravessado pela ideologia, justificando a dominação exercida pelos grupos hegemônicos, além de exaurir-se em bajulações que incensam o poder e de extraviar-se numa erudição de fachada. É visível seu fascínio pelos modelos estrangeiros, importados sem qualquer discernimento. Trata-se ademais de uma reflexão que dá as costas para o presente, abstendo-se de estar *na História*, pactuando com ditaduras, formulando suspeitas noções de "nacionalismo," com as quais intenta recompor a estilhaçada identidade cultural do país. Não raro enclausurada numa torre de marfim elitista, ela rechaça o contágio das manifestações de cunho popular, que apreende paternalisticamente e que poderiam macular seu arianismo. Para dizer numa palavra: tendo escapado de se dobrar a uma indagação do conflito e da diferença, a intelectualidade não refletiu criticamente sobre o drama de seu tempo — que é o seu —, como reza a epígrafe deste texto.[5]

Estes traços gerais podem ser depreendidos pelo menos desde a chamada Escola do Recife, nas últimas décadas do século XIX, com seu exarcebado cientificismo, passando pela ação dos médicos higienistas, pela intelectualidade da *belle époque*, pelos ideólogos dos anos 30 (ligados ao tenentismo, ao Estado Novo, ao integralismo ou à direita católica), pelos modernistas, pelo desenvolvimentismo isebiano do decênio de 50 até desaguar na Doutrina de Segurança Nacional, gestada na Escola Superior de Guerra após a campanha da FEB e responsável pelo ideário posto em prática ao longo dos governos militares, sobretudo depois de decretado o AI-5. Ou seja — e deixando de fora o período anterior a 1870 — : um arco que cobre cerca de 100 anos de fórmulas autoritárias a congestionar a cultura brasileira, as quais começaram a ser postas em xeque mas que, apesar disso, continuam a ocasionar os seus estragos. Baste recordar que Gilberto Freyre — cujas idéias ajudam a assegurar, por assim dizer, e desde a perspectiva dos estamentos dominantes, o pacto de 30, coagulando a violência da formação social brasileira — foi agraciado como intelectual do sistema durante os governos militares e, apesar dos vários senões apontados em sua prolífica obra, gozou de invejável prestígio até seu falecimento.

O trajeto sumarizado comparece em artigo de Luciano Martins ("A gênese de uma intelligentsia"), no qual ele acompanha as vicissitudes da elite pensante até os anos 40, principiando também com a mesma baliza cronológica, a geração do Recife. Não seria custoso recuperar o que antecede à emergência do grupo que se aglutinou em torno do sergipano Tobias Barreto. A cultura brasileira só se constituiu como sistema por volta do século XVIII.[6] Após a Independência já se esboça o intento de esculpir um Estado nacional, a que o Império dá silhuetas mais nítidas, sem contudo lograr êxito no formato centralizador — o monarca é figura mais simbólica, representando a instância moderadora, visto que o poder está, de fato, nas mãos dos grandes proprietários rurais ligados à exportação de produtos para o mercado externo. Como regra geral, a inteligência do Primeiro e Segundo Reinados se reúne ao redor da corte, mimando o imperador, festejando a "aristocracia" agrária, da qual, quase sempre, fazia parte.[7] D. Pedro II quis ser um mecenas ilustrado das letras e artes pátrias, protegendo artistas, escritores (como Porto-Alegre) e instituições (como o Colégio que leva o seu nome). Sua tarefa coincidiu com o surto romântico entre nós, e cumpre lembrar que o Romantismo brasileiro tomou uma direção diversa do europeu. Se é lícito escrever que na Europa a estética romântica foi uma reação contrária aos descaminhos da civilização burguesa (o que lhe imprime, o mais das vezes, um feitio contra-cultural), no Brasil tornou-se um movimento que, ao ser abraçado pela monarquia, reforçou o *status quo*, se curvando aos interesses dos setores senhoriais. A índole conservadora que Lúcia Lippi Oliveira detecta no Romantismo (Oliveira, "As raízes da ordem: os intelectuais, a cultura e o Estado" 510) se casa à perfeição com o nosso oitocentos: o romance do período, por exemplo, é um auto-retrato das elites patriarcais e o nacionalismo plasmado na obra de um Alencar ou de um Bernardo Guimarães é o que convinha às oligarquias dominantes.[8]

Roberto Ventura, num relevante estudo sobre a intelectualidade do século XIX, mostra como os "bacharéis" representaram um modo de transição da oralidade para a escrita, cuja difusão entra em conflito com os valores tradicionais (Ventura 122). Na virada do século vai se ensaiando a profissionalização do escritor, sendo a fundação da Academia Brasileira de Letras um sintoma deste movimento rumo à constituição da literatura como um campo autônomo, ao mesmo tempo que indicia a agonia da "geração de 1870" (Ventura 112-13). A obra de José Veríssimo, em oposição à de Silvio Romero, privilegiando o estético, seria outro indício desta paulatina legitimação da atividade crítica e literária (Ventura 116), num processo que se consolida, recentemente, com a criação dos cursos universitários de Letras no país e, nos anos 70, com a formação de críticos literários profissionais, mediante a implantação da Pós-Graduação nesta área.

Haveria, mais uma vez, uma continuidade entre a elite letrada da geração de 1870, fundamentalmente reunida em torno da Escola de Direito do Recife, e as décadas subseqüentes ao Modernismo: a fundação da Universidade de São Paulo, por exemplo, propiciará um outro "repensar" o Brasil, nas obras, entre outros, de um Florestan Fernandes ou de um Caio Prado Junior, germinadas já no meio universitário. Na frente propriamente literária, a história da literatura coordenada por Afrânio Coutinho (edição lançada em 1956), de inspiração francamente estética e estilística, calcada no modelo do *new criticism* norte-americano, traduz uma concepção da literatura como um objeto de estudo mais ou menos autônomo, dissociado de outras disciplinas com as quais estivera mesclado no passado. O mesmo, apesar de seu maior interesse pelo aspecto sociológico, poderia ser dito da *Formação da literatura brasileira*, de Antonio Candido (publicada em 1959): a reação de Coutinho, em *Conceito de literatura brasileira* (Coutinho 40 e ss.), revela, sem sombra de dúvida, uma disputa, travada já internamente, pela hegemonia do poder no campo literário.

Segundo Luciano Martins, em fins do século passado os intelectuais se empenham em dois debates: um pela Abolição e outro a favor da República. A maneira como se deu este engajamento diz muito sobre sua origem de classe e sobre a sua alienação com respeito ao próprio país. Filhos de famílias tradicionais, profissionais liberais educados na Europa ou nas faculdades do Rio, de São Paulo e do Recife (às quais só a elite tinha acesso), o que lhes dava o mais prestigioso do que funcional título de bacharel, compunham eles o círculo bastante limitado das pessoas ilustradas da segunda metade do século XIX.

Quanto à primeira causa, logo se desativa, assinada a Lei Áurea. Restaram, todavia, as chagas de uma sociedade de extração escravocrata nos preconceitos raciais disfarçados e no desprezo pelo trabalho manual, tido como degradante e associado à servidão. Boa parte da *intelligentsia* fabrica teses com um verniz "científico" que proclamam o branqueamento social (penso aqui, entre outros, em Nina Rodrigues).

Quanto à República, era concebida como "a panacéia contra todos os males," "capaz de abrir o sistema político a novos atores e às desejadas reformas, ainda que estas fossem muito vagamente definidas" (Martins, "A gênese de uma intelligentsia" 72). A República, entretanto, não corresponderá às expectativas da elite pensante. Os militares, indóceis desde a guerra do Paraguai, desembarcam no poder e, sobretudo a partir do governo Campos Sales, se institucionaliza o mando das oligarquias, que conformam o novo regime à sua medida, adotando-se o modelo capitalista. Os letrados da época advogam para si a liderança moral do país, mas mostram-se incapazes de pensar uma nova sociedade, já que não formulam qualquer projeto de transformação. Sua proposta maior — fruto de uma reflexão abstrata, mitificadora e idealizante, sem nenhuma escora na práxis histórica e social — incide sobre a nação, não sobre a sociedade.

Data destes princípios do novecentos brasileiro a *belle époque* tropical, com seus representantes fascinados pelo Oriente, pelos clássicos, pelo português castiço, portadores de uma erudição balofa e incuravelmente afrancesados. São eles que apóiam a reforma urbana e o saneamento do Rio de Janeiro, durante o mandato presidencial de Rodrigues Alves e sob o ditame de homens como Pereira Passos, Paulo de Frontin e Oswaldo Cruz, este último à frente da campanha pela vacina obrigatória e da erradicação da febre amarela. Pautando-se pelo modelo de Huyssmans, em Paris, são demolidos antigos casarões coloniais, num anseio de se extirpar o passado da cidade ou qualquer vestígio da faceta popular e da herança africana da cultura brasileira. Ruas são alargadas, ampliam-se os limites da capital da República, inaugura-se a Avenida Central, com prédios como o da Biblioteca Nacional, o Museu de Belas Artes e o Teatro Municipal (uma réplica da *Opera* parisiense). Praças públicas, como o Passeio, ostentam estátuas neoclássicas. E as camadas pobres são enxotadas para os subúrbios, morros e periferias, proíbem-se batuques e serenatas, causam asco os pés descalços e os corpos suados. A vida gravita em torno da passarela da Rua do Ouvidor, reservada para o desfile "chic" e elegante destes *nouveaux riches* janotas, que colocam seus filhos para estudar em colégios criados precipuamente com este fim, como o Pedro II (para os rapazes) ou o Sion (para as moças), ou freqüentam sociedades e clubes fechados, como o Cassino Fluminense, o Clube dos Diários, o Jockey Club, ou os braços das cocotes francesas. Aí vamos encontrar figuras de proa como Rui Barbosa, Ataulfo de Paiva, Joaquim Nabuco, a decidirem entre si os destinos de todo o Brasil, entre baforadas de charuto e noites de ópera no Teatro Lírico, onde se ia mais para ver quem estava nos camarotes do que para ouvir os cantores se esgoelando no palco. De acordo com Jeffrey Needell, a cultura serviu para manter e promover os interesses da elite, por meio de uma socialização, de uma legitimação e de uma plataforma comuns, que permeavam as relações entre os poderosos, num contexto neocolonial (Needell 234).[9] Acometidos pela eurofilia, usavam roupas de lã inglesa num clima de 40 graus à sombra.

A causa seguinte que congregará os intelectuais será construir a nação, por meio do Estado, que acabará por assimilar a elite ilustrada no terceiro decênio em seus escalões burocráticos. A partir da impropriamente denominada "Revolução" de 30, a "modernização conservadora" se acelera, não a partir de dissensões geradas no interior de uma sociedade civil, mas mediante um processo gerenciado pelo Estado (Martins, "A gênese de uma intelligentsia" 75). Os intelectuais, de uma forma ou de outra, são cativados por este movimento em direção ao Estado, depois da tomada do poder por Getúlio, participando, sob a égide do estadonovismo, como administradores de uma política cultural para o Brasil. É então que se organizam repartições como a do Serviço do Patrimônio Histórico e Artístico Nacional e o Instituto Nacional do Livro, que escritores vão colaborar com o DIP de Lourival Fontes, com a revista *Cultura Política* , seu principal órgão de divulgação, ou com o Ministério Capanema; que vão flertar com o integralismo, com a direita católica, encarnada no Centro Dom Vital e na revista *A Ordem*, ou com o Partido Comunista.

Nesse complicado e sortido saco, vamos reconhecer nomes como Cassiano Ricardo, Tristão de Athayde, Jackson de Figueiredo, Plínio Salgado, Octávio de Faria, Vinicius de Moraes, José Lins do Rego, Jorge Amado, José Américo de Almeida, Rachel de Queirós, Heitor Villa-Lobos, Carlos Drummond de Andrade, Menotti del Picchia, Oscar Niemeyer, Cecília Meireles, Portinari, Gilberto Freyre, Graciliano Ramos, entre tantos outros. Não seria o caso de separar gregos de troianos, porque, de uma forma ou de outra, em maior ou menor grau — e isso é o que desejo ressaltar —, todos estiveram comprometidos com os aparelhos de Estado.

Sequer um poeta da estatura de Mário de Andrade, tão atormentado pela busca do caráter nacional brasileiro, resistiu à tentação. Sua passagem pelo Departamento de Cultura de São Paulo, como querem alguns, significou uma espécie de suicídio intelectual. Aliás, é oportuno adiantar que esta repartição tentava legislar sobre quase tudo, bisbilhotando até os Parques Infantis, os quais, instalados preferencialmente nos bairros pobres da periferia paulista — onde, segundo então se concebia, a precariedade material se mesclava de maneira indissolúvel com a falta de higiene e de moral —, deviam demarcar "ambientes saudáveis" (Sandroni 94).

A crítica que os intelectuais empreenderam antes de se enovelarem nestes laços movediços coincidiu com o sentido da própria Revolução de 30. É ainda Luciano Martins quem coloca, em arguta análise (intitulada "A Revolução de 30 e seu significado político"), que 30 contestou mais a oligarquia enquanto classe dirigente do que enquanto grupo dominante, sendo antes uma negociação entre elites, uma mudança (de forma alguma uma ruptura) política. Cessada a mobilização popular, os ideais democráticos e liberais constantes no difuso ideário de 30 (que apregoava um sistema político em bases democráticas) são substituídos pelos valores autoritários presentes na agenda do Estado Novo. Só em 37 se assistirá à efetiva consumação do movimento de Outubro. Os novos atores — como os tenentes — que forçaram as portas do poder serão enfim absorvidos pelos aparatos estatais, com a expansão da burocracia.

A ideologia legada pelos intelectuais possuía uma função explícita: guindá-los à condição de guias e arautos a orientar a nação. A gestão Capanema (1934-45), em plena ditadura de Vargas, permitirá que a maioria da elite pensante encontre no Estado o desejado aconchego. Junto com a centralização encetada, vem o paternalismo e o autoritarismo, que jogam uma pá de cal nas pretensões de autonomia daqueles letrados. Em resumo, escreve Luciano Martins:

> uma intelligentsia se constituiu no Brasil, no início dos anos 20, num contexto de renovação e aspiração a reformas econômicas, sociais e políticas. Ela revoluciona os cânones estéticos, contesta a cultura dominante, busca suas raízes, valoriza o que é brasileiro, desespera-se pelo "atraso" cultural do país, interroga-se sobre as estruturas da sociedade, procura sua identidade social e tenta estabelecer uma ponte entre a modernidade e a modernização do país. Ela clama por reformas sociais que não sabe definir muito claramente, mas o que a atrai mais é a construção de uma *nação moderna* . Ela fala em seu próprio nome, reivindica o direito de "ensinar, pregar e interpretar o

mundo" [. . .]. E ela fracassa no momento de estruturar um campo cultural, a partir do qual poderia definir suas relações com a política. (Martins, "A gênese de uma intelligentsia" 85)

Para o autor, as transformações econômicas, sociais e políticas que caracterizaram o Brasil no período estudado permitem crer que de alguma forma se ensaiava um processo de constituição de uma sociedade civil, quando da baldada implantação, encabeçada pelo grupo da Escola Nova, da Universidade do Distrito Federal, por volta de 1935. O intento foi abortado pela reforma Campos e pela reação católica, sob o governo de Vargas. Com o boicote de seus planos de independência, a *intelligentsia* se viu cara a cara com o progressivo gigantismo estatal. A ponte que procurava, entre a modernidade e a modernização, a ele conduz. Com isso, ela não só se aparta da sociedade como também fica sozinha diante do Estado:

> as tentativas de estruturar um campo cultural em que seu *isolamento* poderia converter-se em *autonomia* — pela fundação de sua identidade social e pela definição de suas relações com a política — só podem, portanto, fracassar. A procura de sua identidade passa então, num primeiro momento, pela busca de alianças ao nível da sociedade: ela mergulha na política (com letra minúscula) e suas divisões a empurram quase que para o estilhaçamento. Num segundo momento, o do deslisamento progressivo do campo cultural para o âmbito da tutela do Estado, ela é conduzida a buscar também alianças no interior deste. O sucesso do mecenato do Ministro Capanema mostra-o bem. Mas este sucesso deve-se também, em grande medida, à ambivalência da própria intelligentsia com relação ao papel que cabe ao Estado na transformação da sociedade. Os mecanismos de cooptação com que o Estado atrai alguns de seus membros mais criativos transforma sua ambivalência intelectual numa quase-esquizofrenia durante o *Estado Novo* : eles se situam no interior de um Estado cuja forma autoritária contestam. (Martins, "A gênese de uma intelligentsia" 85)

* * *

O que haveria de autoritário nesta produção cultural? Uma resposta convincente exigiria um mapeamento cuidadoso das marcas autoritárias embutidas nas várias roupagens que esta assumiu, o que foge ao escopo deste estudo, no qual, ao invés, estou explorando vias paralelas e complementares, mas nem por isso menos dignas de nota, desta produção, sob cuja diversidade mal se acoberta a inflexão monocórdica e renitente de seu autoritarismo.

Mônica Pimenta Velloso, ao evocar a trajetória dos intelectuais brasileiros desde a Independência, sublinha como eles sempre se elegeram como "consciência iluminada do nacional" (Velloso 3).[10] Será no Estado Novo, todavia, que se fundem o homem de cultura com o homem de ação, quando o Estado coopta a *intelligentsia* e a retira de sua torre de marfim. Personificando a nacionalidade brasileira, auto-outorgando-se a função de tutor de uma sociedade imatura e desprovida de guias, o Estado intervém para salvar e "educar" a coletividade, o que será a missão de órgãos como o DIP ou o Ministério da Educação. Daí toda uma interferência oficial nos distintos escalões da cultura, objetivando doutrinar a população por meio de uma ideologia que atingiu desde os abecedários infantis até o teatro e o cinema, dando o ar de sua graça, inclusive, no carnaval (Velloso 39). Como resultado, a cultura não é vista como reflexão; o intelectual, além de *condottieri*, é encarado como criatura privilegiada, acima do comum dos mortais; e a liberdade de expressão, uma vez restrita aos mais bem dotados e capazes (ou seja: as elites políticas e intelectuais, as quais se arvoram em termômetros da alma brasileira), naturalmente se reveste de um perfil autoritário.

Mônica Velloso ressalta em seu texto a positividade do popular na ideologia estadonovista, uma vez que o povo é isentado de culpa pela crise nacional, cujas mazelas são creditadas às camadas superiores. O povo carente necessita do Estado "pai-grande," que vai referendar não o "errado do morro," mas resgatar o espírito de grandeza inerente às suas manifestações. Claro que se pode contra-argumentar que esta positividade fica abalada pelo fato mesmo de que a ingerência do Estado Novo na cultura nacional procura drená-la para seus propósitos; que ele não acata, por exemplo, o samba que enaltece o malandro; ou que é ele que seleciona as expressões populares merecedoras de serem enquadradas nos estreitos espartilhos dos "legítimos interesses do país," tal como estipulados pelo regime. Porque, não nos esqueçamos, a convergência da elite pensante com o Estado Novo coincide na escolha da solução autoritária e, o corolário é inevitável, da desmobilização social, fazendo com que a positividade do popular indicada pela ensaísta não seja assim tão "positiva." A política cultural do regime louva o povo para melhor arrebanhá-lo ideologicamente e, é lógico, neutralizá-lo. Atitude tipicamente populista e demagógica que, de resto, se repisa nas leis trabalhistas ou na área sindical.

Outro aspecto que gostaria de enfatizar é o detalhe de que, ainda seguindo Mônica Pimenta Velloso, o Estado Novo contrapõe à crise da modernidade a busca do tipicamente brasileiro, com o culto da tradição, dos símbolos e efemérides nacionais (Caxias, Tiradentes), traduzida no ufanismo de um Brasil "impávido colosso." Ora, o impasse deste projeto (no que o Estado Novo muito compartilha com o Modernismo) me soa evidente: enfrenta-se o moderno com o passadismo, com uma volta atrás, conservadora e retrógrada, como se depreende na ficção preferentemente nostálgica e saudosista do período. Não se trataria de exaltar os tempos modernos, à la futurismo, mas de pensar em termos críticos o presente (e o passado), por meio de uma reflexão alicerçada na História. Entretanto, isto seria, em última instância, desmascarar o imenso *tour de force* ideológico destas elites, que recorrem às suas origens — e as decantam — para justificar sua posição de mando atual.

Estas considerações, embora capitais para um correto equacionamento do problema, ainda seriam insatisfatórias para aquilatar o autoritarismo no discurso contemporâneo ao Estado Novo. Por outra parte, em que pese o envolvimento de nomes como os mencionados mais atrás com o DIP, com a gestão Capanema, com o integralismo, com a direita católica, sua adesão ou simpatia, por si só, não bastariam para qualificar sua obra como autoritária, embora minem pela base qualquer veleidade democratizante que porventura pudessem alimentar. Isto não apenas porque não exista relação necessária entre a condição de intelectual e a de ator político (Martins, "A gênese de uma intelligentsia" 65). Como sugeri, o que importaria rastrear seriam as pegadas autoritárias incrustadas em seu discurso, uma vez que não é o bastante repassar os efeitos mais exteriores do autoritarismo. Por esta razão, entendo por autoritário aquele discurso que não franqueia a voz do outro, que é centrado apenas por uma ótica, sem ensejar, em sua própria economia interna, uma pluralidade de sentidos possíveis. Em uma palavra: o autoritarismo, assim enfocado, seria uma *inscrição textual*.

Foi de posse desta convicção que tentei mostrar, em livro recente, a fisionomia autoritária da transição brasileira — a qual funciona, fundamentalmente, como ratificadora da ideologia dos segmentos dominantes —, perseguindo suas ressonâncias em textos ficcionais.[11] Com efeito, a literatura brasileira, em sua configuração mais geral e, em especial, no período aqui focalizado, satisfaz plenamente os quesitos que Pierre

Bourdieu vislumbra na produção de bens simbólicos: ela se presta a endossar as discrepâncias de classe vigentes na estratificação social, a corroborar o domínio das elites.

Estaríamos, a esta altura, tangenciando alguns dos outros aspectos referidos por Edward Said. As instituições, como a escola ou os órgãos oficiais incumbidos da cultura, funcionaram em idêntica clave autoritária. A escolarização na Primeira República deu continuidade às distorções em voga no Império. Os diplomas, tanto os da escola superior quanto os da secundária, são instrumentos que brindam com privilégios uma minoria que tem acesso à educação formal. O título de bacharel (como o de coronel) concede foros de nobreza e confere honrarias e prerrogativas a seus possuidores (Nagle 284), capacitando-os à dominação. Com a política educacional centralizada do Estado Novo um maior contingente atinge a escolaridade. Mas campanhas como a do canto orfeônico, com sua coloração fascista, tendo à testa Villa-Lobos, não escondem, de nossa curiosidade de hoje, o seu matiz autoritário. A educação e a propaganda oficiais veneram a Pátria, Deus, a família e endeusam paternalisticamente a pessoa de Getúlio Vargas.

No mesmo diapasão, entidades governamentais, como o Serviço do Patrimônio Histórico e Artístico Nacional, puseram em vigor uma política de preservação que se restringiu ao tributo ao monumento de pedra e cal. O levantamento sobre a origem social do patrimônio tombado indica tratar-se de edificações vinculadas às experiências vitoriosas da etnia branca, da religião católica, do Estado (palácios, fortes) e das frações superiores da sociedade (sedes de grandes fazendas, sobrados urbanos), da nata política e econômica do país (Falcão 28).

Meios de comunicação massiva, como o rádio, atuaram em consonância com as mesmas diretrizes centralizantes e uniformizadoras (que atualmente se repetem nas redes nacionais de televisão, as quais operam graças a concessões estatais). *A Hora do Brasil*, transmitida em cadeia nacional, se incumbia de venerar Getúlio Vargas e alardear as conquistas do regime, como a legislação trabalhista. Programas de rádio-teatro acendiam a chama do ardor cívico e uma novela policial radiofônica narrava as aventuras de um detetive que, em meio a suas trapalhadas, tinha o mérito de cooperar sempre com as autoridades (Velloso 28). A Rádio Nacional é encampada em 1940 e a seus quadros pertenciam Lamartine Babo, Vicente Celestino, Almirante, Sílvio Caldas, Emilinha Borba, Ari Barroso, Francisco Alves, Carmem Miranda, Heitor dos Prazeres e Donga (Velloso 22). Outros programas reverenciavam datas e renomados heróis da nacionalidade. Em 1942, a Rádio Difusora da Prefeitura abiscoitou um prêmio instituído pela Secretaria de Educação e Cultura por seguir a orientação do DIP, devido à sua programação modelar, na qual se incluíam "Saúde e Música," cujo propósito era o de vulgarizar princípios de educação sanitária, um curso de estudos sobre a Amazônia, ministrado pelo Coronel Pio Borges, e a "Antologia do Pensamento Brasileiro," destinado a popularizar lições de civismo (Velloso 29).

Ao calendário oficial serão anexados os festejos carnavalescos, cujos desfiles deverão obedecer às normas preconizadas e possuir um caráter didático, tendo por assunto temas patrióticos. O próprio samba, por sinal, será amansado pelo regime. Considerado, assim como o frevo e o maxixe, um ritmo selvagem, o samba não escapará dos tentáculos do Estado Novo. Ao invés do malandro, que circulava na Lapa, o "samba da legitimidade" (a expressão é de Antônio Pedro Tota), ao qual se associam nomes como Ataulfo Alves, Benedito Lacerda, Wilson Batista, vai travestir o personagem sambista de trabalhador zeloso, que só faz samba após sair da fábrica (Velloso 33). O local de trabalho substitui a sede da boemia carioca e o malandro vira operário bem comportado e cidadão exemplar. Como é fácil perceber, persiste a mesma aversão às manifestações populares mais autênticas, que já flagráramos na *belle époque* tropical. A única divergência reside em que elas agora são apropriadas e canalizadas para a catequese ortodoxa da cartilha fascistóide do Estado Novo.

Jornais como *A Manhã* (Rio de Janeiro; direção de Cassiano Ricardo) e *A Noite* (São Paulo) ou revistas como a citada *Cultura Política* (direção de Almir Andrade) se constituem nos órgãos oficiais do regime e difundem a nova ordem. Em São Paulo criou-se o "teatro proletário," encarregado de dramatizar "exemplos de comportamento, modelos de cumprimento do dever, forjando assim a figura do 'operário-padrão'" (Velloso 38). Os cine-jornais, tornados obrigatórios, exibem à saciedade festas cívicas, viagens presidenciais, comemorações como o aniversário de Vargas ou o do regime, o Dia do Trabalho, o Dia da Bandeira, a Semana da Pátria (Velloso 36). A arquitetura, com a colaboração de arquitetos do porte de um Oscar Niemeyer ou de um Lúcio Costa e com o muralismo de Portinari, exprime a pujança do Estado Novo, em edificações como o Ministério da Educação e Saúde, o Ministério do Trabalho, o Ministério da Guerra, a Central do Brasil, todos erguidos nessa época.

Em síntese, e ainda como postula Bourdieu, todas as instâncias culturais exerceram o papel de legitimadoras e reduplicadoras da ordem social existente e, por causa disso, adquirindo tamanha feição reacionária, não redundam em genuínos agentes de transformação da sociedade. O resultado é que o discurso cultural brasileiro maquinado pelas camadas dirigentes tem, até hoje, sacramentado o seu poder.

O que ficou escrito pretendeu chamar a atenção para o patamar ideológico que está entranhado, notadamente, nas zonas de sombra do Modernismo brasileiro. Uma larga parcela da crítica literária ficou infensa a estes tópicos não apenas porque evitou tematizá-los — seja por descaso, seja por indigência teórica, seja porque boa parte de seus representantes transita, afinal, nos mesmos estratos sociais. Favorecendo quase sempre o texto e isolando-o em sua imanência, não se deu conta de que a leitura transcende a *leitura da obra* . A produção, a circulação e a reprodução dos bens culturais devem ser levadas em conta; as esferas que autenticam o objeto artístico são outras tantas faces de uma única moeda. O campo em que se insere um livro, um poema, um conto, um romance está atravessado por uma rede complexa de relações e por um intrincado jogo de forças que a mera aproximação da obra deixa de fora.[12]

Daí a premência de se sondar o sistema intelectual, nos parâmetros de uma sócio-crítica, a fim de que se vislumbre melhor a complexa dinâmica do ato de leitura, dos diálogos entabulados entre escritor (enquanto membro de um dado grupo social), texto e contexto, articulando-se este com os outros discursos que conformam o espaço da cultura e com as instituições às quais inextricavelmente se imbrica. Embasado em tais premissas, o gesto interpretativo se conota politicamente e o *lugar da crítica* passa a ser aquele em que ela se converte numa *crítica do lugar.*

Em síntese, o conceito de política precisa ganhar maior guarida na crítica que se dedica a deslindar o *corpus* literário brasileiro. Com uma perspectiva apolítica do discurso, literário ou não, ela corre o risco de reduplicar o autoritarismo que intoxica a cultura brasileira e, assim, em nada contribui para que trevas como as de 37 e 64 se desanuviem de vez. Redimensionamento que deve ser acompanhado de uma indagação das elites letradas e das diversas instâncias e instituições que entretecem o emaranhado complexo do campo intelectual. Um gesto desta envergadura colocará o crítico como um corrosivo problematizador do discurso autoritário, a vergar-se sobre seu próprio drama (ou o de seu tempo, ou o de seu passado), numa fabricação que não arma álibis nem se aparenta com a exuberância inócua dos fogos de artifício.

Notas

[1] Seria o caso, entre outros, dos trabalhos de Nicolau Sevcenko, *A literatura como missão* ; Sérgio Miceli, *Intelectuais e classe dirigente no Brasil (1920-1945)* e Jeffrey Needell, *A Tropical Belle Époque.*

² Os textos de Simon Schwartzman, *Bases do autoritarismo brasileiro*; Carlos Guilherme Mota, *Ideologia da cultura brasileira (1933-1974)*; Jarbas Medeiros, *Ideologia autoritária no Brasil - 1930-1945*; Marilena Chauí, *Conformismo e resistência*; Sérgio Miceli, cit. e Roberto DaMatta, *Carnavais, malandros e heróis* e *A casa e a rua*, insistem na vocação autoritária da política, da cultura, da ideologia, dos intelectuais, da estrutura social brasileira.

³ Uma delas seria a versão canônica que enxerga o Modernismo apenas como "ruptura," sem atinar com as problemáticas contradições embutidas no movimento e na própria modernização brasileira como um todo. A indagação do Modernismo a partir do prisma de uma sociologia da vida intelectual sem dúvida incita toda uma revisão do movimento, de seus êxitos e malogros. Para o exame da inteligência modernista, consultar, de Sérgio Miceli, *Intelectuais e classe dirigente no Brasil (1920-1945)*; de Mônica Pimenta Velloso, "Os intelectuais e a política cultural do Estado Novo;" de Luciano Martins, "A gênese de uma intelligentsia;" de Randal Johnson, "The Dynamics of the Brazilian Literary Field;" de Silviano Santiago, "O intelectual modernista revisitado."

⁴ Sobre os intelectuais brasileiros, além dos livros dos autores citados nas notas anteriores, v.: Dante Moreira Leite, *O caráter nacional brasileiro*; Francisco Iglésias, *História e ideologia*; A. L. Machado Neto, *Estrutura social da República das Letras*; Brito Broca, *A vida literária no Brasil - 1900*; Caio Navarro de Toledo, *ISEB - fábrica de ideologias*; Bolivar Lamounier, "Formação de um pensamento autoritário na Primeira República. Uma interpretação;" Sérgio Miceli, *Poder, sexo e letras na República Velha*; Gilberto Vasconcelos, *A ideologia curupira*; Carlos Guilherme Mota, "Cultura e política no Estado Novo (1937-1945);" Hélgio Trindade, "Integralismo: teoria e práxis política nos anos 30;" Reginaldo Moraes et alii, *Inteligência brasileira*; Luiz Costa Lima, "Da existência precária: o sistema intelectual no Brasil;" Simon Schwartzman et alii, *Tempos de Capanema*; Vários Autores, *A Revolução de 30 - seminário internacional*; Lúcia Lippi Oliveira, *Elite intelectual e debate político nos anos 30* e Oliveira et alii, *Estado Novo - ideologia e poder*; Luciano Martins, "A geração AI-5;" Roberto Reis, "O carpinteiro das letras." O estudo de Roberto Ventura sobre Silvio Romero e outros pensadores da geração de 1870 é um dos primeiros a explorar a ideologia de intelectuais que se dedicaram à literatura.

⁵ Luciano Martins faz uma impiedosa descrição da elite intelectual contemporânea — ou imediatamente anterior, não fica esclarecido — ao AI-5. Após acentuar a falta de rigor e de acumulação intelectual e de reparar que é sobretudo no Rio de Janeiro que o pensamento mais tende a deixar de ser crítico, devido à ausência de uma verdadeira universidade, ele

escreve: "tudo se passa como se houvesse uma permanente hemorragia da percepção social e do talento, da matéria (inacumulada) de uma obra que jamais será realizada. Matéria essa que se esvai através da frase de efeito, através do descontrole do nível de abstração pelo gosto do paradoxo de brilho ou através da crônica fácil de jornal. Esse é o domínio do intelectual convertido em *frasista* e que acaba esvaziando, aos poucos, o eventual romancista ou pensador que pudessem existir dentro dele, numa espécie de subversão do princípio de Lavoisier: tudo se perde e nada se transforma. O esforço de reflexão tende a ser substituído pelo fascínio da gratificação social imediata (o que certamente inclui o mercado), gerando uma imensa necessidade de 'ser aceito,' de ter que se adaptar às modas e ao salão da moda, coisas que, sobretudo numa sociedade em rápida transformação econômica, se sucedem em ritmo vertiginoso. Ser incluído na categoria do 'já era' parece então ser percebido como uma sentença de morte. Em decorrência, esse bovarismo intelectual tem que ser alimentado pelo jogo de espelhos do elogio recíproco, com a conseqüente liquidação do rigor e da capacidade crítica" (Martins, "A geração AI-5" 77).

[6] Tenho em mente as colocações de Antonio Candido sobre o sistema literário brasileiro nas páginas introdutórias do primeiro volume da *Formação da literatura brasileira* (Candido 23). Seria indispensável consultar o estudo seminal de Flora Süssekind sobre o Sapateiro Silva, no qual ela delineia o surgimento do cânon da literatura brasileira entre os árcades do século XVIII.

[7] Jeffrey Needell descreve a elite ilustrada romântica: "these founders of a self-conscious Brazilian literary culture generally indulged in literary pursuits as a kind of part-time passion. Born to relative wealth and closely associated with the urban elite and middle class sectors as liberal professionals and state bureaucrats, they had the education, contacts, and leisure to write and publish. Typically, they were the sons of educated planters or urban-based families and enjoyed a classical schooling, European education or travel, a professional degree, and a career in the bureaucracy, the Colégio Pedro II, the parliament, political journalism, and diplomacy. Their early years might involve some hardship, but only because they *choose* to eschew law or medicine to pursue the Muse. That they had the choice was a measure of their favored status" (Needell 185).

[8] Cf. o capítulo inicial de meu *A permanência do círculo*. V. também Reis, "The Self-Portrait and the Back of the Portrait."

[9] O livro de Needell é indispensável para uma compreensão das diversas instituições — desde as mais exteriores, como os clubes, às mais domésticas, como os salões e a família — em voga na *belle époque* brasileira. Para um estudo específico da *belle époque*, consultar os já

mencionados estudos de Brito Broca, A. L. Machado Neto, Nicolau Sevcenko, Sérgio Miceli (*Poder, sexo e letras na República Velha*) e Roberto Reis ("O carpinteiro das letras"). Por outra parte, vale frisar que Needell discorda de Gilberto Freyre, que entendia a re-europeização do país como um reingresso do Brasil no circuito ocidental, depois do insulamento provocado pelo período colonial. Para o historiador norte-americano, a influência européia nunca se interrompeu, tendo se agravado com a maior inserção do Brasil num mercado mundial que tem por eixo o Atlântico Norte (Needell 153).

[10] Vale a pena transcrever como ela sintetiza o périplo da elite pensante brasileira: "nos momentos de crise e mudanças históricas profundas — instauração do Império, Proclamação da República, Revolução de 30 e Estado Novo — as elites intelectuais marcaram sua presença no cenário político, defendendo o direito de interferirem no processo de organização social. Logo após a Independência, quando estava em curso o processo de construção da jovem nação, os intelectuais portaram-se como verdadeiros guias, sentindo-se particularmente inspirados pela idéia nacional. Assim, os escritores românticos acreditavam ter uma missão sagrada: a de criar um temário nacionalista, destinado à autovalorização do país. Na passagem do regime imperial para a República, os intelectuais voltam a atribuir-se o papel de guia na condução do processo de modernização da sociedade brasileira. Eles aparecem como verdadeiros 'mosqueteiros intelectuais' que, munidos do instrumental cientificista buscam remodelar o Estado, lutando contra a incapacidade técnica e administrativa dos políticos. Na década de 20, quando se fazem sentir os efeitos críticos do pós-guerra, com a derrocada do mito cientificista, o ideal cosmopolita do desenvolvimento cede lugar ao credo nacionalista. A busca de nossas raízes, o ideal de brasilidade, passam, então, a construir o foco das proposições intelectuais. Agrupados no movimento modernista, os intelectuais se julgam os indivíduos mais capacitados para conhecer o Brasil. E é através da arte que eles pretendem atingir a realidade brasileira, apresentando alternativas para o desenvolvimento da nação" (Velloso 1-2).

[11] Cf. Reis, *The Pearl Necklace*, no qual trabalho com José de Alencar, Machado de Assis, Humberto de Campos, José Lins do Rego, Graciliano Ramos, Galeão Coutinho, Carlos Drummond de Andrade e Érico Veríssimo. Entendo por *transição* o período que se estende, aproximadamente, de 1850 (data da proibição definitiva do tráfico negreiro, que abala pela raiz uma economia calcada na mão-de-obra escrava e nos latifúndios) a 1950 (quando a instalação de um parque industrial detona o início de uma produção que pouco a pouco atenderá a um mercado interno em crescimento). Nesse ínterim, o Brasil assiste, ainda que

atabalhoadamente, à urbanização, ao afã de se modernizar as arcaicas estruturas herdadas da Colônia, com uma maior presença das camadas médias no cenário político e o despontar de um tímido proletariado.

[12] Remeto o leitor para estas pertinentes considerações do sociólogo francês: "given that works of art exist as symbolic objects only if they are known and recognized, i.e socially instituted as works of art and received by spectators capable of knowing and recognizing them as such, the sociology of art and literature has to take as its object not only the material production but also the symbolic production of the work, i. e. the production of the value of the work. It therefore has to consider as contributing to production not only the direct producers of the work in its materiality (artist, writer, etc.) but also the producers of the meaning and value of the work" (critics, publishers, gallery, directors). "So it has to take into account not only, as the social history of art usually does, the social conditions of the production of artists, art critics, dealers, patrons, etc., as revealed by indices such as social origin, education or qualifications, but also the social conditions of the production of a set of objects socially constituted as works of *art*, i.e. the conditions of production of the field of social agents (e.g. museums, galleries, academies, etc.) which help to define and produce the value of works of art. In short, it is question of understanding works of art as *manifestations* of the field as a whole, in which all the powers of the field, and all the determinisms inherent in its structure and functioning, are concentrated" (Bourdieu 318-19).

Bibliografia Citada

Bourdieu, Pierre. "The Field of Cultural Production, or: the Economic World Reversed." *Poetics* 12 (1983): 311-56.

Broca, Brito. *A vida literária no Brasil - 1900.* Rio de Janeiro: José Olympio, 1975.

Candido, Antonio. *Formação da literatura brasileira.* 4 ed. 2 vols. São Paulo: Martins, 1964. Vol. 1.

Chauí, Marilena. *Conformismo e resistência.* São Paulo: Brasiliense, 1986.

Coutinho, Afrânio. *Conceito de literatura brasileira.* Rio de Janeiro: Pallas, 1976.

DaMatta, Roberto. *Carnavais, malandros e heróis.* Rio de Janeiro: Zahar, 1979.

---. *A casa e a rua*. São Paulo: Brasiliense, 1985.

Falcão, Joaquim Arruda. "Política e democracia: a preservação do patrimônio histórico e artístico nacional." *Estado e cultura no Brasil*. Ed. Sérgio Miceli. São Paulo: Difusão Européia do Livro, 1984. 21-39.

Iglesias, Francisco. *História e ideologia*. São Paulo: Perspectiva, 1971.

Johnson, Randal. "The Dynamics of the Brazilian Literary Field, 1930-1945." Mimeografado, 1989.

Lamounier, Bolivar. "Formação de um pensamento autoritário na Primeira República. Uma interpretação." *História geral da civilização brasileira (O Brasil Republicano)*. tomo III, 3 vols. Ed. Boris Fausto. São Paulo: Difusão Européia do Livro, 1975-77. 2: 343-73.

Leite, Dante Moreira. *O caráter nacional brasileiro*. 2 ed. São Paulo: Pioneira, 1969.

Lima, Luiz Costa. "Da existência precária: o sistema intelectual no Brasil." *Dispersa demanda*. Rio de Janeiro: Francisco Alves, 1981. 3-29.

Machado Neto, A. L. *Estrutura social da República das Letras*. São Paulo: Grijalbo, 1973.

Martins, Luciano. "A geração AI-5." *Ensaios de Opinião*. Rio de Janeiro: Paz e Terra, 1979. 72-102.
---. "A Revolução de 30 e seu significado político." Vários Autores, *A Revolução de 30 - seminário internacional*. 670-89.
---. "A gênese de uma intelligentsia." *Revista Brasileira de Ciências Sociais* 2.4 (1987): 65-87.

Medeiros, Jarbas. *Ideologia autoritária no Brasil - 1930-1945*. Rio de Janeiro: Fundação Getúlio Vargas, 1978.

Miceli, Sérgio. *Poder, sexo e letras na República Velha*. São Paulo: Perspectiva, 1977.
---. *Intelectuais e classe dirigente no Brasil (1920-1945)*. São Paulo: Difusão Européia do Livro, 1979.

Moraes, Reginaldo et alii, ed. *Inteligência brasileira*. São Paulo: Brasiliense, 1986.

Mota, Carlos Guilherme. "Cultura e política no Estado Novo (1937-1945)." *Encontros com a Civilização Brasileira* 7 (1979): 87-94.

---. *Ideologia da cultura brasileira (1933-1974).* 4 ed. São Paulo: Atica, 1980.

Nagle, Jorge. *Educação e sociedade na Primeira República.* São Paulo: Editora Pedagógica Universitária, 1974.

Needell, Jeffrey. *A Tropical Belle Époque.* Cambridge: Cambridge University Press, 1987.

Oliveira, Lúcia Lippi et alii. *Elite intelectual e debate político nos anos 30.* Rio de Janeiro: Fundação Getúlio Vargas, 1980.

---. *Estado Novo - ideologia e poder.* Rio de Janeiro: Zahar, 1982.

Oliveira, Lúcia Lippi. "As raízes da ordem: os intelectuais, a cultura e o Estado." *A Revolução de 30 - seminário internacional.* 506-26.

Reis, Roberto. "O carpinteiro das letras." *O miolo e o pão.* Ed. Roberto Reis et alii. Niterói: EDUFF, 1986. 39-50.

---. *A permanência do círculo.* Niterói: EDUFF, 1987.

---. "The Self-Portrait and the Back of the Portrait." *The Pearl Necklace.* Gainesville: University Press of Florida, 1992.

Vários Autores. *A Revolução de 30 - seminário internacional.* Brasília: Editora da Universidade de Brasília, 1983.

Said, Edward. *The World, the Text, and the Critic.* Cambridge: Harvard University Press, 1983.

Sandroni, Carlos. *Mário contra Macunaíma.* São Paulo: Vértice, 1988.

Santiago, Silviano. "Alegria e poder" e "O intelectual modernista revisitado." *Nas malhas da letra.* São Paulo: Companhia das Letras, 1989. 11-23 e 165-75.

Schwartzman, Simon. *Bases do autoritarismo brasileiro.* Rio de Janeiro: Campus, 1982.

---. "O intelectual e o poder: a carreira política de Gustavo Capanema." *A Revolução de 30 - seminário internacional.* 365-97.

--- et alii. *Tempos de Capanema.* Rio de Janeiro: Paz e Terra, 1984.

Sevcenko, Nicolau. *A literatura como missão*. São Paulo: Brasiliense, 1983.

Süssekind, Flora e Valença, Raquel. *O Sapateiro Silva*. Rio de Janeiro: Fundação Casa de Rui Barbosa, 1983.

Toledo, Caio Navarro de. *ISEB: fábrica de ideologias*. São Paulo: Atica, 1977.

Tota, Antônio Pedro. *O samba da legitimidade*. USP, Dissertação de mestrado, 1980.

Trindade, Hélgio. "Integralismo: teoria e prática política nos anos 30." *História geral da civilização brasileira*. 3: 298-335.

Vasconcelos, Gilberto. *A ideologia curupira*. São Paulo: Departamento de Ciências Sociais da USP, 1977.

Velloso, Mônica Pimenta. *Os intelectuais e a política cultural do Estado Novo*. Rio de Janeiro: Fundação Getúlio Vargas, 1987.

Ventura, Roberto. *Estilo tropical*. São Paulo: Companhia das Letras, 1991.

CONTRIBUTORS

Severino J. Albuquerque is Associate Professor of Portuguese at the University of Wisconsin-Madison. A member of the Modern Language Association's Executive Committee on Luso-Brazilian Literature, he has contributed articles and book reviews to *Hispania, Latin American Theatre Review, Modern Drama, Luso-Brazilian Review, South Atlantic Review, Romance Notes,* and other publications, and is the author, most recently, of *Violent Acts: A Study of Contemporary Latin American Theatre* (1991).

J. Richard Andrews is Professor of Spanish and Portuguese and Professor of Anthropology at Vanderbilt University, where one of his courses is a graduate seminar on the Renaissance Theater in Portugal. His book-length publications include *Juan del Encina: Prometheus in Search of Prestige, Introduction to Classical Nahautl,* and a translation and study of Hernando Ruiz de Alarcon's *Treatise on the Heathen Superstitions and Customs that Today Live amoung the Indians Native to This New Spain 1629* (co-edited with Ross Hassig). He has published articles and read numerous papers on both Portuguese and Nahuatl topics.

Milton M. Azevedo is Professor at the University of California, Berkeley, where he teaches Hispanic linguistics in the Department of Spanish and Portuguese. He has published *Introducción a la lingüística española* (Prentice Hall, 1992) and he is currently doing research on the literary representation of nonstandard speech.

Bobby J. Chamberlain is Associate Professor of Hispanic Languages and Literatures at the University of Pittsburgh. He is the author of *Jorge Amado* (Boston: Twayne, 1990) and *Portuguese Language and Luso-Brazilian Literature: An Annotated Guide to Selected Reference Works* (New York: MLA, 1989), and the co-author (with Ronald M. Harmon) of *A Dictionary of Informal Brazilian Portuguese* (Washington, D. C.: Georgetown, 1984). He is currently researching a book on contemporary Brazilian literary theory and has just completed an English-language critical edition of Lúcio Cardoso's *Crônica da Casa Assassinada* to be published by the Coleção Arquivos/University of Pittsburgh Press.

Mary L. Daniel is Senior Professor of Portuguese at the University of Wisconsin-Madison and Co-Editor of the *Luso-Brazilian Review*. Founder of the Luso-Brazilian Section of the Midwest Modern Language Association (1966) and of the Portuguese program at the University of Iowa, where she taught for twelve years before joining the U.W. faculty in 1977, she is best known for her scholarship in the areas of modern Brazilian and Portuguese literature, especially her studies in XIX and XX century fiction. Prof. Daniel is the author of *João Guimarães Rosa: Travessia Literária* (1968), articles on Eça de Queiroz, José Saramago, Machado de Assis, Alphonsus de Guimaraens, Erico Veríssimo, Guimarães Rosa, Osman Lins, João Alphonsus, Alceu Amoroso Lima, and Luiz Vilela, and several general studies in the field of Brazilian fiction since 1800.

M. Elizabeth Ginway is Assistant Professor of Portuguese at the University of Georgia. She received her Ph.D. from Vanderbilt and has articles in press in *Hispania* and *Brasil/Brazil* on topics ranging from Machado de Assis, Brazilian modernism to contemporary Brazilian fiction.

Lucia Helena is Associate Professor of Theory of Literature, at the Federal University of Rio de Janeiro, Brazil. She received her Ph.D. in Theory of Literature in 1983. She was Research Associate at the University of Rochester in 1988, Visiting Scholar at Brown University in 1989, and Visiting Associate Professor at Florida International University in 1990. She has published extensively in Brazilian and European journal and is author of the following books: *Totens e Tabus da Modernidade Brasileira* (granted the National Outstanding Book Award of 1985), *Escrita e Poder, Uma Literatura Antropofágica, Vanguarda Européia e Modernismo Brasileiro, A Cosmo-Agonia de Augusto dos Anjos*. Some of her recent publications in the U.S.A include "Genre and Gender in 'The Imitation of the Rose', by Clarice Lispector" (*Style* 24.2, Summmer 1990); "A Personagem Feminina na Ficção Brasileira nos Anos 70-80: Problemas Históricos e Teóricos" (*Luso-Brazilian Review* 26.2, Winter 1989), "A Narrativa de Maria Gabriela Llansol" (*Luso-Brazilian Review* 28.2, Winter 1991), and "A problematização da narrativa em Clarice Lispector" (*Hispania*, 75.5, December 1992).

Randal Johnson is Professor of Brazilian literature and culture at the University of Florida. He is the author of *Cinema Novo x 5: Masters of Contemporary Brazilian Film*, *The Film Industry in Brazil: Culture and the State*, *Literatura e Cinema: Macunaíma do Modernismo na Literatura ao Cinema Novo*, and editor of *Brazilian Cinema* (with Robert Stam), *Tropical Paths: Essays on Modern Brazilian Literature*, and Pierre Bourdieu's *The Field of Cultural Production: Essays on Art and Literature*. At an NDEA Title VI Summer Institute at the University of Texas at Austin in 1968, Alex Severino was the professor of his first course on Brazilian literature.

Francisco Caetano Lopes Junior is Assistant Professor of Luso-Brazilian Literatures at the Stanford University. He received his first Ph.D. from the University of Pittsburgh in 1988 and a second from the Pontifícia Universidade Católica do Rio de Janeiro in 1989. He has published several articles on contemporary Luso-Brazilian and Latin-American literatures. He is currently writing a book on Post-Modernism.

William W. Megenney received his Ph.D. from the University of New Mexico in 1969 and since then has taught Spanish and Portuguese at the University of California, Riverside. Among his most prominent publications are *A Bahian Heritage*, University of North Carolina Press, 1978, *El palenquero: un lenguaje post-crillo de Colombia*, Instituto Caro y Cuervo, 1986, and *Africa en Santo Domingo: su herencia lingüística*, Museo del Hombre Dominicano and the Academia de Ciencias de la República Dominicana. His most recent publications include "West Africa in Brazil: The Case of Ewe-Yoruba Syncretism," *Anthropos* 87, 1992, and "El español de los cumbes de Barlovento (Venezuela) y sus posibles vestigios afronegroides: la filtración por la creoloidización," *América negra* 3, 1992.

Massaud Moiés é Professor Titular da Universidade de São Paulo, Professor Visitante de Literatura Brasileira e Literatura Portuguesa nas Universidades de Wisconsin (1962-1963), Indiana (1967-1968), Vanderbilt (1970, fall semester; 1987, spring semester), Texas, at Austin (1971, spring semester), California, at Los Angeles (1982, spring quarter). Dirigiu as Faculdades de Filosofia, Ciências e Letras de Marília (1960-1962) e de Assis (1961-1962), institutos isolados do Ensino Superior, mais tarde integrados na UNESP. Dirigiu o Centro de Estudos Portugueses da Universidade de São Paulo (1968-1986). Obras principais: *A Literatura Portuguesa* (1960; 26ª ed., 1991), *A Criação Literária* (1967; 14ª. ed., em 2 vols., 1986, 1989), *Pequeno Dicionário de Literatura Brasileira* (coed. com José Paulo Paes, 1967; 3ª. ed., 1987), *Dicionário de Termos Literários* (1974; 6ª ed., 1992),

Pequeno Dicionário de Literatura Portuguesa (editor, 1982), *Literatura: Mundo e Forma* (1982), *Fernando Pessoa: o Espelho e a Esfinge* (1988), *História da Literatura Brasileira* (5 vols., 1983-1989).

George Monteiro holds a dual appointment at Brown University as Professor of English and Professor of Portuguese and Brazilian Studies. Among his recent publications are *The Correspondence of Henry James and Henry Adams* (1992), *A Man Smiles at Death With Half a Face*, a translation from José Rodrigues Miguéis, and *Double Weaver's Knot: Selected Poems* (1989).

Richard A. Preto-Rodas serves as Professor of Romance Languages at the University of South Florida at Tampa. His Ph.D. in Romance Languages and Literatures is from the University of Michigan. He is the author of *Negritude as a Theme in The Poetry of the Portuguese-Speaking World* (1971) and *Francisco Rodrigues Lobo: Dialogue and Courtly Lore* (1972). With the late Alfred Hower he edited and contributed to *Crônicas Brasileiras* (1971), *Carlos Drummond de Andrade; Quarenta Historinhas* (1985), and *Empire in Transition: The Portuguese World in the Time of Camões* (1985).

Roberto Reis (Rio de Janeiro/Brazil, 1949) is Associate Professor of Brazilian Literature and Culture at the University of Minnesota/Twin Cities. He has published poems, short stories and essays on literary criticism in Brazil, Portugal, Spain, United States, Mexico, Guatemala, Argentina, Peru, Colombia, Germany, Japan, France, Czechoslovakia. He is the author of a collection of short stories, *A Dor da Bruxa* ("The Witch's Pain," 1973), a novel, *A Hora da Teia* ("The Spider's Web Hour," 1982), an essay, *A Permanência do Círculo* ("The Permanence of the Circle," 1987). His most recent publications are *Toward Socio-Criticism*, editor (1991) and *The Pearl Necklace*, winner of the Alfred Hower Prize, a collection of essays on Brazilian literature published by the University Press of Florida (1992).

Ellen W. Sapega is Assistant Professor of Portuguese at the University of Wisconsin—Madison. She received her Ph.D. from Vanderbilt University in 1987 where she wrote her dissertation under the direction of Professor Alexandrino E. Severino. A revised version of her thesis, entitled *Ficções Modernistas: Um estudo da obra em prosa de José de Almada Negreiros*, was recently published by the Instituto de Cultura e Língua Portuguesa (1992). In addition, she organized and wrote the preface to Volume III ("Artigos no *Diário de Lisboa*") of the *Obras Completas* of José de Almada

Negreiros (Imprensa Nacional-Casa da Moeda) and has published several articles on Portuguese Modernism in *Colóquio/Letras* and the *Luso-Brazilian Review*.

Ronald W. Sousa is Professor and Chair of the Department of Cultural Studies and Comparative Literature at the University of Minnesota, Minneapolis. Widely published in the areas of Portuguese-language literature and literary theory, he is editor of *Enlightenment in Portugal* (1984) and author of *The Rediscoverers* (1981) and numerous essays and book chapters on both literary theory and Portuguese-language literature.

Luiz Fernando Valente, Assistant Professor of Portuguese and Brazilian Studies at Brown University, is currently working on a book on José de Alencar and the Alencar tradition. His essays on Brazilian and Comparative Literature have appeared in journals and reference volumes in the United States, Brazil, Portugal and Great Britain. He is Associate Editor of *Brasil/Brazil: A Journal of Brazilian Literature*, Consulting Editor for Latin American Literature of *The Explicator*, and a former President of the Northeastern Association of Brazilianists.